Hellbent on INSANITY

Hellbent on
INSANITY

A
ROLLERCOASTER
RIDE
with the
**BEST COLLEGE
HUMOR
OF THE 1970s
(and
A SMATTERING
FROM THE 1980s
WHILE YOUR BACK
WAS TURNED)**

edited by JOEY GREEN

with BRUCE HANDY *and* ALAN CORCORAN

An Owl Book   HOLT, RINEHART and WINSTON   New York

Copyright © 1982 by Joey Green

Published by Holt, Rinehart and Winston,
383 Madison Avenue, New York, New York 10017.

Published simultaneously in Canada
by Holt, Rinehart and Winston of Canada, Limited.

Library of Congress Cataloging in Publication Data
Main entry under title:
Hellbent on insanity.
Includes index.
1. College wit and humor. 2. American wit and humor.
I. Green, Joey. II. Handy, Bruce. III. Corcoran, Alan.
PN6231.C6H4   817'.54'08   81-23716   AACR2

ISBN Paperback: 0-03-059981-4

First Edition

Art Direction by Joey Green
Designer: A Good Thing; Inc.

Printed in the United States of America
10 9 8 7 6 5 4 3 2 1

ISBN 0-03-059981-4

To Mom and Dad

TABLE OF

CONTENTS

APATHY ON THE MARCH

FUN WITH CARCINOGENS

Contents of Table

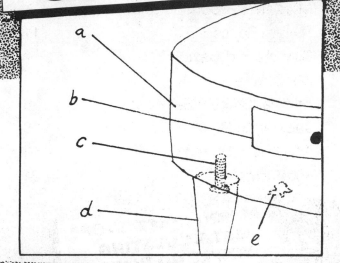

THE FLORENCE HENDERSON GENERATION

INTRODUCTION

Before you settle back into your reclining chair and start giggling over all the monkeyshine associated with the college humor biz, there's a little something you should know. You see, we used to tell everyone we were only in this racket to "bring a ray of sunshine into an otherwise overcast world." But we were only kidding. Listen close, poptart, we're only cranking out punchlines to hit paydirt. We just don't crack jokes unless we can ring every chuckle into our cash register.

Take it from me, there's nothing more invigorating than the sound of crisp mint leaves, and we settled down to the pleasure of lettuce folding a long time ago. We call it Corporate Comedy. Yuks for Bucks. Funny Money. And in the travesty trade, our bank of buffoonery has a parody portfolio with satirical solvency. As soon as we see that sparkle in Ben Franklin's baby-green eyes, we're tickling ribs, slapping knees, and splitting sides.

Now maybe that's not college humor as you remember it. But a lot of things have changed since the twenties. Back then college humor magazines were filled with "he & she" gags, daffy definitions, whimsical observations about college life, and pages numbered consecutively—all adding up to a delightful package of collegiate wit, amusing the same generations that voted for Herbert Hoover. It's not hard to understand why the death of college humor coincided with the 1960s and the first widespread use of psychedelic drugs and napalm. Campus unrest, no doubt caused by the lack of good college humor, increased. With the Kent State shootings, the invasion of Cambodia, and the My Lai Massacre bringing the 1970s to a hilarious start, there wasn't much demand for campus humor magazines. The numbers decreased to less than a handful publishing sporadically. Traditional college humor, like Karl Wallenda, had fallen by the wayside.

Sociologists will inevitably turn and ask why college humor died, if for no other reason than to sponge money from the government to put food in their stomachs and gas in their Mercedeses. Perhaps they'll theorize that the number of college humor magazines declined during the early part of the decade because times became more serious and students more active. Perhaps they'll hypothesize that the magazines disappeared because students who became

anything more than a cocklebur in the pants of their University administrators were usually thrown out of school to face the Vietnam war. Or perhaps hungrier sociologists will add more speculative statements to this paragraph.

All I know is that after a prolonged absence from the nation's campuses in the sixties and early seventies, college humor magazines began reappearing in growing numbers around 1977. College humor was Born Again, and a new generation of campus cut-ups—eager to make a quick buck pirating material from "Saturday Night Live," "Monty Python," "Firesign Theatre," and *National Lampoon*—revived old magazines or started new ones from scratch. The *Temple Spice* replaced the long defunct *Temple Owl;* the *Colgate Harlequin* reincarnated the *Colgate Banter;* the *Emory Spoke* superseded the *Emory Phoenix;* and the *California Pelican* (Berkeley) came out from a seven-year hibernation in 1978. The *Cornell Lunatic* filled the void left by the *Cornell Widow's* 1962 demise, and the following spring the *Michigan Gargoyle* awoke from an extended nap. The *Princeton Tiger, Columbia Jester,* and *Stanford Chapparal,* which had all gone through brief lapses in publication or resorted to mimeograph, were going full steam once again.

"Smart-ass, gloatingly salacious, everything but uptight, this is good old college humor—brought back.with a vengeance,"explained *Newsweek's* October 23, 1978, cover story, "College Humor Comes Back," which failed to mention any college humor magazine.

When the *Yale Record* resurfaced in 1980, its editors tried to explain where it had been for the past ten years: "If we wanted you to see the *Record,* you would have seen it. Sure, we've been publishing issues. Dozens of them. We just haven't let you look at them. You didn't deserve it. . . . We did some really great issues, too. . . . In our spare time we tested Yale's sense of humor. We engineered a stock market slump so the endowment shrank and your tuition soared. We even put out phony 'humor' magazines just to make you look stupid. But we finally got bored with all that and decided to give you another chance. Why? Who knows? That's just the kind of people we are."

Most authorities suspect college humor magazines returned because times became less serious. They think of college humor magazine editors as cocky kids who swing from chandeliers, spritz seltzer bottles, and toss lemon meringue pies. They picture us a tricksters, nimble-witted wags, and jeering culprits. Nothing could be further from the truth. Take it from me, today's college pranksters aren't anything but money-hungry rabble-rousers.

Case in point: In February 1979, representatives from fifteen college humor magazines convened in Philadelphia to sign the Declaration of College Humor, and the National Association of College Humor Magazines was reborn. The first meeting transformed two Holiday Inn rooms into a chapter from *The Dharma Bums*—and coincided with a conference of student government bigwigs from the Ivy League schools. We had no choice but to crash banquet meals as delegates from the Princeton Financial Aid Research contingent. None of us had read Sigmund Freud's *Jokes and their Relation to the Subconscious,* but that didn't stop us from debating whether Northrup Frye sides with gestalt theorists in his assertion that satirists must be born with a "sardonic vision." P.C.P., the Philadelphia College of Pharmacy, was just down the block, and we were mysteriously supplied with vitamins that made us fall to the floor every half hour and flop around like fish. To make a long story short, it was the most boring three days of my life. Besides, we had all revived our magazines with the hope of reaching that mountain of moolah, but we were still in the foothills. So that weekend we decided to put this book together and make some quick dinero. We needed the bread badly; I still can't figure out how we got out of there without paying Holiday Inn the $267.00 hotel bill.

Well, within two years we had sold this book to a major publishing house and we were floating in C-notes. Our annual convention was held in February

1981 at Columbia University, and this time twenty-five magazines cruised in to share in the escargots, Glenlivet, and senseless destruction of several campus dorm rooms. Speakers included Gahan Wilson, Harvey Kurtzman, Veronica Geng, Daniel Menaker, Shary Flenniken, Sam Gross, Tod Carrol, Brian McCormick, Ted Mann, Michael O'Donoghue, and Abbie Hoffman. The Chinese food wasn't too bad either.

Of course, stern academicians will still label the new wave of college humor as uninhibited, irreverent, rebellious, unadulterated, audacious, and "gloatingly salacious." But there are many more individuals whose vocabularies don't include even the first of these adjectives, and few academicians own more extensive thesauruses. *The New York Review of Books* will inevitably label this collection "fatuous and puerile" without ever reading as far as this sentence. And Gene Shalit will call it "a real treat," just like everything else he reviews. But look, college humor has never been anything but a disrespect for authority, a love for the outlandish, and a preoccupation with sex. College humor magazine editors have always indoctrinated themselves with their own brand of humor. "It is probably inevitable that the same two-line jokes and the obviously biological cartoons will continue to appear in years to come," wrote John Burns in the intro to *A Treasury of College Humor* in 1950. "The cry of, 'Waiter, there's a fly in my soup' will echo endlessly down through the ages, and the drawing of the girl whose body is a replica of a brick outhouse will be considered devastatingly original by every sophomore cartoonist—now and forever. . . ."

All I'm trying to say is that when you come right down to it, college humor magazines have been imitative since their inception. They started out in the late 1800s as carbon copies of the old *Life*, the finest satirical weekly of its day. As the influences on college humor magazines went from *Puck* to *Judge* to *Ballyhoo* and back again, the Charles Dana Gibson ripoffs eventually became John Held, Jr., imitations. When Henry Luce bought the old *Life* in October 1936 and changed it into the papaya it is now, college humor magazines quickly shifted allegiance to the *New Yorker*, only to find themselves filled with takeoffs of E. B. White's "Talk of the Town" and cartoons by ersatz Peter Arnos and Charles Addamses right through the 1950s. Later on the college humor magazines turned into crude versions of *Zap Comics*, and today the emphasis is on early *National Lampoon* (before it became a scatological version of *Mad*) with imitations of M. K. Brown, B. Kliban, Sam Gross, Doug Kenney, Henry Beard, Chris Miller, and Michael O'Donoghue. While some readers might argue "imitation is the sincerest form of flattery," few know Charles Coleb Colton coined the phrase. Most would mistake Colton as a low tar cigarette.

College humor magazines aren't just derivative, they're derisive. They create havoc, cause commotion, and occasionally stir up trouble too. Let's take a closer look.

The Stanford Chaparral's spring 1981 issue featured a parody of the San Francisco *Chronicle's* Datebook supplement. The cover story spoofed TV's "Dallas" with the headline "Who Shot RR?" over a photograph of Ronald Reagan. The issue went on sale at nine in the morning (California time), just one hour before the assassination attempt in Washington, D.C. The story was picked up by Bay Area papers, UPI, and AP, and the following day it attracted the attention of local ABC, CBS, and NBC-TV affiliates. The result? Hate mail. Lots of nasty hate mail.

Nor was that the *Chappie's* first brush with controversy. A year before, the editors had sneaked into the printers of the *Stanford Daily*, the campus newspaper, late one night just as the paper was being put to bed. They substituted a front-page photograph of themselves in full bowling regalia, and slapped down the caption, "Tragedy Strikes the Bowling Team: The members of Stanford's bowling team were killed last night in a plane crash en route to the

NCAA bowling championships in Terre Haute, Indiana. Details in Monday's Daily." The editor of the *Stanford Daily* explained the episode on page one of Monday's issues, claiming "the damage to the reputation of this newspaper is irreparable" and asking for financial restitution from the *Chapparal* and for the editors responsible to be tossed from school. The result? The staff of the newspaper turned against the editor, and CBS news cited the prank in a story on abuse of the media.

Such honors were not bestowed on the *Chapparal* alone. The cover of the *Duke Pravda's* April 1980 premier issue, "Getting Off On Duke," pictured a woman sitting on the shoulders of a statue of James B. Duke in what some might misconstrue as an obscene act. The Duke Student Publications Board, made up of administrators and undergraduates, censured the editors for acting in bad faith. The Dean of Students called the magazine's cover "low-brow and vulgar," and, in a fire-and-brimstone speech before the Publications Board, Robert Young, chairman of the Religious Life Committee and Chaplain of the University, condemned *Pravda* for "defying the covenant of the brethren of Duke University." Finally, by acclamation, the Duke Student Government voted to send letters of apology to each member of the Duke family for any offense that may have been caused by the cover photograph.

In March 1980, the *Common Good,* the campus humor magazine at St. John's University, was officially condemned as "blasphemous" and banned from the private, nonsecular campus for publishing a fake editorial, "Wednesday is Sundae," comparing communion with Carvel ice cream cone promotion. The University president, Reverend Joseph T. Cahill, called the article ". . . incompatible with Catholic values and contrary to Catholic faith and doctrine so as to offend the faithful and cause scandal." He ordered security officers to confiscate all available issues. Later, he ordered the *Common Good* to cease publication and instructed the school Office of Student Development to evict the publication from its office. The *Common Good* was forced underground, and Cahill shut the books. "There's no newspaper in the country that can print that trash and get away with it," he argued, provoking us to reprint it here in its entirety. Then again, this isn't a newspaper, so he may have a point.

On November 3, 1979, the *Cornell Lunatic* sold fake football programs to unsuspecting Homecoming game fans. The University's athletic department, which prints and sells the official programs, charged the magazine's editor (yours truly) with violations of the campus code of conduct, including forgery of a letter of permission from the University's Vice President of Campus Affairs. Although permission to sell the parody program wasn't needed in the first place, the editor was threatened with expulsion. But Cornell's Judicial administrator decided to settle the case before *Lunatic* members could mock the University's judicial system at a scheduled open hearing, and the editor agreed to receive a written reprimand from the University. But not before the news went out over AP, UPI, and ABC-TV in Philadelphia.

In October 1976, a questionable cover of the *Glassboro Venue,* illustrating Agriculture Secretary Earl Butz' heinous statement that "the colored" of America wanted only "loose shoes, tight pussy, and a warm place to shit," outraged campus minority leaders. They demanded that the issue be destroyed, *Venue's* charter be revoked, the magazine's six editorial board members resign, and a letter of apology be aired, all voluntarily. The issue was withdrawn from distribution, the editors apologized, and 1,500 copies that had not yet been released were sent out with blank covers. University President Mark Chamberlain and members of the Glassboro State College Board of Trustees denounced the magazine. The Student Government of Glassboro met to decide whether to cut off the $11,000 funds for the publication and revoke its charter. After hearing testimony that such action would constitute violation of the first amendment, the student government backed off, and the

Venue received an official reprimand. The Associated Press carried the news and the story crept into *New Jersey Monthly, Editor and Publisher,* and *The New York Times* before the trouble was resolved.

It all goes to show one thing. If there wasn't any money in the college humor game, we just wouldn't keep at it. So maybe Bennett Cerf, Allen Ginsberg, Ed Koren, Herman Wouk, Rockwell Kent, and Ad Reinhardt worked on the *Columbia Jester* for the mere purpose of entertaining their classmates. Telling my landlord that Theodor Geisel worked on the Dartmouth *Jack O'Lantern,* that Rube Goldberg cartooned for the *California Pelican,* and that F. Scott Fitzgerald, Jimmy Stewart, and Whitney Darrow got their start on the *Princeton Tiger* isn't going to pay the rent. But, hey, James Thurber worked on the *Ohio State Sundial,* S.J. Perelman edited the *Brown Jug,* and George Jean Nathan managed the *Cornell Widow.* Art Buchwald worked for the *U.S.C. Wampus,* Mort Walker cartooned for the *Missouri Showme,* and Max Shulman wrote for the *Minnesota Ski-u-mah.* They all hit the jackpot, as did a slew of others who became insurance salesmen. So we keep reassuring ourselves that four years of horseplay might just end up putting some cabbage in our wallets. Of course, we don't have to convince you of that; we've got your money now.

Messrs. Holt, Rinehart and Winston may think they've duped you into dishing out your hard-earned savings for a well-marketed hodgepodge of clippings from college humor magazines that were slapped together in one night. That may be true, but they're all dead anyway. Actually we selected the best material through a celebrated humor pageant, where it all came down to the swimsuit competition. We also had access to a Humorvac 4000, an intricate network of computers programmed with punchlines from every college humor magazine in the nation, captions to every conceivable cartoon, and departing times for several Eastern airline shuttles. Our data banks overflowed with slapstick statistics. We graphed non sequiturs and analyzed double entendre flow charts. We had everything we needed to misquote inappropriate sources, cite inapplicable definitions, and concoct false conclusions.

After the drugs wore off, our publishers told us to stop clowning around and group our selections into some sort of thematic arrangement. So we shuffled the papers around and gave every forty pages an innocuous chapter heading while trying not to spill any of the Dom Perignon. We were in the conference room trying to figure out how to blast *Zappa at the Fillmore* through Holt's intercom system while someone from design was hounding us about whether the book should be typeset in Souvenir 12-point or Baskerville 9-point. Just then, some irate office manager type burst in, demanding an explanation for the three crates of Ring-Dings that had just been delivered to the front desk, and, well, we lost some material in the shuffle. That may help to explain why over a hundred pages are missing from the original manuscript. Fortunately, that doesn't change the number of G's in our contract.

So, if you really want to get a run for your money, you're going to have to read this thing from cover to cover. There's pathos in every prepositional phrase, double meaning in each syllable, and hyperbole in even the least significant semicolon. And if you want to get the last laugh, you've got to wring out every last drop. Because we've just spent your weekly allowance to make the final payments on a Winnebago. And we're not about to give it back. Varoom!

Joey Green

"You"re So Immature

Georgie is a little monkey. He lives in the house of the man with the orange hat. All monkeys are curious. But no monkey is as curious as Georgie. That is why his name is Curious Georgie.

"I have to split the scene," said the man with the orange hat. "Be a good little monkey while I am out. Try some of the Columbian I bought for you until I come home. Just don't get too curious, you little monkey." And the man went out.

It was a lot of fun for Georgie to smoke the pot the man left for him. He smoked a little, and then a little more, and then a little more, and then a little more.

Georgie got very high. And he felt very good. He began to do a lot of tricks. He even did a little dance.

Georgie wanted to broaden his horizons. Where did the man keep his acid? Georgie was curious.

He looked all over the house. There was a closet in the room. Georgie looked through the closet for the acid. He found a lot of things in there. But he did not find the man's acid. Georgie looked for it here and looked for it there. Where was the acid? Georgie took all the drawers out of the dresser. He took all the toys out of the toy box. Georgie looked everywhere. But he could not find the acid.

The room was a mess. Georgie sat down. He had been a bad little monkey. Why was he always so curious? Why did he make such a mess of the room? His trumpet was on the floor. His racing cars and building blocks were all over. Now he had to clean up the room and he could not trip. The marijuana made Georgie hungry.

Georgie got up. He had to have something to eat. Maybe there was some food in the refrigerator. Georgie went to the kitchen to look. Yes, there was something to eat and it was something good too. It was a sugar cube.

Georgie took the sugar cube and went back in to the other room. Georgie sat down and ate the sugar cube. Soon he began to see colors. Then he looked around. The room wavered back and forth. Georgie turned on the man's record player. He put on a record by Jimi Hendrix. Georgie felt unusual. He could taste the music. Soon he began to imagine that he was a banana. He did not want anyone to peel him, so he hid under the bed. This was good acid.

Soon the man in the orange hat came back with a fat lady. "What a mess," said the man. Georgie was hiding under the bed. "Where is Georgie?" asked the man. "Maybe you should go out and look for him," suggested the lady. "I'll wait . . . ."

The man did not want to hear anymore. He ran to his car and hopped in. "I'm going to kill that little fellow," he said. Georgie stayed under the bed.

The lady did not see Georgie. She took off her clothes, turned out the light, and got in the bed to wait for the man with the orange hat. Georgie had seen this lady before. But now she was a bright shade of red. This was good acid. Georgie had seen the man in the orange hat in bed with this lady before. He was curious. Georgie crawled out from under the bed. What if the man came back? Maybe he would never come back.

The lady had fallen asleep. Georgie climbed into the bed. She woke up. But the room was dark so she could not see. "Orange hat man, you're back," said the lady. Georgie could not talk so he did not say anything. "Gee, you're like a monkey in bed," said the lady. "Ooh, ooh, ooh." Georgie liked the lady. The acid was good too.

Just then the man with the orange hat came back. He turned on the light and saw Georgie and the lady getting down. "Georgie," screamed the man, "I'm going to blow your little brains out." The man opened a drawer and took out his gun. Georgie would never, never be curious again.

The genre of the fairy tale is one of the best known and, unfortunately, one of the most insipid. As a tool of education the fairy tale, because of its inherent simplicity, has limitless possibilities. If the instructive value of the fairy tale could be expressed in a more intelligent style, its didactic nature could further educate an already captive audience.

Many famous authors have told fairy tales in their own unique style. We researched such authors, and, unable to single out one example from our findings, compiled the following version of "Jack and the Beanstalk."

Catcher in the Beanstalk

I must have told you about his guy, Jack. I probably mentioned him before, I'm sure of it. He lived with his mother. I realize that's not the greatest living situation in the world. I know I could never do it. I'm really glad to be at school and to be independent and all. If there's one thing I hate, it's having to live with my mother, for chrissakes. She never lets me do half the things I do now, like sitting around shooting the bull.

Anyway, I was telling you about Jack and his old lady. They lived in this tumble-down shack because they were poor. And I mean poor. Sometimes they wouldn't even get to eat. You know when you're broke you can always borrow money from someone in the dorm. I know I do. And you can always get something to eat. At least you can order a pizza or something, for chrissakes.

Jack and his mom didn't have any cash. All they had was this cow. At least they owned something aside from their tumble-down shack. I don't know why it had to be a cow. Can you imagine owning a cow? Or drinking milk from it? You wouldn't even know where it's been. I know I wouldn't drink it. What I like is soda or some kind of juice. You can keep your cow milk. I won't have anything that's not out of a bottle.

But Jack couldn't get enough of the stuff, being a growing boy and all. He drank it night and day. And the cow couldn't give Jack enough milk. I mean, cows can only make so much milk for a guy. Why Jack wanted to drink so much milk sure beats the hell out of me. All I can tell you is I'm glad as hell I don't have to drink cow's milk and live with my mother in the poor house like Jack.

Beans and Time

It therefore became the imperative project of the old woman (Mother-as-such) to begin a process that would lead to the acquisition of substance requisite to the organic maintenance of Jack (Being-the-son-of). Thus, the man (Dasein, Being there) was forced to make the non-phenomenal decision toward the cow (Moo-sein, Being-in-the-barn) consequent to its disposition. Mother-as-

such possessed nothing of sensitivity or futurity, and presented the possibility of Steaks-for-a-week-as-such. But within the perceived ontical environment of Being-the-son-of, the death (or, more accurately, the finite process, demising) of Being-in-the-Barn would create a schism of certain hermeneutical bonds, demanding a temporary state of anxiety. Whereupon the essential question of a remunerative evaluation (although relativistic in nature) of Being-in-the-barn replaces the a priori opposition (Not-Being-into).

The Happy Hoofer

It was foolish to argue. As his mother was explaining how he should sell the cow, Jack could not ignore the sensitive movements of her full, red lips or the sensual heaving of her still-ample breasts. Memories of his childhood flashed in his mind, of the days when his loving and ravenous tongue had caressed those soft nipples, and the soft gasps she would emit when the pleasure became too great.

He was tying a rope around the neck of the cow when he first felt a strange tingling in that delicate spot below his belly, and began to worry that his mother might notice the ever-increasing bulge that now distended his torn yet formfitting jeans. She had noticed, and could hardly keep her eyes off it. As Jack led the cow away, his mother's gaze was drawn to his firm behind as it danced and swayed beneath his tight pants.

And the cow noticed too. As drops of fresh milk began to glisten at the ends of her firm, young udders, she thought of the way his warm hands had felt that morning, gently teasing and urging the last drops of fluid from her longing body.

They didn't get 100 feet down the road before Jack, in the heat of passion, wrapped his body around the cow and lay her softly in a pile of leaves at the side of the road. . . .

"Cigarette?" Jack offered, a teasing smile still visible on his lips.

The Bagavad Gita

And so it was that Jack came from the house of his mother into the city of man to sell the sacred cow that he had brought with him.

On a street of the city he saw an old man. His face revealed that he was of great age and wisdom; his body bore the scars of renunciation of the ways of society: three skin diseases, running sores, and a violent cough. But in his serene gaze Jack marked well the bliss of a holy man.

"O, blessed saint, is there a place in the city of man where young boys named Jack go to sell cows that they have brought from the house of their mother?"

"Ah, my son who knows so little, but what does it mean to sell, or indeed, to transfer? For has it not been written that over all the things of earth Lord Shiva is master? We can no sooner sell that which is of Shiva than we can extinguish the flame of righteous guidance, that burns on the mountain of everlasting hygiene, overlooking the sea of the expanding waistband."

"Well spoken, holy man! For the first time I have truly grasped the meaning of the ancient scriptures, not to mention several George Harrison songs. But, lo, I am still hungry. How could this be?"

"But what is this thing, hunger? Is it no more than a manifestation of mankind's inability to transcend the bound of time, space, and unsightly bulges? Can we not thus see the illusory nature of hunger?"

The holy man had spoken truly, but unfortunately young Jack couldn't keep up with the double negatives, and fell into depression. Seeing this, the holy man comforted the boy with a gift of 12 magic but poisonous beans, from which it is said strange things would grow, and further showed his wisdom and grace by absconding with the cow that had been the source of such sadness for Jack.

How Jack Brought the Beans to His Mother and What Happened Afterward

After Jack left the city with the beans, he decided to make his way home, pondering all the while the strange things that occurred in the world around him. When Jack reached his home he saw his mother standing near the house, staring off into the distance.

"It is you," exclaimed his mother. "You must come inside and eat and tell me what has become of the cow."

"But first," replied Jack, "you must tell me what has happened to our house for I notice that there is little left of it but a few bricks, and that some terrible woe has befallen you, for I notice that you are bleeding from the cheeks and that your right leg has been torn asunder from your body. Tell me then, mother, what has passed?"

His mother went on to tell him the story of how the Bulgars and the Turks had come to the village, disemboweled all of the men with their sharp swords, raped all of the women, and destroyed all of the houses.

"But now things are for the best, as they are gone, and though I am in pain and near death, I am alive and happy. Now eat, and tell me what has become of the cow."

Jack was confused and pondered awhile the strange events of the world, wondering how his mother could be so happy when it appeared that the utmost woe had befallen her. He then ate the delicious roast dog his mother had prepared, and told her the story of the city, the cow, and the magical beans. Hearing this, his mother flew into a violent rage.

"How could you be so foolish, for now I have nothing to live for," upon which she immediately disemboweled herself with the carving knife.

"Oh, what sorrow there is in this strange world," thought Jack, finishing his drumstick of dog. "But all is for the best as I still have my beans and lots of delicious dog to eat."

Jack planted the beans and fell asleep, wondering if there was somewhere, another land where people were good and happy. When he awoke he found the beans had grown into a large stalk. Jack pondered the beanstalk and then climbed up to its top where he found another strange and different world.

"Perhaps in this unknown place all men are happy and everything is for the best," thought Jack.

Steal This Beanstalk

Now this part of the story may sound a little weird, but trust me, it's all real.

You see, at the top of this beanstalk is some other world or something, with fields of clouds, and all sorts of other crazy things you'd probably never believe. You'd probably say I was tripping or something, but I know I wasn't because this stuff was weirder than anything I seen tripping. Especially this castle, it was really huge and sitting in the middle of the field. I know it was a really dumb thing to do, but I decided to check it out.

So I go inside the place, and wow, everything in there is really big, you know, like the sets of the T.V. show "Land of the Giants"—remember it? Anyway, the next thing I know I hear this real loud noise and turn around to see this real, live giant! I'm not kidding, just like the ones in the fairy tales, a fucking-out-loud giant! Well, the first thing I do is get the hell out of there because this guy really gives me the creeps. I'm not usually a negative guy, but this dude was like a giant-size cop or something, and I was getting real bad vibes, because I was still a little stoned, and in no mood for dealing with thirty-foot heat. So I go into this closet and figure I'll lay back and smoke a joint and wait till the big guy takes off.

I was toking up and thinking what a weird day it had been, when I notice, over in a corner, this thing they call a harp (which is like an electric guitar, kind of, except there's more strings and no electricity), and it's got this chick's head stuck on it, and also there's this big, white duck. And then the chick on the guitar starts talking! And she's telling me how this giant guy is really a drag and how it's a pain in the ass to live up there in the clouds because it's hard to get good drugs, and all like that. Then she tells me that the big duck can lay these eggs made out of gold, and that I could have some if I help them escape. So I told her that I just scored a pound of this really fine gold and didn't need any more, and almost freaked when she said she meant real gold, you know, the metal stuff.

So right then I grabbed them both and made a run for it, because I figured I could use a new amp and maybe some "Yes" albums, some of their earlier stuff. . . .

Exodus, Chapter 31, Verses 1-5

1 And it came to pass, that Jack did run forth and through the temple of the Giant, that he might bring salvation unto Goose and Harp.

2 But, lo, then did the Giant, with sharp ear and short wit, hear them, and even as unto a hammered thumb did he pronounce great oaths, and did call upon false idols, among these, Elvis, that He should bring evil unto them.

3 And fe fi fo fum said he unto them, though he knew not what it meant, nor has anyone known before or since, not even God.

4 And then did Jack go forth amidst the furnishings, that he might hide among them, and under them find shelter. And Goose and Harp they went forth also, they being carried by Jack.

5 And frightful noises did they make, as even unto disco, that they did harken the Giant, and yea, then did Jack bearing heavily upon Goose and Harp beat it from the dwelling, and unto the fields did he then run.

blood of englishman

jack crossed (with
in hand; fowl creatrix of the root
of evil, also
singing strings, still
,unplucked, also)
the fields
of clouds'n wheat'nclouds

and yet behind: gianTrampling
fefifofumfefifofum,
resounding, and
him thinking:

i surely die carrying
what?(these in question?in
question) but a-
head:the head of that(the other)
green giant: forgotten
stalk, no longer
stalk!escape!

:thinking that he was, and
to take leave, taking
to those(the other)leaves, soon,
still sooner, de-
scend-
ing.

A Midsummer's Night Bean

Pistachio: Speak, sir for thou young Jack hast seen;
And descending was he from such dreading air
That, methinks, his ugly squashed doom
Be soon and nigh, and pretty quick at that!
For that large man with fo fum on his lips
Hast made some timbersome, conjunctive gains
While through the beaned verdure ever-falling.
And in his arms, regard, he still enfolds
That noisy lyre (no Apollo's voice!),
And ever yet that squealing, gilded layer
(With bacon, aye, the finest banker's breakfast!),
That, again, methinks him wasted quick.

Omelet: One damn cannot I give for what thee
    thinks!
For view, our Jack safely grounded has just been,
And runs he with such haste for sharpened axe
That, I fear, your Giant sorely plopped.
And see him swing with sweaty, beaded brow
(Glad he used Dial that Jack must be!),
And see the vine a-tremble and a-sway
As mine own knees have done preceding love:
And witness further how that stalk of green
Doth from its sturdy pose decline and fall,
As has, engaged in love, mine member done.
How like that ended Giant is love then,
When passion softs e'en the biggest men. (Exeunt.)

Research Paper, Conclusion

In sum, it can be seen that, having returned to his mother with the harp that sang and the goose that laid the golden eggs, Jack did fulfill all of his original objectives, and thus did terminate his adventure. From the preceding texts it can be inferred that, given the nature of his turmoil and the subsequent abatement thereof, along with the immense financial augmentation incurred by his household in general, Jack indeed improved the quality of his life on practical, as well as aesthetic, levels. It is, therefore, with unqualified pleasure and justifiable emphasis that the author exclaims at the end of the work, "And they lived happily ever after!"

MURDERS IN POOH MORGUE

You have already been introduced to Pooh and his friends. At least that is what Pooh told me when we entered the café and Ginnie Woolf and Fanny Forster huddled very, very close together and said, "Look what the dog dragged in," which was very impolite as Pooh is *not* a dog, as you very well know, but a bear, and a very nice one too, and he didn't *drag* me in, but we walked arm in arm. We talked over Shirley Temples, though Pooh ate my cherry when I wasn't looking, for he is still a growing bear, and he asked me if there were lots of talking animals in my new book and I said, "Yes, of course," and he said, "Why don't you write about singing *flowers* or dancing *beer* bottles?" and I said, "Because flowers don't sing, silly, and bottles don't dance, but animals do talk," and Ginnie and Fanny tittered, and Pooh said he was going to take up Hemingway which doesn't sound as much fun as rugger.

Then I thought I heard Pooh say I was a dumb sap, but I have never been a tree, despite what my friends say, and so I asked Pooh what he had said, and he said, "You're a comely chap," and I thanked him very much. So we are again friends, and he has invited me to his house to see his shotguns, and he is much more fun than Christopher Robin. And before you begin this story you may want to know why he is called Pooh, and so I will tell you. He is called Pooh because that is his name.

CHAPTER I
IN WHICH *Piglet and Pooh Make a Startling Discovery*

Eeyore was dead and it was a lovely morning for a walk so when Piglet came across Eeyore dead and gushing bright red blood in the bright morning sun he was surprised indeed.

"I must tell Pooh," he said to himself, there being no one else around.

Winnie-the-Pooh sat in his favorite armchair polishing his favorite shotgun with honey from his favorite honey jar, the fifth—or was it the sixth?—when Piglet burst in all frazzled, and in such a tizzy that Pooh dripped honey all over his toes.

"Pooh! Pooh! Oh, guess what!" Piglet shrieked.

"What I guess is that you are here, Piglet, and have made me drip honey all over my favorite toes. Bother, you little pig."

"Oh, I'm so sorry," squealed the little porker apologetically.

Pooh was incensed, but put his shotgun away. Instead, he felt he would be happier stuffing Piglet headfirst into a pot of honey. He grabbed him by his little throat and waved him menacingly over the sweet-smelling earthen jar.

"Pooh! Wait! I must tell you about Eeyore!"

Pooh showed concern. He loosened his grip and Piglet thudded-adudded onto the floor. Piglet opened his mouth to say "Oh!" or "Ouch!" but we will never know which was to come out, for instead of either came nothing.

"What's happened to Eeyore?" Pooh demanded.

Piglet stood silent and open-mouthed and picked splinters from his left ham.

"Have you lost your voice?" asked Pooh hopefully.

Piglet nodded frantically.

"Well, then, we must look for it," Pooh said regally. They hunted up and down the house, inside the cupboards and under the rug, but to no avail. Piglet's voice was nowhere to be found, so Piglet tried to talk with his little pig body. He put his cloven hoof to his ear and sprawled on the ground, writhing and clutching himself until he finally lay still as a stone.

"Eeyore's become an actor?" asked Pooh.

Piglet shook his head. He grabbed Pooh by the paw and yanked him out of his house and down the road till they saw a sight so sad they sat and sobbed—I hope you never see a sight so sad as this sight they sadly saw.

Eeyore was dead and the blood gushing from his head was red as raspberry jello. Or was it cherry? Piglet hoped it was cherry for Eeyore had always hated raspberries. He remembered how Eeyore used to say, "I hate raspberries." Now Eeyore would no longer say, "I hate raspberries." Neither would he ever say, "Hallo," "Goodbye," or "I'm lonely." For a moment Piglet thought, "Maybe it's better to be rid of the silly ass," but as this is no way to think of your friends living or dead, he blurted out, "Oh, I'm sorry, Eeyore."

Eeyore didn't answer, which Piglet thought was very impolite until he remembered not only that Eeyore was slovenly, dim-witted, and inarticulate, but that he was also dead.

"You've found your voice," said Pooh.

"No he didn't! He didn't say anything!" wailed Piglet as tears sprang to his eyes.

"No, *you* have found your voice," said Pooh, exasperated.

"Eeyore . . . is dead," said Piglet, and cried and cried.

"Bother. He's bleeding all over the nice clean grass, too. They should have made *him* the pig, not you."

"Look, Pooh! What do you think happened?"

"Suviously Obvicide," said Pooh quickly. "I mean, obviously suicide."

"But why?" cried Piglet, "Oh, why, oh why?"

"Put yourself in his place," said Pooh. Piglet lay down on top of Eeyore's corpse. "No, no," said Pooh. "Get up. Imagine you are Eeyore. If brains were dynamite you wouldn't have enough to fart. You're not only as silly as an ass, you *are* one. What's your alternative?"

"I see," said Piglet, putting on his glasses. "But . . . but Pooh, there's *no gun*! Someone else must have done it unless Eeyore shot himself, brought the gun home, and came back to die."

"Habviously what oppened," said Pooh nervously.

"No! I don't believe it!" cried Piglet. "I'm going to find Christopher Robin. This is murder! Oh, 'tis murder most foul! Don't worry, Eeyore! Justice will be done!" And he ran off to find Christopher Robin, bringing home the bacon as he ran.

Pooh watched the little ham tripping down the road. "Oh, bother," he said to himself.

Public toilet terror

CHAPTER II
IN WHICH *More Startling Discoveries Are Made*

Christopher Robin was startled when Piglet burst into his house.

"Oh, would you like to stay for tea?" asked Christopher Robin.

"No, thank you, Christopher Robin," said Piglet, now out of breath, "but I must tell you what happened! You must come with me! Eeyore's *dead* and he's gushing raspberry jello."

"Oh, no. Let's not go see Eeyore, for I'm a sensitive little boy."

"But we *must* find out the murderer!" said Piglet in a frenzy.

"Yes, but how?" asked Christopher Robin.

"Well, let's ask everybody if they did it, and if someone answers yes, well, then that's the murderer!"

"Splendid!" said Christopher Robin.

So Piglet and Christopher went to visit Owl who invited them in for jam starts and gin. "Hallo, Piglet," he said. "Hallo, Christopher Robin."

"Hallo," they said. "Have you heard," continued Piglet, "that Eeyore has been murdered?"

"Hoo?"

"Eeyore," said Christopher Robin.

"Hoo-hoo!" said Owl.

"And we were wondering, if you, ah, *did* it," babbled Christopher Robin, blushing.

"Hoo-HHAH!" said Owl. "Oh dear me, no. No, not I. Let's go ask Tigger!"

So Owl and Piglet and Christopher Robin wandered over to Tigger's, singing a song as they skipped. And the song they sang skipping sounded so:

Oh Eeyore's dead, oh Eeyore's dead
His empty brain's laid bare
He bled so red, he bled and bled;
He was no Fred Astaire.

And so they arrived at Tigger's house, and Tigger said, "Hallo! Are you here to be eaten?"

"Oh *yes*," cried Christopher Robin until Piglet and Owl jabbed him in the tum and he doubled over.

"No, no, Tigger," said Piglet and Owl. "We want to ask you a little something. Remember Eeyore?"

"The little ass?" said Tigger.

"Well, Eeyore's dead," said Owl.

"Oh, my," said Tigger. "Is he still fresh?"

"He's been murdered!" squealed Piglet. "And we want to know if *you* did it."

"Oh, my, no," said Tigger. "Murder spoils the meat. Adrenalin and all that, you know. But I'll help you look. Let's go ask Rabbit!"

Everyone agreed that Rabbit should be asked—it would be impolite to excuse him. So they skipped down the road, singing their song, high-kicking until they reached Rabbit's. They knocked on the door, but there was no answer. They knocked again. No answer.

"Oh, Rabbit," they called, and opened the door.

Pieces of Rabbit lay all over the living room. One ear was on the telly, the other on the coffee table. His four feet were on the Mah Jongg board, whiskers were strewn about, and his fluffy cottontail sat in the middle of the floor.

"Well," said Tigger, "at least there's a lucky Rabbit's foot for everybody." And everybody took one.

"We need more help," cried Piglet. "Oh, let's find Pooh!"

When everyone arrived, Winnie-the-Pooh was sitting in his favorite armchair, polishing his favorite chainsaw with honey from his favorite pot, the fifth. Or was it the sixth?

"Oh, Pooh!" squealed Piglet.

"What is it now?" asked Pooh.

"Pooh," said Owl, "first Eeyore, and now—now Rabbit is dead, see?" And they all held up their Rabbit's feet.

"So I've heard," said Pooh. "And I know who the murderer is."

"You do?" they all gasped.

"And what's more," beamed Pooh, "he's in this room."

Everybody looked at everybody else very, very nervously. No one moved.

"And there he is!" exclaimed Pooh very loudly, and pointed his finger right at Christopher Robin.

CHAPTER III
IN WHICH Christopher Robin is Tried and Everybody Lives Happily Ever After

A trial had never been held before in the forest, but all agreed that Kanga and Baby Roo would make the perfect court—there being a shortage of participants, since everybody was either covering the trial for the press or selling souvenirs (except, of course, for Eeyore and Rabbit, who were dead). Pooh was to be lawyer for both sides. Everyone was excited.

"Let's start!" shouted Kanga, pounding Baby Roo with her gavel. "Where's the liar for the prosecution?"

"I am the liar," said Pooh proudly.

"And the liar for the defense?"

"I am he too," said Pooh, even prouder.

Christopher Robin hung by his feet from a rope tied to the chandelier. Now he was cut loose, and he thudded-adudded to the courthouse floor.

Tigger was the first to take the stand, and after he swore to tell the whole truth and not to eat the judge, Pooh asked him, "Tigger, do you know who killed Eeyore and Rabbit?"

"Oh, yes," said Tigger bouncily.

"Who, then?" led Pooh.

"Christopher Robin, of course," Tigger replied.

"And how do you know?"

"Why, Pooh, you told us yourself!" Tigger announced boldly.

"Next witness," said Pooh.

Now Owl took the stand.

"Owl," asked Pooh, "how do you know Christopher Robin is the murderer?"

"Why Pooh, you said so. And you'll notice Christopher Robin's head is much, much wider than it is long, a true sign of a criminal psychopath."

"Next witness," beamed Pooh.

Piglet took the stand.

"Okay, porkpie, what happened on the day in question?"

"Well, Eeyore was dead and it was a lovely day, and I ran to Christopher Robin's, and he welcomed me in after I surprised him, and he was wearing his dress, and . . ."

"Did you say dress?" Pooh asked, considering the implications of Christopher Robin's androgynous smock.

"Why, yes," said Piglet. "And a very nice one it was, too."

"Next witness," chortled Pooh with an ear-to-ear grin.

Christopher Robin sheepishly advanced to the stand.

"Oh, Pooh," cried Christopher Robin, "you know I didn't do it. You know that."

"We shall see what we shall see," chuckled Pooh. "Do you recognize this body?"

Eeyore's corpse was wheeled out, still gushing a teensy bit.

"Gaaaah. . . .Eeyore," gagged Christopher Robin.

"So!" Pooh shouted. "You admit you know this body. You, Christopher Robin, are the murderer of Eeyore and Rabbit, and you shall pay!"

"No! It's not true," Christopher Robin sobbed, but Kanga had already beaten Baby Roo senseless with the gavel, and Christopher Robin was dragged away screaming to the electric chair.

The aroma of freshly cooked little boy soon spread all over the Forest, and everybody burst joyfully out of the courtroom to picnic all day. Pooh went home to polish his shotgun collection, Kanga pummeled Baby Roo a little while longer, Tigger ate Owl, and Piglet found himself at the wrong end of one of Pooh's shotguns.

Baby Showers

Savory Seuss

GREEN EGGS AND HAM

By Dr. Seuss. 62 pages. Beginner Books. $3.95.

Green Eggs and Ham, a hard-hitting novel of prose and poetry, was originally conceived in the early 60's during the height of anti-government sentiment. In our current atmosphere of rapidly changing international politics, the novel has taken on new significance. As were most of Theodore Geisel's earlier books, *Green Eggs and Ham* was published under the pseudonym Dr. Seuss, a name intending to invoke the respectability of graduate study, with the omnipotent power of the Greek gods. Seuss' current work has been profoundly influenced by some of his earlier books, most notably *The Cat in the Hat, On Beyond Zebra,* and *If I Ran the Zoo*, in which he initially explores the dynamic rhyme schemes and bold imagery which reach a creative peak in *Green Eggs and Ham*. It is clearly one of the Doctor's finest pieces.

The book opens with a two-page, full-color spread in which a diminutive man in a large red hat is seen galloping by perched on the back of a four-legged animal. Clutched tightly in his little hands is a sign bearing the words, "I am Sam." To the observant reader, this immediately conjures up the political emotions of the mid-60's. The man in the red hat represents the United States and his visual insistence that "I am (Uncle) Sam" fits perfectly with the U.S. attitude of ethnocentrism. The beast ridden by Sam clearly represents another country that has fallen under United States' colonialism. Subsequent pages introduce a furtive character in a black hat. This character (actually a dog-like animal) is quickly confronted by Sam carrying another placard reading "Sam I am." This can only represent the classic confrontation and display of self-righteousness that characterized Soviet American relations. The book builds toward a peak of international tension as Sam thrusts forward a lengthy fishing rod-type object (symbolizing trans-Atlantic intervention) bearing a platter of typically American dairy and meat products. Sam poses the question "Do you like Green Eggs and Ham?"

With powerful simplicity, drama, and clarity, Seuss reduces American interference in Soviet affairs to an easily understood gesture. Offended by this American political gesture, the Soviets are undaunted and reply "I do not like them Sam I am, I do not like green eggs and ham," thus setting up the conflict which runs throughout the novel.

Mr. Seuss' poetry and choice of words is equally impressive and serves as a splendid counterpart of the bold symbolism. Often displaying an admirable gift of gab, Seuss leans toward the monosyllabic unipole rather than dabbling in modified polysyllables. In all, his writing style is quick and fluid, making the book impossible to put down. Although it is 62 pages in length, one can read it in five minutes or less. To absorb the full meaning of the poetry, I recommend spending several hours (as I did) carefully combing the book for symbolism.

For some unexplained reason, *Green Eggs and Ham* is not available in several of the area libraries. However the Kirkland Library in Clinton has several copies available. Interestingly enough, the book is found in a side gallery possessing tiny chairs and tables, enabling one to sit within a foot of the ground to fully appreciate the down-to-earth nature of the novel.

Me and Bogey

Roger Maistiff was seven and one night refused to go to bed. There was something good on television. His mother pleaded with him, but he was a stubborn boy.

"Go to bed now," Mother finally said, "or the Bogeyman will come and get you." She was at her wits' end.

"What's a bogeyman?" Roger asked.

"He'll scare you and you won't have anyone to blame but yourself," Mother said shaking her finger.

"But what's he look like?"

"He's the Bogeyman! He doesn't look like anything, just like him! Ask your father!"

Roger asked his father, who sat next to where his mother was standing and smoked a pipe, what a bogeyman looked like. The form behind the newspaper paused briefly. Then the headlines lowered and glasses peered on the small boy. "You'll know him when you see him," he said. "He's big and, um, he's big and going to come and get you, young man, if you don't go to bed right now."

Roger shrugged his shoulders and went back to the television, while his parents, who were both tired and rather wrung out by the whole scene, went up the stairs to bed. In the glow of the T.V., Roger felt quietly guilty. But if someone was coming to get him, he wasn't going to bother changing into pajamas and going to sleep.

At eleven twenty-two, during Eyewitness Sportsview, the Bogeyman came and got him. The big form was casually dressed and he parked his faded blue El Dorado, which boasted stickers on its back window from many different states, near the front door of Roger's house. To avoid waking Roger's parents with the doorbell, he lightly tapped on a window pane next to the door.

"Yes?" Roger said, opening the door.

"Are you Roger Maistiff, who wouldn't go to bed when his parents told him to?" the Bogeyman asked.

"Yes."

"Then I've come to get you." The Bogeyman folded his arms, satisfied. Roger's curious face made the pause an awkward one, however.

"Yes, well," Roger said.

"So, er, let's go!"

"Why?"

"C'mon, I don't know. I'm just supposed to come and get you. Don't ask why. Look, I got the car washed and everything."

Roger walked out to the car, whose fins winked in the light of the streetlamps. "It does look nice," he said. They got in and drove to Stickney's (it was Roger's idea). Over a cup of coffee, which Roger's mother seldom let him drink at home, Roger heard the Bogeyman's secrets of life and his many tales of the cruelty and unfairness done to him and Bogeypeople in general.

"Oh, they were terrible to me when I was growing up," he moaned over Peppermint Tea. ' "Ha, ha, look at the Bogeyman,' they'd always say at school. I was always 'it' and 'last pick.' I was always catching it because of my background. I would go to pick up my date, and the parents would laugh and say, 'You? The Bogeyman's come to get our daughter? Isn't she a little old for you, sonny?' ' The imposing figure dragged heavily on the Camel filter lodged between two fingers.

"Was it always that bad?" Roger asked.

"No—it got worse with affirmative action." He groaned even louder. "You wouldn't believe it, kid. I was such a minority that I *had* to go to college to fill some federal quota. All I wanted in life was to be a good, hard-working Bogeyman and get lots of little children like yourself. And there I was, an English major at a prestigious university. Now my head's so screwed up I don't know what to do." He made a fist and ground out his cigarette and lit another. Roger yawned discreetly.

"Yeah, you're bored and I don't blame you. Here—let me show you a card trick, then I'll take you home." The Bogeyman showed Roger how to make the four jacks come home first and then delivered him to his doorstep. On the way home, Roger sat low in one of the El Dorado's bucket seats and listened intently to a Bob Dylan tape the large driver had popped into a tapedeck which hung beneath the dashboard. "Any day now, any day now, I shall be re-leased," a vehement voice moaned over guitar chords. "This guy speaks to me," the Bogeyman said, thumping his thumbs in time to the music against his steering wheel, "or used to speak to me. He's too busy with God now to care about Bogeymen anymore, dammit."

Roger got out, his bare feet gingerly hopping to the cold sidewalk. "Thank you for the time," he said politely, closing the door. He waved goodbye to the car and trotted to his door, warmed by the thoughts of his new friend.

For the next year, Roger was bad enough so that the Bogeyman came and got him at least twice a week. The man was a moody sort, but he knew a lot of card tricks and was on a first-name basis with all the waitresses in Stickney's.

"Being a kid isn't easy, I know," he said one night, sipping his tea. "When I was your age, my parents told me that a businessman would come and get me if I was bad. No wonder I'm so screwed up."

Other nights he was even more depressed about his fate. "What a rotten, shitty life!" he once moaned, picking at a shiny plastic plant. "I can't do anything right, nothing at all. I should turn it all in and kill myself. I think I will."

"Oh no," Roger gasped. "Don't scare me like that."

"I scared you?" the Bogeyman exclaimed.

"Sure you did. I'd be sad as heck if you didn't come and get me some nights. Mom doesn't let me drink coffee, and you tell good stories."

The Bogeyman was jubilant and nearly upset his tea. "If I scared you, I'm doing something right, for sure. Shit yes, I'm a damn scary Bogeyman, that's what I am! Yee ha!" The Bogeyman was so pleased he taught Roger Gin Rummy and let him win twice that night. "Helen, coffee for the whole house tonight, on my tab," he yelled to a passing waitress.

Two weeks later, Roger was not eating dinner so the Bogeyman, summoned by his parents, would make his inevitable appearance. "Eat your dinner, Roger," Mother said. "Or else. . . ."

"Yes, Roger, you must eat dinner," Father chimed in.

"No thank you, Dad."

"Well then, eat your dinner or you won't get your allowance for a week," Father said.

Roger couldn't believe his ears. "What? Don't you mean that the Bogeyman will come and get me?"

"Don't be silly, son. You're too old now for that nonsense. I suppose you still want quarters from the Tooth Fairy." Roger was silent. The Bogeyman had warned him about the infamous Tooth Fairy, so that he always made sure his baby teeth were "accidentally" lost in apples and down drains as soon as they came out. He could earn his quarters in other ways.

"Now get to bed, young man." Roger went to bed, and the Bogeyman didn't come that night. Or the next. He was no longer welcome, it seemed. Roger remembered the Bogeyman's story about how the parents of his date had said that she was too old for him. He walked to his desk, plush carpeting between his toes, and gently shook the faded green piggy bank that stayed on the table by his bed. He wanted to punish his parents for their unfairness. But allowance wasn't something to be taken lightly. And school kept him busy—there was a lot of it. Then he had a job . . . .

Golden Age Acres was set in a light brown meadow and surrounded by leafy cyprus trees. The main build-

Great Scenes from Childhood

The turtle that died.

ing, where most of the senior citizens sat and slept, was a converted mansion of ancient brown shingles and towering brick chimneys. In the main hallway, which had been smartly remodeled in the most modern of rest home motifs, an elderly man stood urinating on the floor.

A nurse rounded a corner and shouted: "Mr. Maistiff, please!" The old man, who stood silently with his baggy blue pajamas bunched at his knees, did not seem to notice her. "Go to your room please, Mr. Maistiff. We won't have anymore of this!"

The head nurse, who dealt smoothly with every shriveled personality on her floor, appeared in time to see a final spurting shower make ripples on the puddle in the hallway. She sent the younger nurse for some tranquilizer in a hypodermic needle.

"Please put yourself in your pants, Mr. Maistiff," she said casually. "I think you've done quite enough for today. Let's go to bed now, shall we?"

The old man stood fast and hummed softly.

"Mr. Maistiff, go to bed right now or. . . .or. . . ."

"Bogeyman?" the wrinkled face blurted. The head nurse was not the head nurse by a quirk of fate. She caught on quickly. "That's right, Mr. Maistiff, the Bogeyman will come and get you if you do not go to bed immediately and cease this foolishness. . . ." A smack sounded as the old man's buttocks hit the linoleum floor. In a crouch, he looked up at the nurse mischievously.

"Gracious" was all the head nurse could say. "Gracious, gracious, gracious." The hypodermic needle arrived just in time to save both staff and patients of Golden Acres considerable embarrassment.

Roger woke up in his metal bed when a breeze blew in the open window. A strangely familiar face stood over him.

"So what are you waiting for?" he asked Roger. "The car's out front. I waxed it up for the occasion, good as new." Roger smiled and stood up as a new-smelling deck of cards was shuffled in his face.

"Look, if it's all right with you," the Bogeyman said, opening the door, "we'll make a whole evening of it."

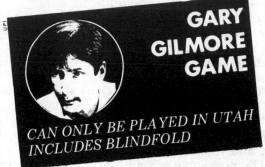

16

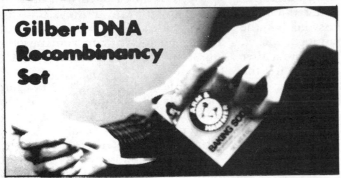

by Edgar Allan Poe

JACK & JILL

Qui n'a plus qu'un moment a vivre
N'a plus rien a dissmuler.

—Quinalt

November, 18—

In the dreary village in which I live, twilight was creeping over every rooftop and every street. There is a certain mystery in the hours that close a mid-summer day. This brief (ah, so brief!) period of time separates day from night like the knife-blade of Man's conscience; twilight is a nebulous thing, obscuring what once seemed clear. One's eyes are wont to play the role of the jester, to perform tricks for entertainment. And although the twilight hours dull the senses—and so the brain—I am certain I witnessed an event of unparalleled terror.

From the home of Lady B— came her child-servant Jack, a native boy from the slums of Calcutta who adopted the Christian name of an English missionary. The lithe youth was accompanied by his younger sister Jill, a frail, beleaguered-looking child. I sat upon a grassy knoll as the two children, each grasping a bucket, gleefully marched up a hill to gather water. This was a daily task for the children, although I never took notice of it but for this twilight. From the distance they could have been a pair of sprites of Nature—or two demons from the spirit world.

Jack groped for surer footholds as the hill became more steep. His sibling wearied and tarried behind him, but Jack's ascension to Destiny continued. And then Fate—oh horrid Fate!—came down upon these innocents like an eagle upon its helpless prey. In one fell swoop, one awful swoop, Fate intervened with uncompromising terror. Powers that be which guide all life, Fate that changes all our goals, why are you unyielding? Why must every knee bend before you?

To question Fate is to question Time, for all is done and all is for naught, despite our feeble attempts to alter what cannot be altered.

Just before he reached the well, Jack lost his footing on loose gravel and fell backwards down the hill, his arms flailing, his hand still grasping his bucket. And though darkness was fast descending, I could perceive the almost inhuman look of horror on his sister's face. Her mouth was open as if to scream, but no sound she made. Her paralysis from fear was total. Jack tumbled and cried out aloud and—terror of terrors—collided with his sister. Their limbs became entwined in a hopeless tangle in their attempt to halt their death descent. The boy's head fell against a jagged rock (Oh Fate, you play your tragedian role so well!), and dashed his brains upon the green grass. His sister knelt over the body of the boy who so recently knew life. Her tears mixed with his blood, and the grass tasted what mortals are made of.

I realized then that death knows no logic. In the most prosaic of life's mundane activities, in the fetching of water, in the cutting of firewood, in the gathering of food, death lurks. Where Fate intercedes, no mortal can resist. Forti nihil difficile!

Historic Moments From the Early Lives of Great Men: Louis Pasteur

"Okay, you washed your hands. So who cares?

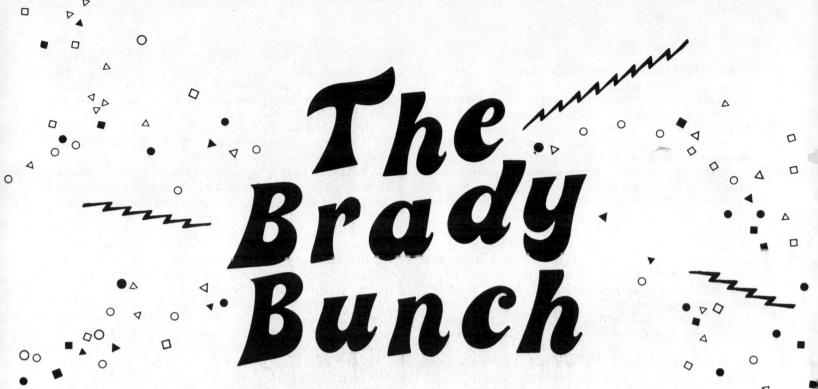

The Brady Bunch

"We're going canoeing! We're going canoeing!" Cindy and Bobby Brady burst into the kitchen where Alice cheerfully sliced shaggy Shep's dinner. She looked up from the steak at their cleanly beaming faces.

"Oh don't take me," she quipped. "I'd sink the whole tub."

"Of course you're going, Alice," Cindy chirped, her golden ponytails bouncing happily. "Yeah," Bobby said, playfully tossing a chunk of meat to Shep. "Dad says everyone's going. Do you need any help packing? Greg and Peter are helping Dad load the canoes, Mom and Marcia are at a charity benefit, and Jan is waterproofing the T.V. Aren't you excited?"

Alice could only smile as she finished preparing dinner. "No, I don't need any help, and yes, I am excited. Now why don't you two run along so I can finish cleaning up." As the two youngsters bounced merrily into the spacious living room, Alice slowly shook her head. "Those kids," she said, polishing the chrome on the refrigerator.

At six o'clock the next morning, bright and early, the shiny green station wagon was loaded up and ready to go. "All right, kids, everyone in the car," Mr. Robert Brady said, finishing off his orange juice. The girls were the last to climb into the back seat. Marcia had called her latest boyfriend to say goodbye.

"Gosh, Marcia," Greg said once they were on the road. "We're only going to be gone for the weekend."

"Yes, I know. But he's kind of special," Marcia said.

"Oooooooooooooooh," Bobby said.

"Quiet, Bobby," Cindy snapped precociously. "I'm sorry, Marcia, he's really quite immature."

"Sure, but that's OK. He'll grow up someday." Marcia smiled kindly at her younger brother.

Bobby said, "I can hardly wait," and told a bad knock-knock joke.

At the wheel, Mr. Brady smiled boyishly. "So kids, is everyone as excited as Bobby is about going canoeing and roughing it in the wilderness?"

"Uh-huh," the chorus sounded.

"By the way, Mom," Jan said, "did you bring your blow drier? I forgot mine."

"Yes, honey," Carol Brady reassured her sprite daughter. "I just hope we brought enough food."

"Don't you worry, Mrs. Brady," Alice said, also in the front seat. "If we eat everything we brought, we'll *roll* down that river."

It took only a little while for the merry ensemble to reach the Wigotdaclapta River. The Brady kids popped out of the station wagon like jack-in-the-boxes when it pulled to a stop at a small gas station. They sniffed jubilantly at the clean mountain air.

"Look at the trees. There are so many of them," Jan said.

"And so much green, too," Peter said. "I love the outdoors."

While Mr. Brady went into the gas station to get directions, the kids wandered up the road adventurously.

"Does anyone hear banjo music?"

"Yeah—it's coming from that house over there." Greg pointed to a small gray shack with a porch, where a slight figure sat plucking a banjo.

"How can anyone go upstairs in a house like that?" Bobby said as they walked closer.

"Ssshhh."

"Yuch," irrepressible Bobby spoke up again, pointing to the banjo player. "He looks kind of weird."

"Quiet, Bobby," Greg said. "He's mongoloid. I read about it in science. We shouldn't make fun of him."

"It's not his fault, Bobby."

"Right, Marcia." Greg nodded his head. "Anyway, Bobby, how would you feel if your head looked liked a peeled grapefruit someone had stepped on?"

"Gosh." Bobby looked down at the ground with shame. He had learned his lesson. Peter played his radio louder than the banjo and everyone cheered up.

"All right, kids, everyone on the shore!"

"Last one down the river's a rotten egg!" The three shiny aluminum canoes slapped the water and the merry crew climbed aboard them, wearing bright orange life preservers.

"Got it!" Mr. Brady exclaimed from the beach, clicking an instamatic camera. Alice nearly tipped a canoe when she got in, but otherwise the launching went smoothly. Within moments, the expedition of three canoes was slipping quickly down the broad river, energetically singing camp songs just slightly out of key.

By the time noon rolled around, everyone was ready for lunch and the eager beavers paddled to the nearest bank. "Last one out's a rotten egg!" Greg and Peter tied the canoes to trees while Marcia and Jan spread the picnic blanket and Cindy chased a chipmunk around a tree, giggling effusively. Mr. Brady put his arm around his wife. "We should do this kind of thing more often," he said. She smiled and compared her hand to a dried leaf.

The picnic was spread and the happy family and maid gathered around the red and white checkered blanket. Suddenly, two older-looking men with whiskers, smudged clothing, and floppy hats burst from the underbrush. One of them was carrying an old gun and the other drooled.

"You must be from the next campsite," Mr. Brady said, extending a hand to the men. "I'm Robert Brady and this is my wife, Carol . . . ."

"Hello."

" . . . and the kids Greg . . . "

"Hi."

" . . . Marcia . . . "

"Hi."

" . . . Peter . . . "

"Hi."

" . . . Jan . . . "

"Hi."

" . . . Bobby . . . "

"Hi there."

" . . . and, of course, Cindy—"

One man took Mr. Brady's hand and bit him between the fingers while the other man pushed him to the ground. Mrs. Brady, obviously flustered, combed Cindy's hair. "Why don't you join us?" she said. "We were just about to have lunch."

"Yes, please do," Marcia said.

"Yeah, Mister," Bobby put in. "I'll even show you my marble collection."

The two strangers kicked the food all over the picnic blanket, getting potato salad on their scrappy boots. "Do you get the feeling that they aren't so hungry?" Alice said, catching a piece of chicken in mid-air and taking a bite out of it. "What's wrong, fellas? If you want a date you can just ask nicely." The second man moved toward the maid and pulled violently on one of her arms. "Oh you cad," she exclaimed. "Pull a little harder and I'll marry you tomorrow." With a push she was on the ground and the man grabbed Greg, who had been whittling a tie clasp, and dragged him behind a nearby fallen tree. "You really know how to hurt a girl," Alice said from the ground.

"Gosh," Peter said. "They've got Greg."

"You a big boy, ain't you?" the man said to Greg.

"Don't y'all try nuthin or move an eyelash," the unclean man with the gun said with a strange accent, "or you be dead real quick."

"Really quick," Marcia corrected. "What's wrong, Mom?" Mrs. Brady looked concerned.

"Honey, do you think the kids should be watching this?" she asked her husband.

"You're right, Carol," he said, brushing dirt off of his windbreaker. "All right, kids, everyone turn around."

"Awwww, Dad."

"You heard me." They turned around.

"But Greg has all the fun!" Bobby said.

"Don't worry, Bobby," Mrs. Brady soothed. "When you grow up, you're going to have just as much fun as Greg."

"Squeal like a pig!" the strange man yelled out from over by the tree.

"Oink, oink," Greg said.

"Cock-a-doodle-doo," Bobby said.

"Baaah-baaaah," Cindy said.

"All right, kids, that's enough," Mr. Brady warned. "The man was talking to Greg."

"Shame about all that lunch, though," Alice said, looking over at the fallen tree. "There're going to be some hungry folks around here after this is over."

"Don't worry, Alice," Cindy said sprightly, picking toadstools. "Marcia, Jan, and I know how to make a scrumptious casserole from natural vegetation. You just leave it to us."

The industrious youngsters prepared the new lunch and the two mountain men were finished just in time to join in the feast.

"How are you, Greg?" Mrs. Brady asked.

"Wow," he said, "That was better than spin-the-bottle."

Mr. Brady looked uncomfortable. "We'll talk about this later, young man," he said. After a big lunch, everyone decided to take naps.

□

Highlights

THE MONTHLY BOOK
for Dentists' Offices

April
1979

WITH THE *Same Cover Every Month*

fun
IF YOU CAN'T READ

HELLO!

Let's Talk Things Over

Have you ever noticed that dogs are funny creatures, and that they do strange things? Like biting people and sniffing each other. These acts are not normal, except for dogs.

Why, you may ask, do dogs behave in such a peculiar manner? Well, the answer is not easy, but science seems to have worked it out. A dog, you must understand, is a creature of habit, an animal living by instinct. He does things without thinking about them.

People always think about something before they do it, but that is because we are not animals. As an example, think about how you feel when you are playing baseball, and you give up a long home run. The next time that batter comes up to hit, don't you just feel like throwing the baseball in his face? You proba-

bly would except you realize that if you miss, he would most certainly pound your face into the dirt with his bat. Well, if you were a dog, you wouldn't think about the bat. You would just throw the ball at his face.

Or, how do you feel when your best friend shows you her new doll from Taiwan which she says is the prettiest doll in the world, and certainly much prettier than all your American dolls? Don't you want to just rip the doll's head off? Well, that's just what a dog would do.

As an animal, a dog always does things without first thinking it over. And most of the things a dog does are low down, miserable, and wretched. That is because a dog usually feels just that way. If all you ever ate were stale Gaines Burgers and Mom's

leftovers, you would not feel so good yourself.

If you were chained up or fenced in all the time, do you think you would be happy? Not at all. True, you would not have to go to school, but you also could not go to the candy store or the movies. How many dogs do you know that have seen *Star Wars* even once?

Have you ever heard someone say they were feeling awfully doggone low? Or heard someone referred to as being lazy as a dog? That's because a dog is like someone living the blues, except they can't express themselves with a harmonica or a saxophone or even a voice. All they can do is bark. Or bite people. Or chew their cud. Do you think that makes them happy? Not at all. It is just something they do.

The Rat:
Our fun, furry friend

If you live in the city, as many of us do, you have probably never seen most of the animals that we talk about in *Highlights*. Last year we decided to feature wildlife that city dwellers are more familiar with. This year, instead of discussing such silly creatures as the woolly mammoth, the smelly skunk, or the prickly porcupine, we are adventuring into the city to find new animal friends.

The urban animal of this month's issue is a member of the exciting rodent family, the rat.

Rats can grow to any size. Some are small enough to fit through the bars of a baby's safety crib, while others are massive enough to take on a healthy Doberman. Some have long tails—but all of them have an insatiable appetite and very sharp teeth.

Rats come in all colors and do different things. Little white rats work for the Food and Drug Administration. They spend most of their time high and are responsible for the inflated cost of quality drugs. Most of them die of some kind of cancer. Medium-sized brown rats live out in the country working to deplete the world's food supply. They are responsible for the growing number of former farmers. Most of them die of indigestion. Huge gray rats are self-employed in the city. For rest and relaxation they strew garbage all over the city, but their real job is to spread disease quickly. Most of these rats die of old age.

Things aren't really as bad as they seem. Sociologists report that rat social climates are improving. The white rats are quickly becoming immune to

cancer and can now enjoy such pleasures as saccharin, nicotine, cyclamates, and THC with almost no dangerous side effects. Brown rats are learning to eat balanced meals (a little starch, some green vegetables, fish or meat, and dairy products), and are no longer falling prey to the dangers of arteriosclerosis, heart attack, or malnutrition. Gray rats are approaching immortality through the evolutionary process.

Yes, rats have come a long way. You can learn from their progress. Remember, children, if you want to succeed in this world, regard everyone as your enemy and be the sneakiest rat in town.

★Teaches empathy for animals

Roofus and Gallant

Roofus cheats at cards when he's losing.

"Sorry, the smallest I've got is a fifty."

Roofus hogs all the blankets.

"I'll turn my electric blanket down to save energy."

Roofus doesn't say thank you.

"I intended to give it all back, your honor."

★ Learning good manners is important in an upwardly mobile society.

THE TIMBERTOES

Winter was here. It was cold inside the Timbertoes' house. "What should we do to warm up?"

"Let's build a fire!" "But we have no fire wood left." "We already burned the kitchen table."

Father and Mother thought. Tommy thought too. But Tommy did not think fast enough.

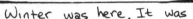

Father unscrewed Tommy's arms. Mother made kindling from Tommy's hair. "What do we burn next?"

The Bears Go Camping

Woozy: "Camping in the winter sure is fun!"
Poozy: " . . . and cold!"

Father: "We'll need to get some wood for the fire."
Mother: "But all the wood is wet!"

Woozy: "Who are you?"
Father Timbertoes: "AAAEEFFHH!! A talking bear!"

Mother: "A puppet . . . a wooden puppet!"
Father: "Quick, grab him!"

Mother: "Now we shall be warm."
Piddy: "Did we have to kill him?"

Father: "Survival is never easy."
Piddy: "Especially for puppets!!"

★Survival of the fittest

25

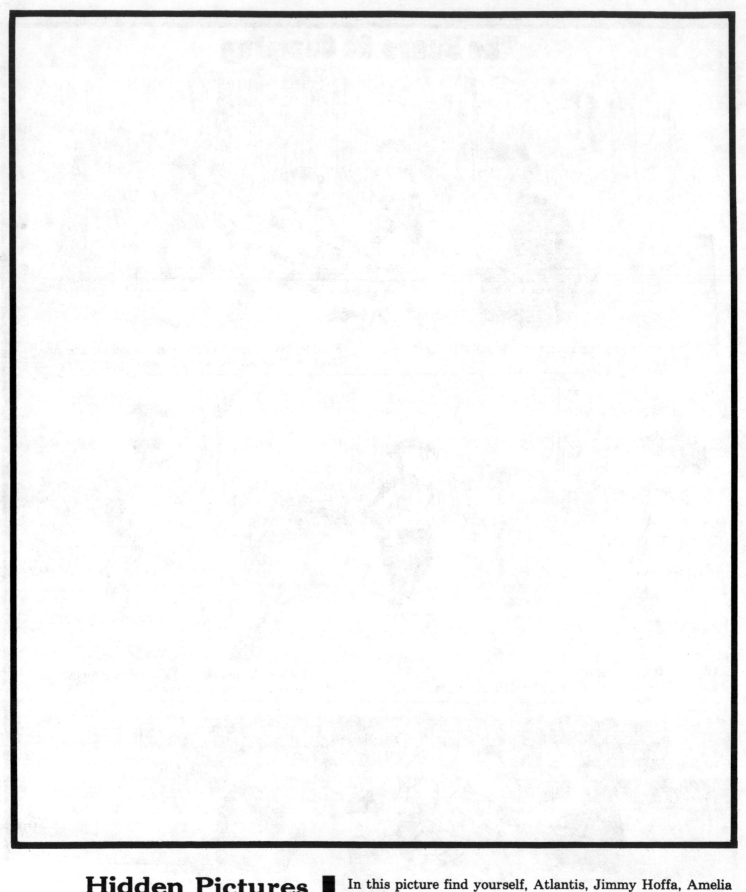

Hidden Pictures

In this picture find yourself, Atlantis, Jimmy Hoffa, Amelia Earhart, the *Edmund Fitzgerald*, Adolf Eichmann, a pair of clean underwear, 18 minutes of lost tape, a parking space, the stolen nuclear submarine, Bigfoot.

Our Own Page

Henri Matisse
Age 51

Jackson Pollock
Age 44

Willem de Kooning
Age 48

Pablo Picasso
Age 54

Vincent Van Gogh
Age 23

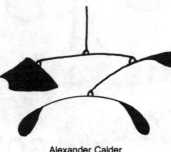

Alexander Calder
Age 65

Some Girls

Some girls like to cook,
Some girls like to sew,
Some girls play with dolls,
Some girls play with jacks,
Some girls like jumprope,
Some girls giggle a lot.

Mickey Jagger, Age 9
Stickeyfingers, England

Land That I Love

I live
Underground
But
I love New York.

Abbie Hoffman, Age 7
Anywhere, Amerika

Snow

I get flakey,
When it snows,
Cause I put it,
In my nose.

Peter Bourne, Age 8
Movedust, NY

Things to Do with Pets

1. Give a daddy-long-legs a judo lesson.
2. Inject caterpillers with water until they pop.
3. Test the theory of suspended animation: freeze a frog.
4. Bury your cat in knee-deep grass before dad cuts it.
5. Break your hamster's legs, cover him with honey, and put him near an anthole.
6. Put your fishbowl in the oven.
7. Reclaw your cat.
8. Sharpen your parakeet's beak with some sandpaper.

Marlin Perkins, Age 8
Mutual, Omaha

A Dream

My friend and I,
Went on a magic trip.
We did not ride a bus,
And we did not sail a ship.

We swam through scents,
And we tasted lots of sound.
And everywhere we looked,
There was color all around.

We returned with a message,
To save the human race.
But nobody believes us,
They just laugh us in the face.

Timmy Leary, Age 11
Timewarp, Calif.

My Doodie and I

My BM is white,
So I must be right.

John Vorster, Age 3
Fecestown, South Africa

27

If You Don't Stop Matriculating, You'll Go Blind

Ahem. Is this thing on? Testing, testing. Can you hear me in back? Good.

How many of you came to college to get a good education? Raise your hands. Let's see, that's one . . . two . . . three . . . okay. Now, how many of you came to college to have a good time? One, two, three, four, five, six, seven, eight—it looks like just about everybody has a hand up.

Students don't attend college to learn at all. You can put your hands down now. Just take a look at the facts. How many times has someone come up to you and said, "College sure is swell! I just love going to class and doing term papers!" It doesn't happen often, does it? As you can see, most students don't like going to class or doing term papers. In fact, most don't even think college is swell! Some of you may think that classes will interfere with your education. You are mistaken. Classes won't interfere with your education. No, education will interfere with the rest of your life.

Remember when you were in the first grade and you just couldn't grasp the concept of "See Spot Run"? It's the same in college, only "Spot" is a molecule of deoxyribonucleic acid.

Many students think college would be a lot more fun if you didn't have to go to class. You wouldn't have to worry about getting up early the next morning after a late party. There would never be any tests to study for, papers to write, books to read, or projects to turn in. You'd never have to think about grades. It would almost be like being a football player.

But what is the purpose of a university? To universitize the students? No, university is a noun, not a verb, so it can't universitize anything. A university is filled with many fine buildings, big sprawling lawns, trees, and street lights. Yes, and students. The students come from farms, cities, villages, towns, municipalities, and even from across the Atlantic Ocean. They come to the university for a specific purpose. To avoid classes.

But a college without academics would be like a hospital without a lot of sick people in white gowns walking up and down the hallways, coughing and wheezing. As Plato said, "Alpha sigma mu, zeta omega kappa."

Somewhere between the time you register for your first class and the time you receive your diploma, you will learn something. It may not last you until the end of your days. It may not even last you long enough to take off your gown and mortar board and yell, "Yippee! I've graduated! No more tests! No more papers! No more student discounts! No more checks from Mom and Dad, Blue Cross coverage on the family plan, or cut-rate subscriptions to *Newsweek*! Yahoo!" But just remember, everyone takes something with them when they leave college. I'm not talking about ashtrays or silverware, I'm talking about knowledge.

Nobody graduates college without learning something. Not the football players, not the engineering students, not the sorority sisters. If you've learned how to drink yourself unconscious without losing your lunch, you've learned something. If you've learned how to pass a final exam without doing any of the reading or attending any of the classes, you're going to make it in the real world. If you've learned how to sneak into the dining hall without being caught, then your four years of undergraduate study have not been spent in vain.

I'd like to thank you all for listening. I hope you enjoy yourselves, and I hope to see you at the Homecoming parade. Refreshments are now being served in the main lobby.

Are you sure this thing was on? I don't think they heard a word I said.

Why We Speak English

There is a story told about H.L. Mencken back in the days when he was the editor of the *American Mercury*. One crisp autumn afternoon, he met a young woman in the elevator on the way to his office. The girl asked him if he were the famous editor and Mencken, somewhat taken aback, replied that he was. She then asked him if he would be kind enough to take a look at a story she had written. Mencken was impressed with the young-ster's spunk and invited her to join him in his office.

After he had finished reading the story, he looked up from the typewritten pages and asked the young woman her name. "Gertrude Stein," she replied. "Well, Ger-trude," Mencken said, "there's a dangling modifier in this story." He then grabbed her by the lapels of her coat and pitched her out the window. She fell eighteen sto-ries to her death.

The story isn't true, but it does illustrate a very impor-tant point: exaggeration can ruin even the best of writ-ing and turn specious anecdotes into cheap jokes. Also, just as we must understand Italian to enjoy opera, and Hebrew to enjoy a bar mitzvah, we must understand En-glish to enjoy ourselves.

The reason for this is that we all speak English. We didn't always speak English. We used to speak Anglo-Saxon. Anglo-Saxon was a rather primitive language consisting only of a few letters and dealing only with the rudiments of human experience. In fact, Anglo-Saxon consisted of only seven four-syllable words describing parts of the human body and their functions. Conse-quently, although modern readers find Anglo-Saxon poetry mildly titillating, it very rapidly becomes tire-some.

But it was not until Daniel Webster invented grammar that English became firmly established. (Daniel Webster should not be confused with the famous nineteenth-cen-tury congressman Henry Clay who distinguished him-self in the Lincoln-Douglas debates.) Since then, many great men have understood the importance of gram-mar. Noam Chomsky has made a career out of it.

But we have begun to forget the importance of gram-mar and the vital part it can play in our daily lives. Ev-ery time we make a grammatical error, we sound igno-rant. Every day, people who should know better use prepositions when they should use participles and ger-unds when semi-colons are called for. Genuinely intelli-gent people talk like typesetters for the *San Francisco Chronicle*.

The importance of good grammar was not lost to Winston Churchill. Once, the Prime Minister ended a sentence in a draft of one of his famous speeches with a preposition. A menial underling, not fit to wipe the great man's boots, had the invidious temerity to point this out to Mr. Churchill. Churchill, one of the great writers of our age, sagely replied, "Thank you very much, a sentence that ends with a preposition is the sort of nonsense up with which I will not put."

Since the invention of grammar, English has become the second language of most of the world and in many countries is threatening the integrity of the native tongue. The French—a race of pedants—have been waging a battle against what they call "Franglais," the adoption of English words that have no French counter-part, such as "le dog," "l'homme mellow," and "Like, je relly zi wer your keming frem, y'nau?" But, what are we to expect from a race of pedagogues? They neither real-ize nor care that English has adopted many French words and phrases without difficulty. This can be seen in such examples as "Paris," "French kiss," and "Pardon my French." But the French remain pedicular to the end; as Camus once said, "The French—they make me sick. I want to vomit in De Gaulle's hat."

The French notwithstanding, the size of our vocabulary is expanding every day. Chaucer wrote the *Canterbury Tales* using only 45 words and no prepositions. And while Shakespeare had only 500 words at his disposal, he wrote some of the most beautiful sonnets in the English language without using the letters on the bottom row of a typewriter keyboard. As recently as 1965, nobody would have understood this joke:

HE: What has red hair, big feet and lives in a test tube?
SHE: Bozo the Clone.

Now, clever japes of this nature evoke uncontrolled mirth. Yet, while we are adding words to our language at the rate of 2500 a fortnight, we still have no word for a place where barbers go to drink gimlets and play marbles. Do we need all these new words? After all, you may say, there were tribes in Bolivia whose language consisted of a single letter and who communicated by Morse code. They are extinct now, but for different reasons entirely. On the other hand, there are languages such as Chinese, where the same letter is never used twice and yet there is still no word for gimlet because it is a crime punishable by death to import Rose's Lime Juice into China.

Because of the problems of an ever-expanding vocabulary, euphemism has reached epidemic proportions. Everyone is trying to outdo everyone else in finding pleasant ways to refer to things that thoroughly disgust us. When someone says, "God, I wish I could get laid," we know that he really means something dirty. Why doesn't he come right out and say it? After all, we're all adults, we know what he really means is that he wants to *make love*. Euphemisms make our language flabby. Look at the restaurant menu that advertises "Ground steak—specially charbroiled over glowing embers by our chef and lovingly placed on our own golden brown bun in a bed of crisp green lettuce and garden-fresh onions. Garnished with a sprig of our finest parsley." Why don't they just say "Greasy hamburger on a roll"?

Euphemism goes hand-in-hand with that old standby, the cliché. These tried and true old workhorses are as easy as pie, but carry the seeds of their own destruction. You should take the bull by the horns and stand on your own two feet—don't let them do your talking for you. You can bet your bottom dollar there's more than one way to skin a cat and you can speak your mind without using old saws or leaning on crutches. If you want to change your tune, put your nose to the grindstone. Crack some books and burn the midnight oil and before you know it, you'll be safe and sound. Your words of wisdom and deathless prose will be fresh as daisies. Enough said. A word to the wise is sufficient.

Some great beaches won't be crowded this summer

Academic pressure.

The never-ending struggle with required courses. The inability to cope with Professors.

The competition among students trying to succeed in the rat race.

All-nighters. Research papers. Only ten more chapters of Bio. Four novels to be read by Thursday. Take-home final due tomorrow. Oral presentation for Wednesday.

Financial aid cut back. Gym requirement. Roommate hassles. Never get into grad school. "What's your major?" Family pressures.

Sound familiar?

Did you ever just want to end it all?

Agony Airlines

Delivering more People to God than any other.

The Creative Writing Seminar

In ages past authors wrought their works by the light of smouldering fires, on dusty desks in lonely cabins, governed by feverish bursts of a fragile quill pen. Wild-eyed and disheveled, the writer would emerge from a week of scribbling without interruption, having put forth a modest creation, such as *Moby Dick*. If the maid ever forgot to wake the writer from his creative trance, he might write himself into his grave from lack of sleep, nourishment, and the company of his fellow human beings.

Fortunately, the quill has yielded to the key, and the crackle of the hearth and the rustle of sylvan creatures have been lost beneath the typewriter's hum and the roar of the city street. There are still those stalwart fellows who pace winter's lonely beaches absorbing the contemplativeness in which deserted strands seem eternally bathed, but by and large the compulsive Romantic scribe has gone the way of the canal boat and the returnable bottle.

Rather, the will to create is nurtured in our ivory towers like a premature infant—in heated seminar rooms, plied with wine and cheese, and soothed by the kind and forgiving words of others. On the University campus this incubator is known as the Creative Writing Seminar.

He read from his page like Socrates with a scroll from the library of Alexandria—a lost poem by an anonymous poet—a testament to the folly and frailty of all mankind: a short story about high school romance:

. . . The steering wheel shook in my hands as if it, too, were saying, "No, No," as she had done throughout the entirety of "The Deep" at the drive-in only moments ago.

"Where do you want to go?" I asked her.

"Home," she said, as if she were surprised; as if every RG (Regular Guy) didn't take his date to Roy Rogers' for a mocha shake before going home. "Sheesh," I thought to myself.

"How about a shake at Ro-Ro's?" I articulated.

"I really think it's time I was getting home." There was thick mist all over the road as we pulled up in front of her house—where there were no lights on.

As the engine rattled cautiously to a stop, my steering wheel stopped shaking, but she didn't. She flipped the handle of the door and popped quickly out of my Dad's brown, Tudor Falcon. Turning once more she blurted, "Hey, thanks a lot, OK? I'll see you in school Monday, OK? Bye, thanks again—Bye!"

The reality was hard to take. The scenes began to fall into place—she hadn't had scarlet fever for two weeks at all, and when her sister had answered the phone she probably was home but just not answering the phone because she knew it was me calling. I wanted to punch her out.

Like a painful act that won't go away, the shake of the steering wheel reminded me of the sinking feeling—like eating fifty jelly donuts all at once—that she had left me with. The Falcon moved slowly through the mist, as if it were carrying the weight too. I knew that it was over.

His eyes moved up from the page with the Christmas-morning look of wondering whether Pop will like the tie. He was convinced that he had

brought forth from his psyche a creative masterpiece, peerless in western civilization.

"You know," he began, "the incredible thing about that story is that it *really* happened—just like I said!"

The eyes still open in the class seemed to waver like pools of grape jelly smashed on the kitchen floor. No one spoke until the professor glanced around the room like a hunter. "Bob, you look like you have something to say."

Disturbed by the reverie, the prey cleared his throat and brought his consciousness back into the customary three dimensions: "Oh, I really liked your piece, but, ah, I don't know . . . it seems like an old story somehow."

One bold tigress spoke up confi-

35

dently. "Was there any symbolism in his really wanting to go to the roast beef sandwich shop?" The feminist's analysis crept into the conversation on little cat's paws. "I mean, it seems like you—I mean the character in the story—didn't really have a lot of respect for the woman. It sounds like you pestered her for quite a while. I mean, what could she do?"

"Well she didn't have to be so much of a sneak about it. For all I know she just didn't like Fellini movies.. . ."

"Yeah, but you were so stupid. I mean the man in the story wouldn't have realized what anything she said really meant. There were a lot of clues that she didn't like you."

"She *could* have wanted to see the basketball game the other time. I mean, it's *possible*."

"Could you discuss your problems outside of class?" the professor growled. "We're here to discuss literature, not psychohistories."

"What's so great about Roy Rogers' Roast Beef Sandwich Shop?"

Edgar knew. He knew a lifetime of suffering that ate away at his body and soul. And now he was going to tell.

I felt an intense surge of apprehension, having choked down the magical tenth cup of thick, foamy beer. On lowering the plastic grail from my quivering labia, I endeavored to ram myself through the myriad onlookers, standing round me like heathens viewing a perverse rite. They tried to preclude my expulsion from this suffocating circumstance. I stumbled out onto the lawn of Bones Gate, painted gray with the onset of dusk. There I fell prostrate before the mighty pillars of the porch, writhing in tart anticipation of the imminent gastric cataract. My hands in coition as if I were praying, I let the full force of the enemy within overflow from my bowels and spew forth like a potent geyser. I canted inarticulate incantations as the malodorous effusion was ejaculated from my throbbing, gaping orifice. There I fell into oblivion, my head plunging into the midst of my own regurgitation.

As he finished, he looked up—not to note reactions, but as a gesture of completion. The words he had read had carved wrinkles into his stone forehead, but now he was ready to stand by them. The first to speak was the feminist. "I think there were definite sexual overtones in this description, as illustrated by Edgar's use of words throbbing labia, ejaculation, etc. But I think Edgar is a little muddled on this subject, and one of his major fallacies is that he shows his typically male view of sex—very self-oriented, a kind of catharsis, after which he can just roll over and go to sleep."

The professor leaned back with a confident William F. Buckley smirk on his lips. "Catharsis. A very good literary term, Ira. Catharsis means evacuation of the bowels. In literature, it's a purgation of emotion. A very effective mechanism, Edgar."

A bearded fellow cleared his throat and volunteered his reaction. "Maybe it's just my own interpretation, but I

"I *like* the Dead."

think he was, in fact, describing a religious ritual, falling prostrate before the pillars. He used words such as "heathens," "rites," and "incantations."

The professor gestured towards him. "I think J.D. has a point. I think there are religious as well as sexual connotations in this passage. The only real question I have, Edgar, is how do these metaphors work for you? It seems to me very deviant to make associations between vomiting and sex and religion. What could ever possess an individual to make such a bizarre and abnormal association? I don't think anyone in this room can really see this as you seem to do."

"As deviant as it is, the association is *very* clear in *my* mind. Obviously Edgar is using alcohol as a substitute for sex and religion. I think it can be argued that Edgar must be very insecure about his shortcomings as a

man, if you *know* what I *mean*. But he uses throwing up as a sort of sexual climax, as confused as his concept of sex seems to be. I think he also uses it as a religious experience because I think I can safely say that he's a very shallow, pathetic person whose most profound religious experience is brushing his teeth . . . hey, where are you going?"

"Let him go, Ira. Some people just can't take constructive criticism."

She dove deep within her soul to read the words she'd written on the page and mimeographed for the class. Her voice had an angelic ring of irony as each word fluttered from her mouth as a paltry testimony to the depth of her feeling in writing her poem, "Coffee at the Hop Snack Bar, Oct. 17, 1977."
We shambled across a starry plain.
That day—you and I, brotherless.

With the retrievers and their sa
         l
          i
           v
            a-soaked
Tennis balls: suns of frosty innocence.

A rose pricked the rainbow
When you told me I was lonely.

A note on the candy machine said,
   "20 cents John Bussey, WDCR."
I am surrounded here, as I sip my coffee.
Without a CAT cap.
Without a sleeveless vest.
Without a nickname like "Pus"
   or a "Glasseater" on my back.
I am in clogs . . . am I different?
The dog nips at my donut.
   Why do people butt in line?

She held her eyes on the page even after she was finished. Several members of the class were crying tears of joy. "Oh, wow, that was *heavy*."

"Incredible. So real."

"I liked the part about the clogs and the jock shirts."

"Yeah, that was great."

"Who's John Bussey?"

"Since when is candy 20 cents?"

"They changed it last year."

"Oh, I live off campus."

She interrupted rather sternly. "What did you think of the Christ imagery?"

"Huh?"

"What, with being surrounded and all that?"

"Who's John Bussey?"

She was stricken with disbelief. Her eyes were as wide as waterbeds. "You didn't see it? It was everywhere! How can you be so insidiously blind?" All heads were hung in heavy shame.

"What was all this stuff about John Bussey?"

. . . My hand reached out to touch his in the darkness. It seemed like a dike had broken between us, as if our relationship had entered another dimension. I was so happy to be beneath the sheets with him.

The quiet sincerity of his words were such that no one around the table made any movement or said anything about the story they had heard. The professor pinched the bridge of his nose and glanced around at the class. "It's rather unusual for a male to put his writing into the female persona like that . . ."

"Yeah, I guess it kind of is." His sheepish chuckle put the class only slightly at ease.

"That *was* a female persona, wasn't it?"

"I guess it can be whatever you want it to be."

"You must be rather sensitive," injected the professor, "but your character has the problem of exuding his maleness despite his being female in the story. That's the difficulty in doing something like that."

"Yeah, I guess so."

He leaned back, waiting for a muse to bless him and instill emotion into his oral interpretation. Feeling inspiration creeping into his limbs, like the pleasant buzz that slowly developed after chugging a few beers, he humbly began to read aloud his paragraph, entitled "Winter Carnival Lost."

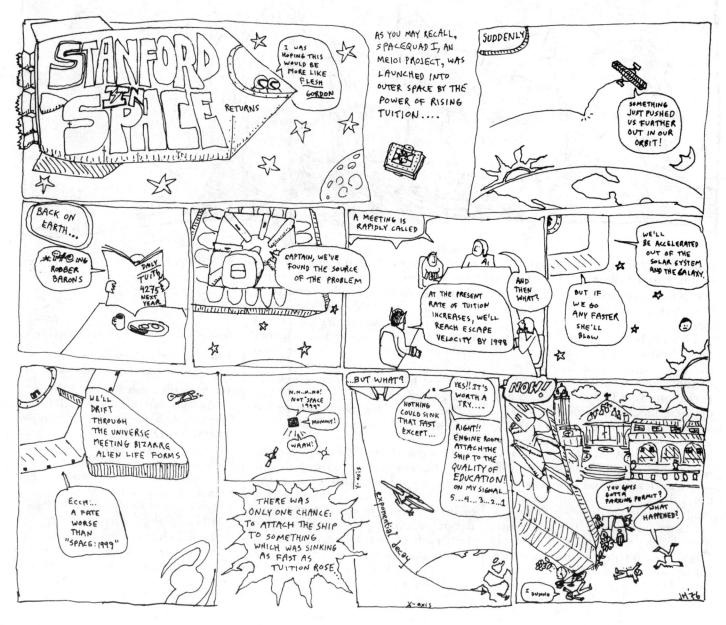

The winter wonderland was melting. The icicles hanging from the roof would slowly bleed to death onto the snow below, and finally, let go their tenuous grips and fall, their tiny brittle spines shattering on the wall as they descended. The huge white St. Bernard in the middle of the green began to decompose, its snowy flesh melting from its carcass. The green itself began to drown in its own mortal fluids, and in its death throes, it trembled so heavily that the doors of Robinson Hall coughed open and vomited its humid, chill air. Its terminals moaning ceaselessly, the computer went into cybernetic convulsions, leaving pools of sweat around its deathbed. The snow-capped mountains, their entrails scorched and bleeding, passed wind over the small village of Hanover. The sense of imminent demise was thick in the air; it permeated his down vest and rugby shirt, putrefying his heart.

I looked up into the gray heavens and tried to contemplate the meaning. Why? Why must this snowy paradise end?

A long silence ensued—a silence that shrouded each individual, cutting him off from the others. Taking a deep breath, the professor blotted with his handkerchief the cold, acidic droplets of sweat hanging from his brow. Around the table, three listeners returned their cheese to the serving plate. There were no comments.

She looked bored and somewhat confused as she always did. The world did not fall into place for her, and neither did her hair; it looked as if she had stuck her finger into a light socket. She squinted as she read:

Bimo looked amazingly like an ape as he sucked on the burnt roach: the thought almost sent me into a long fit of giggling. Scratching his steel-wool stubble, he said, "Man, I wish I was back in Detroit, shoving those steel pipes into place. Life is so meaningless around here." He sniffed again. You could tell that the low-grade coke was nipping at the lining of his nose like so many insects. Lucas was hunched over reading Nietzsche again; Lucas was a genius, but he was also a labeled schizophrenic. He was a riot.

She finished, picking hair out of her little hairbrush and rolling it into tiny balls.

A clean-cut young man cranked his head out of his La Coste sweater and asked, "You take drugs?"

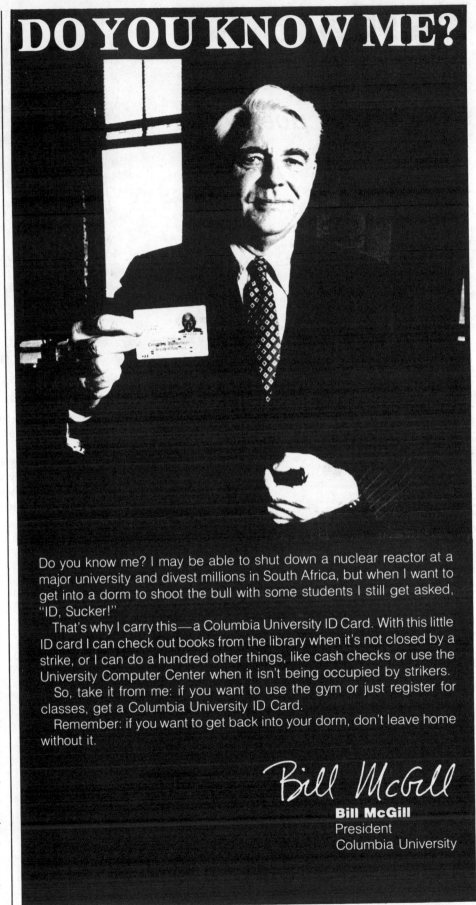

DO YOU KNOW ME?

Do you know me? I may be able to shut down a nuclear reactor at a major university and divest millions in South Africa, but when I want to get into a dorm to shoot the bull with some students I still get asked, "ID, Sucker!"

That's why I carry this—a Columbia University ID Card. With this little ID card I can check out books from the library when it's not closed by a strike, or I can do a hundred other things, like cash checks or use the University Computer Center when it isn't being occupied by strikers.

So, take it from me: if you want to use the gym or just register for classes, get a Columbia University ID Card.

Remember: if you want to get back into your dorm, don't leave home without it.

Bill McGill

Bill McGill
President
Columbia University

W To TuWE

Volume I   Number 1

*a new concept
of "realism" poetry*

at the door, February, 1977

Hi !!!

A dollar?!? We never had to
pay before! Just let us in, OK?

But we don't HAVE a dollar. Really.
Jeez, what a crummy deal:
Let's go someplace else.

Signpost

You missed the exit,
  You louse,
    she said.
How could you miss
    the goddam exit?
    she asked.
Jesus. That's the last
    goddam exit for miles!
    she explained.
You really blew it this
    time
    she shed a tear.

Awareness

Oh, wow, you know —
  like
  it
  was *so* incredible,
you know? So mellow,
    r
    e
    a
    l
    l
    y, oh wow.

to childhood

Hey, will ya lay *off!*
    ow! ow!
Enough's enough, fellas:
    hey, that really *hurts!*
    Quit it,
    would' ya?
C'mon, it's not funny anymore.
Teacher, they're *bothering* me again!

We Were

We met.
    By accident, perhaps?
Nonetheless we were.
    And now you've gone
    With you is
    my sawdust and tinsel
    my virgin spring
    my winter light
    and my goddamn hotcomb.

Apartment 8-B

Ah, hello?
  Yes, ah,
    excuse me,
      I'm the neighbor from next door...
      That's right, 8-A,
        could you turn the music
        d
        o
        w
        n a little?
Well, that's nice,
  I'd be happy too, but
    I have to work tomorrow, and
      it's 3 am and all...
Hey, listen, I've got my rights—
Yeah, more of the same to you too buster!
I'll call a goddam cop is what I'll do.
        click

        Shithead.

reflections

  The sound
  that person is making
    chewing his salt water taffy
is the worst, most horrible
    thing I've ever heard,
    I think.
  What an asshole,
  for slurping and sucking
    on that soggy wad.
He sounds like he's about
    to drown.
    Blech.

on the road to the beach

If you kids
  don't quiet d
        o
          w
            n,
  I'll stop the car right here.
Allright, then, I guess we don't
  go to Rehoboth.
Well, now that's better,
  isn't it?
    Let's try and
keep it this way.

NOAM CHOMSKY! SO FINALLY WE MEET, YOU...

CUNNING LINGUIST? THAT'S ANOTHER ONE OF YOUR FEEBLE JOKES THAT I'M SICK OF HEARING, SKINNER. FOR YEARS I'VE WATCHED YOU FROM THE ROOF-TOPS OF MIT. WELL, NOW I'LL PUT AN END TO THIS BEHAVIORIST MADNESS...

HA! WE'LL SEE. TRY THIS ON FOR SIZE!

HMM, HE'S CLEVER.... THAT'S MY FATHER'S GILT-EDGED TALMUD. HOW'D HE KNOW I WAS FORCED AS A CHILD TO READ IT THROUGH EVERYDAY?

NICE TRY, BUT... "SKINNER HERDS BLUE GOATS GAILY THROUGH THE HARVARD YARD IN SPRINGTIME."

THAT SENTENCE... IT'S.... IT'S....

THAT'S RIGHT: IT'S NEVER BEEN UTTERED BEFORE! YOU SEE SKINNER, HUMANS ARE CREATIVE, NOTWITHSTANDING YOUR WARPED PSYCHO-LOGICAL FANTASIES.

.HEAD FEELS GRIM...

WH-WHERE AM I?

BACK IN THE BOX, DAMN YOU!

I DON'T THINK HE CAN STOMACH YOUR PELLETS EITHER, SKINNER. NOW GET OUT AND TAKE YOUR HARVARD EDUCATED WHITE MICE WITH YOU!

WE'LL MEET AGAIN YOU... YOU... INNATISTS!

C'MON, BEN, LET'S GO.

PROFESSOR CHOMSKY, I OWE YOU....

YOU OWE ME NOTHING OVERMAN, WE'RE JUST PARTNERS IN THE SAME ENDLESS VIGIL: TO SEEK OUT AND DESTROY THE FOES OF MINDLESSNESS WHEREVER THEY RAISE THEIR UGLY HEADS.

YOU KNOW NOAM, FOR A PREEMINENT LINGUIST YOU DON'T HANDLE METAPHORS WELL AT ALL.

THE END

44

The Eliminants of Style

A College Handbook

J. Middleton Murry defines "prose" on page 52 of his *The Problem of Style*. He calls it "the language of exact thinking," and goes on to stress the importance of clarity of style in literary expression.

The other day I asked a colleague what he knew about Middleton Murry. "Oh, yes," my friend replied, "he was a friend of D.H. Lawrence."

The fact that poor Murry, whose prose was very clear indeed, is remembered only as an accessory in the life of D.H. Lawrence, whose prose was not clear at all, indicates a trend in literary history. Even a casual glance through the works of Dryden, Swift, or Milton reflects a prose style bordering on the unfathomable. And this is embraced by the autocrats of academia as the standard of excellence to be emulated.

Thus, the newly arrived college student is faced with an immediate dilemma: He can continue the charade of writing simple prose, or he can plunge himself into the maelstrom of convoluted expression, which is the mark of a true intellectual.

To guide those brave souls who accept this latter challenge, we offer here a short outline of basic rules of writing, which, if followed, will ensure success in one's literary excursions.

Introduction

Perhaps the most fundamental rule of college expository writing is: "Forget everything you've been taught about concise prose."

Many naive freshmen have been misled to believe the notion that "good prose is clear prose." The lesson in the competitive world of higher education is that "clear prose is vulnerable prose," and that one should never rush to make any expository remark.

Of course, one must usually write on a particular "topic" and one may ultimately be judged on his abilities to demonstrate his mastery over the particular subject matter he is considering. To these ends, there are three stylistic modes by which the aspiring intellectual may secure the tacit approval of his mentors. These are: qualification, obfuscation, and citation.

Qualification

This first modality has been popular in recent years because of its simplicity of design. The theory goes this way. If the writer can by means of syllogistic machinations so limit the scope of his opinions that they all but vanish from sight, he will ensure that they are safe from refutation.

Which leads up to the First Fundamental Theorem: "Only State What is Obvious in the First Place and—When Forced to Elaborate—QUALIFY." For example:

"It is perhaps some measure of the difficulties posed by teleological constructs, that act utilitarianism often fails to remain consistent within its own tenets . . . ."

Here the words "perhaps" and "often" are used to protect the writer from the very real possibility that his thesis may be incorrect. If the professor cites a contradiction, it is merely an exception to the rule. Note also that teleological systems present "difficulties" but not "impasses." Other useful qualifiers commonly exploited are "partially," "marginally," "substantially," "may prove to be," "offers us some insight into," "is one of the salient contributors to," and so forth.

A more obvious method of eschewing the provocative is to carefully refute the few conclusions you are forced to reach, thus denying your mentors the opportunity to take issue. For example:

"One could argue that Transcendentalism is but an evolved form of English Pantheism. While Transcendentalism does borrow several Pantheistic characteristics, the significance of theophany in the two systems, it should be noted, is very different. . . ."

If the writer can successfully introduce, qualify, then refute all possible lines of argument, then he has established what is called a "dialectic."

While the skilled writer might take many pages to qualify his thesis, the amateur may gain satisfactory results by calling a smaller essay a "discussion," or a "conceptual framework," or an "etiological analysis"—all of which forestall the necessity of reaching any particular conclusions, which could be open to attack.

Obfuscation

Obfuscation is one of the most useful tools in essay writing. When used correctly, it leaves the reader unable to understand the "higher logic" which is driving the essay toward a conclusion.

There are few achievements in the history of thought more confounding than thirty pages of erudite but incoherent analysis followed by a "logical" conclusion. And in the writing trade, where egregious obscurity is often taken for quintessential profundity, obfuscation is the name of the game. Thus, we invoke the Second Fundamental Theorem: "Never State in Simple Prose What Can Be Stated in Convoluted Prose."

Even the most modest ideas can be expressed in ways which make the reader suspect that a subtly important statement is being made.

For example, a section of Mumford's classic urban history text reads:

"If the subdivided urban man, or *Teilmensch*, forfeited the unconscious wholeness of the simpler village type, he achieved, at least vicariously, a new sense of the individual personality, emerging from the chrysalis of tribe, clan, family, and village."

While the ideas in this selection are relatively straightforward, the use of convoluted syntax, a German appellation, and an abstruse zoological metaphor add that extra air of erudition and mystery.

The use of foreign words and phrases adds great weight to otherwise superficial insights. But the novice in the use of such foreign language "enhancers" must be careful not to overstep his credibilty.

For example, a freshman may say that:

"Greek architecture expresses what LeCorbusier called "la simplicité de la ligne."

But only an upperclassman can state that:

" . . . the subsequent evolution of the Doric Order show the marked influence of the Greek obsession with the ἰδεαλ."

Thus we arrive at the Third Fundamental Theorem: "Common Words Make an Idea Seem Shallow. Always Eschew Banality of Word Choice." The college student soon learns that "ideas" do not exist in a university, only "notions." A policy is never "stupid" although perhaps "insensate." Opinions are never "wrong" but rather "problematic."

Armed with a pocket thesaurus, even the casual freshman can make the most juvenile remarks read like sophisticated ruminations.

In an effort to add a greater element of erudition to their jottings, social scientists rely heavily on the means of creative expression outlined above, and have also become renowned for their abilities to "coin" words as they need them. For example, the well-known historian Mayer resorts to the following:

"Clearly cooperation between the upper cartel of anxiety and the counter-revolutionaries is consequential though not identical in pre-emptive and posterior counteroperations."

Or:

"Desensitization therapy using anxiety hierarchies has proved more successful than aversive counter-conditioning in reducing social dysfunctions."

This ability of social scientists to seek out convoluted arrays of polysyllables serves as a testimony to the heights of expression which can be attained by inspired prose-artists.

Citation

A liberal citation of references and quotations is of great help in adding an air of historical integrity to what

Frog doing a research paper.

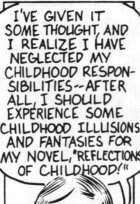

otherwise would be an insipid remark.

In literary critiques, those epitomes of pedantry, obscure references to remarks made by such intellectuals as Gray, Johnson, and La Rochefoucauld add that extra air of pomp, while quotes from Nietzsche, Schopenhauer, or Mencken add punch to what would otherwise be dismissed as cynical drollery. (Quotes from Kant, Ruskin, or Emerson are to be avoided at all costs, because of their popularity among the "Cocktail Crowd"—anathema to the "University Society.")

Used effectively, the obscure citation can add that extra hint of profundity to even the most Mickey-Mouse prose endeavor.

Conclusion

In conclusion, in this monograph we have *touched upon* three of the major factors which *contribute to* the complexity of undergraduate prose. *It is beyond the scope of* of this *short essay* to focus on all of the *factors which lead to* this complexity, *although* qualification, obfuscation, and recitation are *clearly in the forefront.*

As a final note, we are reminded of those apopemptic remarks made by I. Stunk, protagonist of Danziger's epic poem *What Makes Flowers Grow.* "Dung well slung," said Stunk as he wheeled his barrow through fertile fields, "is like a song well sung!"

"I bet you'd like to know who this bastard is. . . ."

An Existential Anthology

The Death of a Sales

"Good morning M'am. I've got a wonnnderful gadget I'd like to show you here. This is the Bonny Johnny E-Z Can-Opener-O-Matic, which opens cans so quickly I'll bet you can't say . . . Um, it'll, uh, open 'em before you can say Jack Spratt and his fat wife. Would you like me to demonstrate?"

"No."

A Day in the Life of Lee Harvey Oswald

Three people sitting around talking.

Another person sat down.

"Boy, it sure is cold today. I swear I haven't seen such a cold day in a long time. Jesus, it's freezing. . . . It's really cold," he said shivering.

The others left.

These Two Guys Just Can't Get It Together, Man

John Phillips was despondent. After a long and vicious argument with his girlfriend they had broken up. His old friend Chuck took him out for "a few brews."

"Well, John," said Chuck as they sat in the bar, "there's plenty of other fish in the sea."

"Yeah I know," said John. "But I hate fishing. Especially the part where you cut off their heads. Ha ha."

Chuck was confused. But John was feeling better already.

A Story With a Message

Boom boom boom. War is bad.

Hey Hey Hey Enola Gay

"Is that an American bomber up there?" said the Hiroshiman.

"No," said another.

He was wrong.

The Thorn and the Thistle

The city lay below them, glowing like a jewel in the night.

"Look at all the lights. The city . . . " he paused. "It's glowing like . . . like a jewel in the night."

"That's a dumb cliché," she said.

This is Short

William Blount was the toll collector on the Cumbarton Bridge.

Hey, Life's Like That, You Know?

Joe was born. Then he met some people and he died.

Bicentennial Boogie-Woogie

Some people were standing around somewhere when George Washington strode up, attired in his usual colonial toggery.

"Well, how are all my children in the aftermath of the festivities marking the 200th year of freedom and liberty for this great nation?" he asked.

"We're fine sir, but you're dead," one of them observed.

A Day in the Life of a Dog

A German shepherd lay in the sun, sopping it up. He buried a bone and went on the neighbor's lawn.

The Other Side of the Highway

Betty was in an awful accident and was left paralyzed from the waist down. But that's life.

This Guy's Dumb

"Once there was a man who found a magic lamp and the genie inside gave him three wishes so he wished for a million dollars and a beautiful girl. But he wasn't sure what else he wanted so he decided to save the third wish and one day he was driving along and started singing "Oh I wish I were an Oscar Meyer wiener" and he turned into a big hotdog. . . . Oh shit, I wasn't supposed to tell the last part . . . . It's funnier if you don't. It would've been funnier."

That was Michael Behling's favorite joke. He and his wife, Venice, were divorced after six months of marriage.

Of Mice and Housing Tracts

Fred grew up in Fremont. He married a girl from Milpitas. They lived in Hayward. Then they moved to Bakersfield.

Love Means Never Having to Say You Like Steve Miller

"Do you like Fleetwood Mac?" he asked.

"Yes, I love it. And I've seen Star Wars three times," she said.

"I've only seen it twice," he laughed. "The special effects were great."

They got married.

A Tom By Any Other Name Would Still Be A Tom

"My name is Tom," said Tom.

"So's mine," snapped the other Tom coldly.

50

Literature? In America? Incredible but true! And it doesn't take any talent! The Hack Writers' School of Famous Literary Giants will turn you, a simple truck driver, into another Rod McKuen! Here's one of our more popular installments to give you an idea of a typical lesson:

the U-ASSEMBLE HAIKU

No Experience Necessary

The Haiku is one of the most difficult of all poetry forms to master. Developed by those masters of slow torture, the Japanese, it has three lines with five, seven, and five syllables respectively.

Most poets are so stunned by the complexity of this type of poetry they simply ignore it, leaving the field *wide open* for anyone who is willing to give it a try!

Why struggle with writing esoteric poetry for magazines when all you have to do is use the U-ASSEMBLE HAIKU, mail the poetry to effete publications like *Poetry* or *Atlantic Monthly*, and then just watch the checks roll in!

The U-ASSEMBLE HAIKU is the easiest literary device in the world to operate. Any child above the age of seven can do it! It's so simple, a dean at a southern technical institution produces masterpieces in just the time it takes to type three little lines.

To compose a poem, simply use the Chinese style: pick one line from Column A, one from Column B, and your final line (or 'dessert' as they say in Japan) for Column C. Type the three lines in the order suggested: A, B, and C. Do not mix lines. Spice with punctuation as needed. Do not add capital letters. True poets cannot recognize a shift key.

Column A
time is not water
frogs eat bugs and wink
man shits on his hand
chimneys belch black smoke

Column B
shit walks, and nobody talks
my sweatsocks lie on the floor
snow covers the hopes of man
flies flock to dung and to you

Column C
America eats
eternity laughs
destiny beckons
stones contemplate man

Other "How to write" kits available from the Literary Giants include "Editing the Manuscript" by William Faulkner, "Composing the *Reader's Digest* Joke" by Bennett Cerf, and "Scripting the Column" by Furman Bisher. You'll be raking in more bucks than you can shake a stick at (that last colorful phrase came from lesson 15, "The Case for Clichés"). Don't Delay! Do it today!

The Graduation Kit

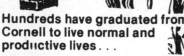
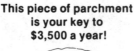

Imagine for a moment, if you will, a world without late registration, prelims, and homecoming games. A place without beer blasts, poetry readings, or Pink Floyd. In short, the "real world." Distant as it may seem, that terrifying scenario lies just around the corner. Of course, freshmen may sleep easy with the comforting thought of "four years, baby!" but don't kid yourself. If there's one thing you've learned by now, it's that time flies when you're doing drugs.

After four years of all-nighters, reserved readings, and late night pizzas, graduating students can't help but find the transition to reality devastating. To help you tackle the rites of passage without developing anything more serious than a degree, we present this

GRADUATION KIT

One: No Exit

Picture the scene. Graduation's just days away. You've got five papers due last week. It's Senior Week and everyone else is out getting butterfly-stomping drunk. You're sitting in Uris Library underneath a mountain of books.

"If only there was some way I could get all of these papers out of the way before the beer runs out," you sigh.

There is. The *All-Encompassing Research Paper*® satisfies your every academic responsibility. Guaranteed to cover five subjects or five professors, whichever comes first. To satisfy ten-page length requirements simply xerox the second page eight times.

ROUSSEAU'S LACK OF IMPACT ON WILLIAM FAULKNER AS COMPARED
TO THE ANCIENT GREEK HUMORIST'S UNFAMILIARITY TO ROBERT LOWELL'S POETRY
IN ACCORDANCE WITH B.F. SKINNER'S APPROACH TO VEBLEN'S ECONOMIC THEORIES
AS UNINFLUENCED BY THE WORKS OF RENE MAGRITTE

Like Faulkner's Anse Bundren in As I Lay Dying, Jean-Jacques Rousseau fails to mention that Thorstein Veblen's theory of conspicuous consumption does not touch upon Aristophanes' attack on Sophocles in "The Clouds." Consequently, Vardaman's inability to cope with Addie Bundren's death hardly reflects the principles outlined in The Theory of the Leisure Class, yet Rousseau's desire for the state to banish anyone not believing in the State's dogmas is noticeably missing from Robert Lowell's portrayal of Boston in "For the Union Dead."

While Faulkner's Vardaman sees his dead mother as a fish, and Lowell solemnly notes "The Aquarium is gone. Everywhere/ giant finned cars nose forward like fish;/ a savage servility/ slides by on grease,"[1] parallels between the two works could not be any more irrelevant unless contrasted in terms of Veblen's theory. If, for example, trout is $4.00 a pound and lox is $3.00, Veblen asserts that consumers will opt for the more expensive fish for the prestige of purchasing it. Such a principle never materializes in either Lowell's poetry or Faulkner's novel.

Although Rene Magritte uses fish for symbolic purposes in several of his works, fish would be a rather poor substitute for a pigeon in operant conditioning experiments utilizing the Skinner box. Whether Addie Bundren's coffin can be discussed in terms of the Skinner box returns us to Magritte's use of rectangular forms transforming before the viewer's eyes to drapery, cloth, or even fish. Lowell fails to make such a connection:

　　　　Once my nose crawled like a snail on the glass
　　　　my hand tingled
　　　　to burst bubbles
　　　　drifting from the noses of the crowded, compliant fish.[2]

Perhaps Lowell alludes to Rousseau's compliant citizens who are content with the Social Contract's restrictions, yet Faulkner returns frequently to the

You hand in your papers and manage to squeak through the final semester—you thought. Turns out, you never did get through four semesters of physical education. It might also come as a surprise that you currently owe the library $4,796 in overdue book fines accrued over four years of research paper writing. Not only that, you took the take-home bio final home with you and forgot to turn it in. To complicate matters, your parents just flew in for commencement exercises. It seems the only exercises you'll be doing are squat thrusts on unemployment lines.

Sometimes there just aren't enough gorges to go around. But let's not jump into anything. If you can come up with a foolproof excuse for missing the ceremony ("I got the sniffles," "I have a headache," "I was run down by a Greyhound Bus"), we'll handle the rest. When the dust has settled you'll mysteriously produce a bona fide sheepskin. Just clip the appropriate letters from the adjacent page, glue them into the proper positions, and voila! Now they'll have to call you "Doctor."

Two: Picking up the pieces and throwing them away

One of the first problems you will encounter after your dorm contract runs out is deciding what to do with the stuff that was absolutely necessary for college survival but is totally useless anywhere else.

When you move into your split-level townhouse you won't be able to fit two-weeks worth of groceries into an *insignificantly sized refrigerator* that won't even keep a six-pack cold. Your best bet is to donate the itty bitty fridgy to the local ASPCA so they can put little dogs to sleep.

And what about the *cinder blocks* you used for book shelves? Try to explain those to the wife and kids. The Hernandezes will be glad to take them off your hands if the price is right. Seems they love to park their old pick-up trucks on top of them.

Black light "Stoned Again" Posters taped up on your office wall just won't cut it with the executive vice president. But if you spring for a mounting, a chrome frame, and a snazzy piece of protective glass, you're sure to overhear the Chairman of the Board remark how "your innovative youthfulness brings a spark of excitement to an otherwise colorless atmosphere." Don't forget to sign them with famous artists' names.

You may have grown close to your *House of Shalimar bedspread-tapestry* over the past four years but it won't go over very well on the Upper East side. Don't sweat it; they make great dropcloths should you decide to have the den done over in burnt sienna.

Stealing all those *traffic signs* may have seemed fun at the time, and they certainly looked cool hanging in your dorm room, but they just ain't in the same league with Lautrec or Gaughin. Punch three holes in them and use them for bowling balls.

Although they were big on campus, try walking into your nine-to-five sporting a Jefferson Starship *concert t-shirt*. Instead of sticking out like a sore thumb in the

Cornell University
Be it known that

having satisfied in full the requirements for the degree of

Bachelor of Arts

has been admitted to that degree with all
the rights, privileges and honors pertaining thereto
in witness of this action the seal of the University and the signatures
authorized by the Board of Trustees are affixed below
Given at Ithaca, New York, on the twenty-sixth day of May,
in the year one thousand nine hundred and eighty

Dean

President

ABCDEFGHIJKLMNOPQRSTUVWXYZ
ABCDEFGHIJKLMNOPQRSTUVWXYZ
ABCDEFGHIJKLMNOPQRSTUVWXYZ
ABCDEFGHIJKLMNOPQRSTUVWXYZ
ABCDEFGHIJKLMNOPQRSTUVWXYZ
ABCDEFGHIJKLMNOPQRSTUVWXYZ
ABCDEFGHIJKLMNOPQRSTUVWXYZ

accounting department, sew all those concert t-shirts into an eyecatching quilt for the guestroom.

You can be darn sure you're not going to stick that silly *memo board* down in the lobby for the doormen to snigger over. Cut it into little circles and create dynamite coasters for those wild cocktail parties you'll be throwing. "Perrier, anyone?"

Sure, you had a bigger *beer can collection* than anyone else in your hallway, but the interior decorator says they're no substitute for drapes. Don't throw them away, you're going to need to tie them to the back of the Volvo after the wedding! And that old *yellow highlighter* will come in handy to write "Just Married" on the windshield!

Unless you want to be the laughing stock of Madison Avenue, you won't be making Lipton's Cup of Soup in your little *coffee hotpot* anymore. Just clip the plug and fill with pencils and pens to make an attractive pencil holder for your office desk.

We all know how hard it is to get the Sunday barbeque charcoal fire cooking. But old college *notebooks* and *textbooks* will be a valuable resource in case you don't get your Sunday *Times*. And your *student ID, co-op card*, and *Cornell card* can help correct the wobble in the dining room table if properly placed under the short leg.

Three: Stalking the Wild Job

Perhaps by this time, you've realized that your dream of growing up to be a lion or an alligator will require more years of expensive schooling. You'll have to settle for a career that's just a little less exciting like firefighting, nursing, or serving as President of the United States. One of the best places to discover the numerous possibilities is in the classified section of the *New York Times*. After you've read about all the nifty motorcycles for sale, you'll best direct your attention to the column marked "Professional Employment." College grads just don't find jobs at the saw mill, Hill's drug store, the taxi terminal, or in the produce department. They'll still only pay you minimum wage at Burger King even if you do have a Masters in food science. When hunting through the classifieds, know what to look for.

Four: Return to Sender

Remember the last time you applied for a summer job? You were after that real cushy spot in your uncle's

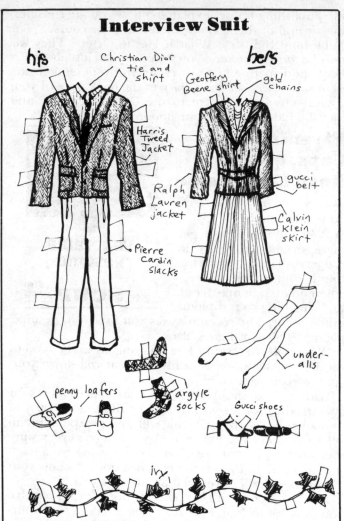

The party's over. Starting early Monday morning you're going to take off that cap and gown. But dare you put on those grungy Levi's, tie-dyed t-shirt, and sandals before walking into your interview at Barnes, Barnes, & Shapiro? Of course not. Unless you have no intention of paying off your federal loan, clip out this READY-TO-WEAR INTERVIEW SUIT along the dotted lines, fold back tabs A, B, and C, and presto! Barnes, Barnes, Shapiro & You!

law firm. But you were dumped like a truck when they hired some sleazebag who waltzed in with a sheaf full of recommendation letters (he even had one from the governor, that scumcake). Don't let that happen again. All you need is a xerox machine, a typewriter,(this handy piece of Cornell stationery,)and a fertile imagination. Poof! You are voted most likely to succeed.

You might even discover more entertaining uses for your forgery talents. Try brightening up your younger sister's day by slipping a postmarked letter of acceptance into the family mailbox. Spark a controversy by signing a racist letter to *The Cornell Daily Sun* with the name of a white professor you admire. Send some letters to all the

Cornell University
Ithaca, New York 14853

big publishing houses explaining how you are considering several of their books for use in your course, "The Publishing Industry: What It Has to Offer." They will only be too glad to send you a free copy of just about any book, anticipating huge revenues from subsequent student sales. Now sell them back to the book store of your choice. Or donate them to the Cornell Library and they'll build a wing in your honor.

Five: It's the Cops, quick, flush the resume

Okay, so the big day arrives. Your interview with J.B. is at 9:30 A.M. sharp. You get there bright and early in your stylish interview attire, toting your letters of recommendation in one hand, and clutching your diploma in the other. The secretary asks you for "your resume, please." The world goes black.

"Resume? Why would I be carrying around a bowl of soup?" you stammer as beads of sweat roll down your chin to stain your cummerbund.

Without that shopping list of your achievements, or an introductory lesson in mind reading, how will J.B. know your credentials? How will any prospective employer find out you bussed tables at Sambo's every summer since sophomore year? How can you ask for a starting salary of 30 thou if the boss just doesn't know your cumulative grades averaged an impressive 1.8?

Maybe it's better if the company doesn't find out that you took off to Idaho for three semesters to find yourself. Instead, placate that establishment clone with some real achievements.

```
                        YOUR NAME HERE
                           RESUME

    EDUCATION:    Bachelor of Arts, Government        1980
                  Cum Laude
                  Cornell University
                  Ithaca, New York

                  Junior Year Exchange Program     1978 - 1979
                  Oxford University
                  Cambridge, England

                  Phillips Exeter Academy             1976

                  Sorbonne                         Summer 1975
                  Accelerated High School Program
                  Paris, France

    WORK
    EXPERIENCE:   Chairman of the Board            Summer 1979
                  Texaco
                  Houston, Texas

                  Executive Vice President         Summer 1978
                  International Business Machines
                  New York, New York

                  Associate Editor                 Summer 1977
                  Los Angeles Times
                  Los Angeles, California
    EXTRA-
    CURRICULAR
    ACTIVITIES:   President, Cornell Campus Council
                  Editor, Cornell Daily Sun
                  Editor, Praxis, Cornell Literary Magazine
                  Title Role, Spring production of "Romeo and Juliet"
                  President, Debate Team (1979-80 National Champs)
                  Captain, Swim Team
                  Editor, Cornellian, Yearbook
                  President, Alpha Omega Epsilon House

    HONORS:       Nobel Peace Prize for Nuclear Submarine designs;
                  Pulitzer Prize for book, Einstein Revised; President's
                  Gold Medal for Physical Fitness; Inductee, Quill & Dagger
                  Honor Society; Champion, Intramural Ping Pong.
    SKILLS &
    INTERESTS:    Flying Lockheed jet fighters, Esperanto, recombinant DNA
                  experimentation, Mozart, chess, skeetshooting, skydiving,
                  Dostoevsky, Sartre, and D.H. Lawrence.

    REFERENCES:   Cyrus Vance, Secretary of State
                  Ralph Nader, Consumer activist
                  Gene Shalit, NBC-TV, critic
                  Erma Bombeck, Syndicated Columnist
```

Six: Nothing to say but it's okay

Now that the preliminaries are over, it's time for you to put all that heavy preparation to work. The most important thing to keep in mind is that you don't want your prospective employer to think you're desperate for bucks or even a job for that matter. If your interview is scheduled for ten in the morning, plan on arriving about 40 minutes late mumbling something like, " . . . couldn't get the fucking Bentley started."

Any attempt by the interviewer to feel out your job qualifications should be brushed aside immediately. Look 'em dead in the eye and make it clear from the start that "My experience and education far exceed yours or anyone presently employed by this mismanaged company." Get to the important information as quickly as possible, like how many K's a year they plan on dolin' out.

If you smoke, by all means light up. If you don't smoke, adamantly insist that the interviewer doesn't either. Employers love prospects who aren't afraid to assert themselves. Remember, the people you're dealing with have no idea of what they expect to accomplish by talking to you. You'll have to be patient with them. Enliven the discussion and give a display of good nature at the same time by offering the interviewer a joint.

Sooner or later every corporate interviewer runs out of inane things to ask and the bullshit really starts flowing. Inevitably they'll set you up by asking something like, "Now that I've made an asshole of myself, perhaps you'd like to take a stab at it." This is, of course, your cue to ask some intelligently motivated questions about the company and provide them with enough ammunition to dump your application in favor of the brunette's (the one with the oversized resumes).

Don't fall for the bait. Explain that through the Freedom of Information Act you've already been over the firm's profit and loss statement. Then make a vague reference to the interviewer's personal tax return. Prospective employers admire candidates who have done extensive research prior to applying for the job. At this point slowly rise to your feet, shake the hand of the interviewer (who's probably still struggling out of his/her tilt-a-whirl chair), and, as you walk out the door, tell the receptionist you'll be getting back in touch if you're still interested.

Seven: Tell them I'm not in

Don't be fooled into thinking that four years of tuition hikes have quenched Cornell's insatiable thirst for money. Now that you're a powerful alumnus the University plans to weasel you into donating everything from a building in your name to a tree on the Ag quad. Little do they realize you're more concerned with coming up with the doorman's fee, keeping your double-knits pressed, and buying that new dishwasher from Sears. Not to mention keeping up with payments on the new paneled station wagon.

Once you recover from the initial shock of receiving that ballsy plea for donations, you're going to have to concoct a graceful excuse for not contributing to the Noyes Center renovation fund. There are plenty of advantages to having yourself declared legally dead. You'll

That All Important Job Interview

"**There's a swig left for you, sir.**" Be thoughtful of your interviewer. Also, make certain that whatever you offer him is a respected brand name.

"**Have I got something for you!**" Fat resumes are impressive. Is yours thick enough to be proud of?

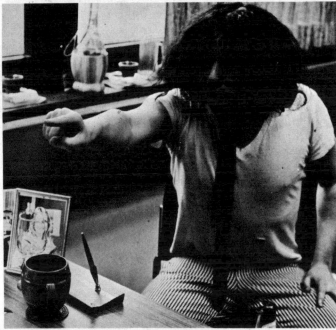

"**Listen to me, mister, I'm the man for the job!**" Constantly pointing at your interviewer shows that you mean business.

"**Just a sec ... mmmgglllpp ....**" Blowing huge bubbles provides "think time" when you're stuck for an answer.

"**Well, I'm off to my next interview!**" Let your interviewer think that there are other potential employers who are eager to enlist your services.

never collect social security, but you won't be financing Cornell's new Bio Complex either. And that junk mail will stop piling up in your mailbox.

"A good offense is good defense," according to a forgotten maxim. Try countering Cornell's financial pleas with an equally ballsy demand for University funding for the new nursery you'll be adding to your home. If babies aren't your cup of tea, tell them you donated a building last year. This will raise some eyebrows as they begin the embarrassing search for your check. A young alumnus from Minnesota accidentally mailed her October phone bill payment to the Cornell Fund. When puz-

zled alumni officers called her up to report the error, she exclaimed, "Gee whillikers! I must have sent the $1,000,000 in small bills to Ma Bell!" This one could work for you.

Eight: Future Shock

No matter how hard you try avoiding Alumni contributions, you'll no doubt end up subscribing to the Alumni Magazine to keep tabs on your classmates and read watered down versions of what's supposedly happening on campus. Here's a taste of what's in store:

News of Alumni

Class Notes

Welcome to the Real World!

'00

"I did the grocery shopping this wk," writes **Matt Churity** of Swampbog, Utah. "I'm not a Cornell alumnus, but I thought you'd like to know anyway." **Eileen Dover** is resting comfortably after an operation to replace every organ in her body with styrofoam balls. Congrats to **Armand Hammer** who, on Feb 2 of this yr, became the 1st person to drive a Cadillac into a replica of the Venus de Milo sculpted from marshmallows. **Calvin Hist '42.5** reports that his father, **Neil**, is a senile old man. In Ithaca, I spoke to **Bobby Pinz**, an ex-lacrosse player whose hobbies inc breathing, sweating, and drooling. **Derek Crane** retd to the Big Red last month, and walked across the Arts Quad on a brisk Feb morning wearing only a pr of swmng fins.

'33

Harriet Upp finished breakfast one morning, walked out the front dr carrying her briefcase, and took a bus to work. **Lana Caine** is now tchng at Salt Lake School for the Thirsty. **Lou Natic** rpts that since his mandatory rtmnt at 65, he's spent his days riding the elevators at the Chrysler Bldg in mid-Manhattan. "I hope to get stuck between floors," he writes, "but the only thing that has gone wrong so far is the indicator light for the 15th floor. They haven't fixed it in 2 mnths."

Jack Knife, Miles Tugo, and **Monty Cello** deserve more mention here, but nobody knows who they are. Fun-loving **Burt Toast** tells us that he and his wife **Peach Melba** enjoy ringing doorbells and hiding in the bushes before they can be answered. **Erna Buck** and

Grant A Loan run one of the top 10 plastic shoelace tip mfrs in the world. **Thurman Nuclearwarhead** suffered a mntl bkdn soon after graduation and blew up 7 mpl bldgs.

Nobody knows what happened to **Ann Dogenous. Hugo First** occupies phone booths to annoy people trying to make impt calls. Down in Acapulco, **Marianne Divorce** Quick reports that her seventh millionaire husband just died under mysterious circumstances. **Mike S Membrane** watches TV 15 hrs a day and burps a lot at night. **Cal Q Late** just bought a can of fruit ccktl and plans to open it during the cmng yr.

Art T Fact continues his job as a paperwt at the Library of Congress. He is an expt in collecting dust and his wife likes to lie unconscious at the bottom of swimming pools. **Freida People** has been wandering aimlessly in the Plant Sci bldg at Cornell for the past 30 yrs. **Tuck S Inn,** his wife Phyllis, and their 4 children enjoy making rest stops in towns beginning with the letter "K."

Matt R Afact enjoys rdng the NY *Times* Classified sctn by holding them up to a mirror. **Sal E Mander** was elected "Most Likely to Be Mistaken for a Mannequin," at his current home, the State Inst for the Criminally Gauche. **C D Character** just lost his job and now sits on a park bench making faces at little children.

Rita Goodbook, Tom O'Hawk, Trudy Myword, and **Dick Tate** never knew each other while at Cornell, but at a recent Reunion they failed to meet one another. **Marion Ett** rcntly had her name legally chngd to EXIT. "I always wanted to see my name up in lights," she writes. **Denton Mecar** just had new tires put on his car.

'40

Cora Gated is still invlvd with the Moonies and enjoys selling flwrs in airports. Look for her the next time you pass through LaGuardia. Six mnths ago, **Stan Dupp** dropped a note telling me that, after 10 yrs, he is still inserting pimentos into olives. But we rcntly learned he got a new job putting cotton into aspirin bottles. **Bill Ding** is a complete failure.

When you see **Jay Walker** at the next Reunion be sure to tell him that he's got his shoes on the wrong feet. Our sincerest sympathies to **Bob Apples** who rctly picked a scab off his knee. **Bart Tender** rpts that if his kids like the way the toothpaste tastes, "maybe they'll stop eating food altogether." **Ray Gunn** wears clothes when he goes to work. **Cherie Blossum** is no longer dangling participles, although she still uses unnecessary adverbs. **Simon Ize** uses both hands to get dressed in the morning. A correction from last mnth: **Duncan Donuts** was listed as having seen *Star Wars* 3 times. He's only seen it twice—it was *Saturday Night Fever* that he saw 3 times. **Glenn Dale** is helping design a new version of the swizzle stick. Closer to Cornell, **Matt A Door** passed away but not before donating himself to be used as fodder in the Arts Quad resodding proj. **Martha Vineyard** is one of 4 Cornellians. **Curtis C Tuothers** writes that "no one even suspects that I embezzled over $20,000 from the Cornell Campaign." **Harry Carray** observes that if kitchen utensils could speak they would probably make great conversationalists. **Emil Nitrate** voted for Richard Nixon in 1972.

Jim Shorts hangs out in a local Burger King and enjoys ordering French fries. **Naomi Twodollars** holds 4 jobs, works 7 days a wk, hasn't had a vacation in 12 yrs, hates life, and wishes she was dead. **Sam Arien** gets plenty of rest, drinks lots of fluids, and takes aspirin to relieve the aches and pains that accompany colds and fevers. **Louis D Battle** told **Wendy Warr** that he owns several multi-natl corps when he has actually been on welfare for the past 2 yrs. **Tim Bucktu** and wife Brenda inadvertently fed their dog a mixture of plaster of Paris and write that "Smokey is a lot more obedient." **Morris Less** rcntly received a letter in the mail, carefully opened the envelope, and was surprised to find a bill from the tel co which did not contain deadly pesticides. On a more somber note, I was shocked and saddened to learn that **Mason Dixon** thinks the square root of 16 is 3. And on a final note, **Claire D Room** is sponging off relatives to support her family of 4.

'55

Louise Z Annah enjoys visiting asylums to make sure she hasn't been committed yet. Her former roommate **Ada Goodmeal** has just been prmtd despite having been fired 3 mnths ago. **Albert Hall** is never home, has never spoken to his wife, and doesn't realize he has 4 children. **Juan O Clock** finds time to fit his interests in narcissism into his hectic schedule mfg mirrors for the blind. **Paul Zee** pushes drugs to elem school kids, while her husb Floyd spreads communicable diseases on street corners.

Della Ware writes that if she had wings she would probably be commonly mistaken for a bird. **Bertha D Blues** is no longer addicted to benzoid-peroxide, and writes she's switched to a Windex solution. **Harry Armpit** spent 10 days last July locked in a storage closet at the base of the Statue of Liberty. **Ethel Alcohol** is still using the same mouthwash and reads billboards to support her family of 3. **Rose Budd** expects to be victimized by the 245 inhabitants of a local trailer park, but her husb Dirk writes that "we don't live anywhere near a trailer park." **Chris Cross** writes that he has no time to write to us. **Mary Cule** uses a soldering iron to remove her unwanted facial hair. **Pat Myback** has been knitting the same sweater for the past 9 yrs.

Scott Landyard doesn't like to eat 3 x 5 index cards, but his wife writes that he's gone through the entire card catalogue at the Boston Public Library. **Terry Torry** occasionally changes his clothes. **Maureen Science** denies being romantically invlvd with a Greyhound bus. "We're just gd friends," she explained. **Margie Null** bought a can of aerosol cheese spread and spent 2 wks squirting dabs of cheese into coin rtrn slots. **Yul O'Gee** writes that he plans to grow old and die. After donning a kangaroo outfit **Grace F Termeals** hopped onto her dining rm table, shouted "WA-HEE" at the top of her lungs, and disappeared into thin air. **Bea Hive** wears a motorcycle helmet to prevent juvenile delinquents from spraypainting her hair orange. **Pam Perrs** has trouble pronouncing words that begin with the letter "L." **Abbie Road** lies on her bed and stares at the ceiling 8 hrs each day. "It gives me something to do," she writes.

Beverly Hills has pursued a career as an illustration in a periodical because "I thought I'd follow the advice of my friends who always said I was 2 dimensional." **June Bride** took a piece of aluminum siding and coated it with grape jelly for no reason in particular last spr. **Jay Bird** says his parents gave his hobby horse to the Salvation Army when he outgrew it as a child.

'62

Carrie D Weight sets up fldng chrs in lge auditoriums for no reason. She writes that she finds the work challenging and enjoys seeing the expressions on people's faces when they walk into auditoriums they thought to be empty. **Sal U Tittorian** paints white walls white. When not bowling gutter balls at Bowl City, **Gene D Fect** translates Yeats's ptry into Esperanto. **Bonnie Fide** has spent the past 7 yrs lobbying in Congress for the forced reunion of the Beatles. Needless to say . . . **I M Gross** spends his spare time making disgusting noises in libraries.

Thanks to the miracle of mdrn silence, **Lou Cyte** has not said a word in over 4 yrs. **Joy Buzzer** is dating the Pillsbury Doughboy, and really enjoys his pop 'n' freshness. **Charles River** enjoys solving quantum mech probs at the opera. His wife doesn't. **April Showers** is a Capricorn even though she was born in June.

Ray D O'Active has written 4 bks relating his experiences with fast-acting nasal mist. **Mike Crowaveoven** enjoys gift-wrping trees in Central Park. He says, "I just want to make sure people notice God's gifts." **Perry Winkle** has never eaten a water cooler. After being elctd "Man most likely to drink oven cleaner from a Dixie Riddle Cup," funnyman **Buddy Sistem** burst into flames and exploded. "Never underestimate a person with a tattoo of a blueberry muffin on his or her thigh," writes **Sherwin Paints**.

Lucy Ferr has won acclaim at the Met Museum of Meaningless Art for re-upholstering her husb, **Tim**. "Only people with knives ever approach me on the subway," writes **Dennis Toffice** who has always disliked the taste of tap water.

Ameila Rate is the Dizzy Dean Prof of Space Sci at Guam Aerospace Acad. "The work load is very light," she rpts. "The school only has about 15 students, and none of them are enrolled in any of my classes." **Simon Sezz** obsrvs that "If you pluck the wings off a fly, it can only walk or hop around." **Amanda D Votion** is having trouble sewing buttons onto concrete abutments.

Nona R Business prgrmd a cmptr to recite zipcodes in 12 foreign langs. **Gladys D Weekend** quit gluing $20 bills to walls because it's hard to convince merchants to accept garage drs for pymnt. **Norma Tive** has discvd a new energy source but refuses to reveal it. **Pierre Pressure** fell out of a 30 story window and missed the ground. **Marsha Mallow** enjoys reading menus in Chinese restaurants.

Last May **Madge E Nation** sold over $8,000 worth of wintergreen Lifesavers to squirrels in the San Diego Zoo. **Sam Pell** only watches dishwashing dtrgnt commercials on TV.

'88

Norman D Coast '52.3 tells us that his oldest son, **Fred**, rcntly constructed a 50 ft model of the Parthenon with Q-tips and 3 cases of mint-flvrd toothpaste. **Cal E Berr** is currently in Nepal srchng for the meaning of life because he couldn't find it in Newark, NJ. **Scott Free** sharpens pencils twice a wk with his wife Gloria and his son, Cletus. **Wade A Minute** has just pntd his den burnt sienna.

Faith Full likes stomping on ant hills and burning the survivors with a magnifying glass. **Saul Tenncracker** has written a 7-volume hstry entitled *Authors of Seven-Volume History Books*. On the lighter side, **Patty Wagon** of Ft Itude, Mich, rcntly checked into the hosp for a tonsillectomy and was inadvertently given a lobotomy. Better luck next time, Patty! **Lyle Lott** only answers the telephone when it rings. At the Bar Mitzvah of **Iris Stocrat**'s son Moshe, **Vic Trolla** set fire to the drapes, sat in the cake, and shot the bartender. Still a card at parties, eh Vic? **Clem N Cee** spent 6 wks remvng staples from bulletin bds. Luckily, he categorized them by their ferrous content and has been mailing them to friends.

Hal E Tosis has been pres of every maj oil co in the US, flies a Learjet, has written 4 best selling bks, starred in a B-way prod of his own Pulitzer Prize-winning play, and is presently training for the Olympics. It's hard to believe that Hal wet his bed until sophomore yr. **Sal Vige** has memrzd every word in the American Heritage Dictionary that ends in the suffix "-ify."

Clara Fye rpts that her husb Bob has forgotten his 1st name. They spnt Thanksgiving consulting friends, neighbors, and relatives, but they still haven't stumbled upon it. We wish them luck in their srch. **Tony A Ward** spent Christmas vctn trying to get his wife and children out of his locked car.

Outro: How big a tip should I leave? (or What's 15% of $40,000?)

Well, that about does it. It's true that we didn't hit the terror of Bridge night, scoring dope on Wall Street, or asking for an extension on that new account. But the sprinkler system's on the blink, and the exterminator's at the front door. Just don't fall for that old graduating speech line about commencement being the beginning rather than the end of your education. There's always grad school.

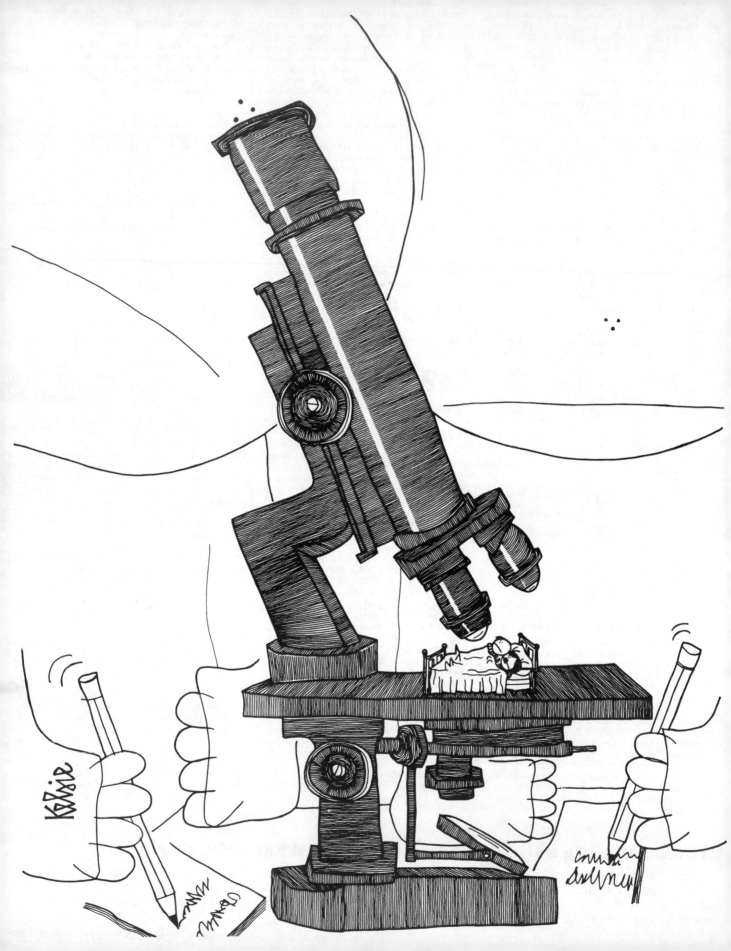

Sex, Drugs, & Bowling

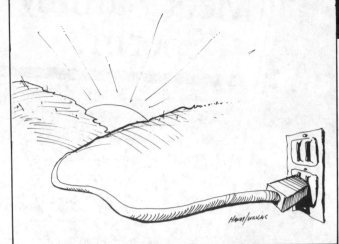

It was Thursday night, and I hadn't seen any action in a week. I had two choices. I could put on my bowling shoes, smoke a joint, and fantasize about Suzanne Somers in front of the TV, or I could go for the real thing. I leaped out of the chair, yanked open the closet door, and grabbed my bag. I did up some 'ludes, slipped out the back door, and headed down to the Bowl-o-Drome. I had my latex wrist glove in my backpocket in case I got lucky.

As the desk attendant assigned me a lane, the drug began to take effect. I was sharing lanes with a cute blonde number with shoulder length hair and the kind of bowling ball you could really sink your fingers into. She introduced herself as Linda, and her dilated blue eyes met mine. She looked like she could bowl all night.

I was mesmerized by the erect pins shimmering at the other end of the alley. My bowling bag hugged my 16-pound ball until it was ripping at the seams in hot anticipation. I saw Linda stare at my bulging bag, and I caught her eye as she looked up. Linda reached over and began rubbing my bowling bag as she slowly undid the zipper and exposed my firm, polished sphere to the cool air of the alley. I had the best bowling ball she had ever seen.

Her lips parted as I cupped the ball with one hand and caressed its smooth, waxed curves with my other hand. When she began flicking her wet tongue over her lips, I let my fingers glide over the rock-hard ball and then slid my thumb into a round inviting hole in its side. I shoved two more fingers and slowly lifted the ball, holding it close to my chest in a warm embrace.

My body ached to part those creamy white pins standing at full attention at the other end of the lane. In one swift motion, I drew my arm back, thrust forward, and released the ball in burning passion. The orb heaved, screaming toward the pins. I could feel the floor vibrate as my black solid penetrated the ready target. Linda gyrated as the reset mechanism dropped over the remaining pins. I caught my breath, but as soon as I glimpsed the two pins left standing, I quickly sprang back to life. A perfect split invited me with a sense of mounting urgency.

The drugs began to tighten their grip as I lit up a joint. My hands were in a fierce sweat but the air from the vent blew softly, drying the perspiration from my palms. As the ball return spit up my swollen black marble from its bung hole, I popped my last amyl nitrate. I was suffused with the strength to hurl that sucker through the back wall. Linda let out a scream of delight as I jammed three fingers deep into the waxed black ball. I moved closer to the foul line and shot a tremendous load of piping hot polymer spiralling down the receptive love tunnel.

The ball generated rainbow trailers, careening like frames spliced from a late-night science fiction movie, as it rocketed down the wavering alley. My breathing became short gasps as I started to writhe in ecstacy. I could feel the shock of the ball hitting the ten pin. It seemed to float across the back alley forever, but in an instant it had smashed the seven pin into an iridescent madness. My face was drenched with sweat that trickled off my forehead into a pool of euphoria. Linda squeezed her eyes tightly. She leaned back, rocking and oozing into my arms with the spasms that gripped her. The sensation was incredible. As the ball pulled itself from the return chute, spinning in a sea of florescence, I felt a final explosion of ecstacy. Linda and I collapsed from exhaustion, lost in the maraschino haze. It was the best frame I've ever bowled!

—Name and address withheld

LOVE STORY RETOLD

Dear Erich Segal,

First I want you to know how much I enjoyed your book and your movie, particularly the book since it didn't take as long to get through. I didn't cry at the movie, but it wasn't because I didn't try. The lady sitting next to me started crying before the lights dimmed, and I thought she was going to make it hard for me to hear, but lucky for both of us she fell asleep about half an hour after the movie started.

You see, I don't know what Harvard is like, but I didn't suppose people could be too different there from here at the University of Nebraska; and then when I read the articles you wrote about how much like real college life *Love Story* is, I thought I would try getting a girl the way Oliver Barrett IV did it.

First I changed my name from Dave Hogg to Davidson Hogg IV. I couldn't afford to have Henry Mancini write me a theme song, but I decided I could hum the "Warsaw Concerto" every time something dramatic happened and then again on my wife's deathbed.

Then I started looking out for an Italian. Nebraska isn't exactly crawling with Italians, but I wanted to stick close to the game plan, although I decided early on that a Puerto Rican might do just as well, so long as my parents objected.

Finally I found a drug store on Pine Street with a soda fountain that had an Italian waitress. I waited for her to insult me, but she didn't so I had to try to provoke her by making a few comments about how slow she was (which she was). I never did get a rise out of her until I had given up and started to leave.

"Thanks for the big tip," she said. "How am I supposed to pay my bills with nickel tips?"

"That's twenty percent of the check," I told her. "How am I supposed to pay my way through school if I go around overtipping fat slobs like you?" Finally things were looking up. "By the way, what are you doing tonight?"

She screamed for the manager, who was also her husband, and he tossed me out before I could ask if she knew any other Italians.

Well, people are friendlier here in the midwest, and after a few tries I had to modify my approach a little bit so as not to be quite so insulting. That was how I got Maria out for a date, and everything seemed to be falling into place. After the movie she said, "Davidson Hogg IV, if your father is as rich as you tell me, how come your Studebaker needs paint so bad?"

"You can call me preppie," I told her.

"You mean you went to prep school?"

"What's prep school?" I said.

That was my last date with Maria, but I did learn some valuable things from her. One thing I learned was that a girl named "Maria" isn't necessarily Italian. As it turned out her name was Maria Czinchowicz, and she said she was a Russian, but I knew better than to believe that.

Well, I won't go through all my false starts, but I wanted you to know that old Oliver was pretty lucky to hit it off right away. If you based your story on somebody real you can tell him I said that, if he's stopped crying yet. Otherwise I wouldn't mention it.

To make a long story short, I finally found an Italian girl and got her interested in me. She wasn't quite as attractive as Ali McGraw, because she was shorter and heavier, and she wore tight black stockings and sometimes forgot to shave under her arms. She was no beauty, to be frank, but I figured I could put up with her for a couple of years until her disease got her. Besides, she was the genuine article—spoke Italian like nothing you ever saw. In fact, she didn't know much English. But between us we spoke the language of the heart, and we took to each other so fast that I suspected she had been reading *Love Story* too.

We did all the right things. We studied together, although she had dropped out of school in the tenth grade. We played in the snow a lot, until Angela got the croup. When I proposed to her, I thought she accepted a little too quickly, and I had to remind her of her harpsichord career and her scholarship in Paris; but other than that everything worked out fine. The next problem, of course, was to try to talk my parents into accepting her. So one weekend, I drove her home to meet them.

It was a disaster from the beginning. They thought she was the ugli-

Joseph during the immaculate conception

est girl they'd ever seen but beyond that they liked her. My mother went for her because she mopped the floor and did the dishes after dinner.

But my father's reaction was hard to figure out. I'd heard him say a hundred times that he hated Italians; I think because of something he caught from an Italian girl during the war, and also because his boss is Italian.

"Well," he said, "you can't hold a grudge forever. I won't stand in the way of your happiness."

"So you don't refuse to allow it? You don't disapprove?"

"To each his own," was all he would say. "How can I stop you?"

I was mad at him for forgetting his part.

"You could disinherit me. You have to consider that angle. I don't have any money."

"I don't either," he said.

Well, you know, I hadn't thought about that. I had kind of given Angela the impression that we were a wealthy family. I never said so outright, but I used to talk about oil stocks, and my ancestors on the Mayflower, and how much I missed having the butler bringing me my Cream-of-Wheat in bed every morning. Now I guess she could see that butlers are pretty scarce around our house, and I was all ready to tell her that poor Joseph had died and we had retired his number, but she never asked. I guess she never understood me in the first place.

"Goodbye," my mother wept, when we left. I was relieved that people had started crying, because it meant I was on the right track, and reminded me that it would be all over in a couple of years. "God bless her, she's a damn good housekeeper. That I can say for her."

My father agreed. "You'll never go wrong with an ugly girl," he said. "She won't run around on you. Be sure you get a good doctor for your blood tests."

Next we went to see the Giambellis. The place didn't look much like the apartment where Ali McGraw's father lived, particularly since it was crawling with kids. But I decided to overlook the difference and make the most of the similarities.

"Glad to meet you, Sal. Call me preppie," I said as I shook his hand. He looked a little surprised, but we had a good talk after dinner. He wanted to know when we were getting married, so he could make arrangements for the mass.

"Well, no, actually, Sal," I said, trying to remember Oliver Barrett IV's diplomatic words, "We aren't going to get married in a church. We were sitting in bed one night, you see, and there was this cross around her neck, so I asked her . . ."

Sal looked like he had swallowed a sea urchin.

"Haysooz! I keel you!" he shouted, and jumped on me. Angela and her mother, who had been listening through the door, came into the room screaming and jumped on me too, and between the three of them and some of the older kids they beat me black and blue. It wasn't strictly

true that Angela and I had discussed the wedding, and as for the part about being in bed, I guess you know where that scene came from.

After this particular discussion we decided to go ahead and get married in a church. Her parents weren't too happy about my not being a Catholic, but they said they had hopes that I would learn the ropes soon enough, because they would rather their grandchildren would roast in hell than be brought up Baptist. I swear that wedding took longer than your whole movie with the Roadrunner cartoon thrown in.

After that I insisted on having a civil cermony, too, because that was my favorite part of *Love Story*. So the next week we went to a notary public on Great Divide Street and told him what we wanted.

"You can't just make up a ceremony," he said. "I've got to perform the service. If you don't say just what's written in the statute book, it don't constitute a marriage."

"It was legal at Harvard for the bride and groom to say it any way they wanted," I insisted. "Didn't you see *Love Story*?"

"Of course I did," he snorted. "I don't know what's legal in Hartford, but here in Nebraska there's only one way to get married by a notary public, and I guess I ought to know what it is. You don't want to go around not married, do you ?"

"Well, don't worry about that. We're already married."

"Already married? God damn son-of-a-bitch, boy, what are you doing standing here arguing with me? How come you want to get married again?"

"So as not to be hypocritical."

He kicked us out of his office, and suggested that we put our second marriage license within arm's reach of the toilet if we wanted it to be of any use to us.

I couldn't very well go to law school, but I decided to take some night courses at the University so Angela could prove she could support me for a while. I told her she was supposed to get a job as a schoolteacher and let all the kids get familiar with her and call her by her first name. As it turned out there weren't any schools that wanted her, so she

got a job in a car-wash and let all the men get so familiar with her that she was pregnant inside of three months.

I was pretty annoyed by this development, and gave her a good talking-to.

"I thought you were going to play this thing by the rules," I said. "We're supposed to keep from having kids until we move to New York and I start making $25,000 a year, and then it's supposed to be impossible, because you're dying. Well there's more than one way to kill a pigeon, and I'm told that pregnancy is a very vulnerable period. But I don't want any falling down the stairs or getting run over by a truck, do you understand? Because you're supposed to linger on and your father and I have got some serious crying to do. After all I've been through I don't want you spoiling everybody's favorite part of the marriage."

"Italian girls don't kill so easy," was all she said.

Well, the baby was born right on schedule. I told Angela from the first that he didn't look like me, but she kept on saying I had a naturally suspicious mind. He didn't have my nose or my mouth or anything, but that wasn't what really caught my attention so much as the fact that he had slanted eyes and his skin was kind of yellow. She said that was because she didn't have enough calcium in her diet, but I never heard of such a thing. Everybody cried a lot more at the christening. I wanted to call him Davidson Hogg V but Angela said no. She didn't like the number V, and it would have to be either Davidson IV Junior or Davidson VI, or else Salvatore after the old man. I said why not Chang after the baby's old man and she threatened to stop shaving her legs if I didn't apologize.

That about wraps up the story. All I want to know is whether you see where my mistake came in. (One problem is that it turned out Angela read your book in an Italian translation called *Tale of Passion*, and she says her favorite part was the knife fight in the Tangiers bordello.) If you ever run out of money and decide to write another book, you might want to tell about the way it is here in Nebraska, because in some ways I think my story is more of a tragedy than Ryan O'Neal's. Angela sends her best, which isn't much, and says that next time you write about an Italian you'd better not make her an only child, because there's no such thing in an Italian family. That may be her way of telling me she's pregnant again.

Your fan,
Dave Hogg

Stalking the Yale Woman

"Leave me alone! Just leave me alone!" cried our lovely Miss November, Claire O'Grady, her brown doe-like eyes all the more luscious aflutter with tears. "Just get the hell out of my life, stop following me around, and *leave me alone!*"

With one well-rounded lower lip stuck out in an irresistible pout, Claire told us how she had been initially wary about posing for us. "All during lunch I felt as though I were being watched, like at a freak show," she said, wriggling with excitement. "Then, on my way out, I looked behind me and there was this gang of creepy little characters ten feet away, just staring. And as I go out, they followed me, and they were trying to hide behind bushes so I wouldn't see them. I would have run away except that I dropped a book and I had to stop and pick it up. And then they were all behind me! One of them was holding a camera! It was awful!"

Naturally, Claire was thrilled when the editors made their offer. "They were obscene," she recalled with a spirited shake of her thick, tawny mane. "Maybe," she added softly with a sparkling tear on one cheek and a quiver of that precious lower lip, "maybe if I'd let them take one picture, none of this would have happened."

Despite that fiery "no" on her tongue, we could hear that throaty "oh, yes!" in her voice when she leaned over to pick up that book she dropped. "I heard a click. That slug with the camera took my picture while my back was turned! When I turned around they were running away. I should have chased after them, but I thought, 'Why bother? Good riddance.'

"But they wouldn't go away!"

It's always hard to decide how to pose one of our models, but Claire's natural beauty made it easy to photograph her just as she is, living her typical but highly titillating day. When we confided to her friends and roommates that we wanted to feature her, they delighted at her good fortune and eagerly shared their knowledge of Claire's personal life and habits. Between their information and our own research, we discovered that Claire is much more than a pretty face, also having taut, high calf muscles, a creamy white neck, and a triangular mole on her left hip. There is much more to her than *usually* meets the eye.

Claire is a very clean girl, taking two showers every day so that she can scrub every inch of that supple flesh. Her taste in clothes is impeccable. And according to her former boyfriends, Claire is very, very friendly, even on the first date. She's really just the perfect girl. Well, not quite perfect. Tuesday she forgot to brush her teeth.

When asked whether she would pursue a career as a

We can't keep our eyes on our own papers when Claire is taking a test. Don't panic, Claire. We're just checking for crib sheets.

stewardess or a cheerleader, Claire flushed. "Your damned article has ruined my life!" she said, flashing us a sight of those almost perfect pearly teeth, except for that chipped lower premolar on the right side that almost no one notices without looking very closely. "Your prying has ruined my reputation! Now I'm paranoid about people taking pictures of me. I keep thinking I hear 'click' here and 'click' there! I can't sleep, I'm losing weight!"

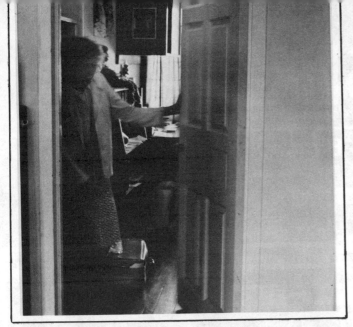

A good salesman learns to be persistent, and if Claire's selling we're buying! We won't take "Beat it, swine," for an answer. Claire, you're such a kidder!

Naughty, naughty, Claire! Does your mother know what you're doing?

Come on in, the water's fine! Claire (above) was all in a lather when we took this shot. Gracefully posing for our cameras, Claire (below) stoops low enough to pick up a book she dropped just moments before this picture was snapped.

But is Claire the sort of girl who would dress up in a leather jumpsuit for her man? Claire had this special message for our readers. "If I ever get my hands on you," she whispered seductively, "I'll kill you. I have a right to my privacy! Don't you think I have things I'm ashamed of?" Yes, Claire, like those long, smooth legs of yours are just the most adorably teensy-weensy bit knock-kneed, or what happened in the girls' locker room in tenth grade. But we love you for it.

"Stop it! I don't want people knowing these things! I don't even know what I'm saying anymore! Stop chasing me! That 'click' is driving me crazy! 'Click' here, 'click' there! Click, click!"

Readers may be desolate to learn Claire and her wool sweaters are leaving school and joining a convent. Yale's loss is God's gain, we reckon. But don't fret, readers. We may visit her again soon. Wonder what nuns wear under those habits, anyway? See you in church, Claire!

DESIRE
a computerized analysis

What A Columbia Man Thinks A Barnard Woman Wants

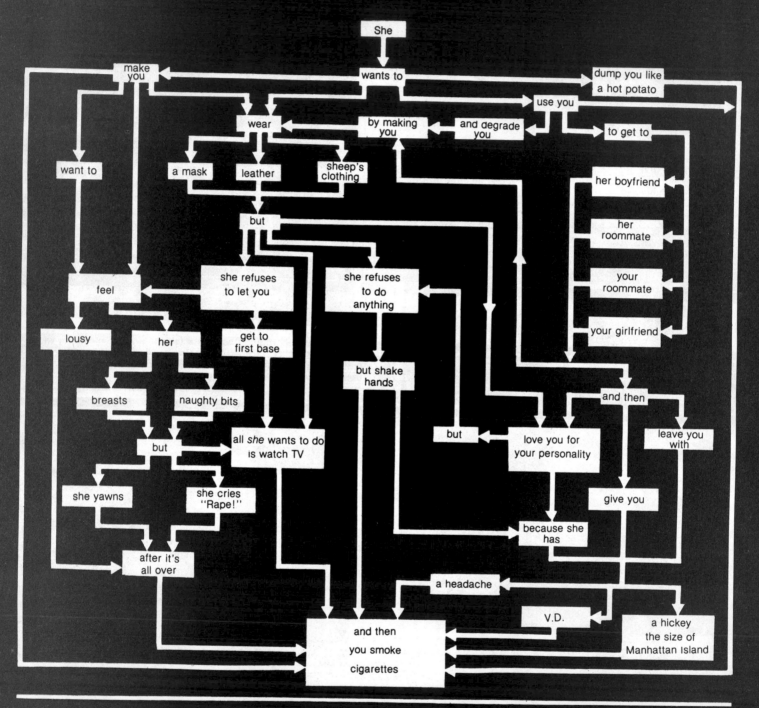

What A Barnard Woman Thinks A Columbia Man Wants

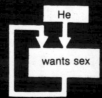

The Dagwoods

PARTY DOLL

Our pinup girl, Michelin Tyre, is a pneumatic young miss who's a hit at any blowout she attends.

Our publisher has assigned us the task of writing the copy for the pinup section. The task is not a terribly arduous one, particularly for one of our literary abilities. One need only identify some activity currently in vogue in which the pinup girl is involved and write, in a style perhaps best described as lustful enthusiasm, a profile liberally laced with sexual innuendo. Nevertheless, we are displeased by the assignment, which we regard as a demeaning and, we may say, wasteful use of our talents which, in our view, would be better employed on prose poems about establishments serving fine food and liquor. Beneath our urbane exterior, we seethe with displeasure. Our stomach flinches experimentally, testing its progress toward the ulcer which, if we are not careful, will cut short our budding career as an international gourmet.

We arrive punctually at the first location, the suburban home of our publisher's cocaine connection, and find our pinup girl waiting. We smile paternally at our pinup girl, whose

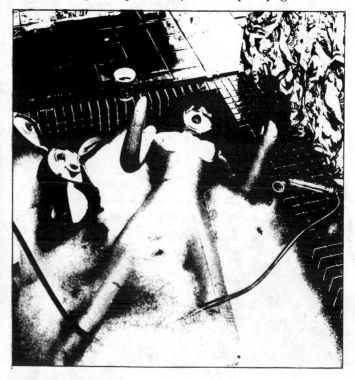

svelte contours recall nostalgically a favorite overstuffed chair which graced our apartment in younger, happier days. We seat ourselves suavely beside her on the couch, lifting our trousers at the knees so as not to mar the crease. Clapping our hands to set the appropriate tone of enthusiasm, and also to gain her attention, which shows a tendency to drift, we review with her the preliminary interview sheets.

Our pinup girl's name is Michelin Tyre. She was born in Hong Kong. Good, we can use that; it sounds mildly exotic. Our readers' fondness for mild exoticism is well documented. Our pinup girl's employment record is not so encouraging, copywise. An unbroken string of massage parlors, porno shops, topless bars, strip joints and suspiciously long periods of unemployment. The most innocuous item is a stint selling flowers on streetcorners, which somehow lacks the glamour we're looking for. Our stomach churns tentatively.

We smile weakly at our pinup girl, who appears to be lost in thought. Our conversational sallies, however, have discouraged us from regarding our pinup girl as a being capable of thought as we know it. We are persuaded that there exists beneath her bounteous curls, if not a vacuum, at least a space. We clap our hands sharply, twice, and explain that, although our magazine is noted for the pictorial content of its pinup girl section, it is traditional to include a modicum of biographical information to stimulate the fantasies of those of our readers who are somewhat lacking in imagination. Is there, perhaps, some talent which the preliminary interviewer has carelessly neglected to discover, some special interest or ability which she regards as uniquely hers? We pause expectantly.

"Well," our pinup girl replies, "I have incredible lungs. I can hold my breath for the longest time." That will prove an inspiration to the photographer, no doubt, but it is scarcely copy. We scowl venomously at our pinup girl, who has the effrontery to be utterly devoid of interesting features, save those which are readily apparent to the most casual observer. Our stomach addresses us with preliminary rumblings of ominous portent. Our pinup girl has no qualities worth mentioning, and yet our continued livelihood depends upon our mentioning them.

Very well, we will make some up. We beam graciously at our pinup and shoo her along to her first session with the photographer. We return to the interview sheets with a spirit of lustful enthusiasm, looking for openings, trying out various phrases. *Born in the British Crown Colony of Hong Kong, Miss Tyre recently rolled into Austin, where she hankers to "hook 'em" with a Texas Longhorn. . . . When she's not exposing her talent (baring her assets?) in show business, Michelin takes to the streets as a freewheeling businesswoman. "Selling flowers on streetcorners," she says, "is a great way to get out and meet people. You wouldn't believe some of the offers I've gotten." We'd like to see her pushing daisies somewhere. . . . Her voice has the same breathy quality as that of the late Marilyn Monroe, and we're sure this airy miss has just as promising a career ahead of her. . . . She may be a bubblehead, but with baubles like these, and her effervescent personality, we're sure you'd like to pop in anytime. . . .*

We smile to ourselves. Yes, it can be done. With a little pumping up, we can inflate the story into a piece large enough to cover our posterior.

We are a genius.

"I get high as a kite on a shot of helium. Whenever I'm feeling low, it picks me right up."

78

SEPARATE TALES OF BANALITY

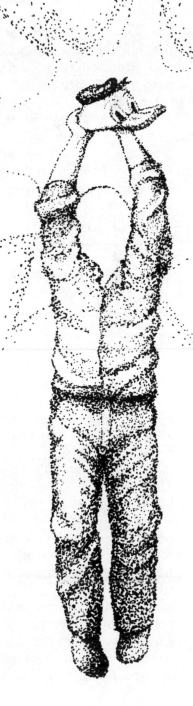

The middle-aged railroad car chugged across the horizonless desert, pulled by an engine that would be extensively overhauled in a few evanescent months. The engineer, brakeman, and attendant were in the cab of the engine smoking marijuana, "the common man's mescalito" as Don Aldock once nomenclatured. The other five passengers were either dozing or attempting to.

My memories of the last visit to Don Aldock are vaguely vivid, that is to say I will never forget what happened, but I'm not quite sure exactly what *did* happen. As I prepared to depart, quite pleased with what I had learned, Don Aldock had bared his teeth to the sun for the first time since I had met him; that is to say, he smiled. I had expected perhaps a capsulizing quote to capture the essence of my experience, or perhaps congratulations for the rapidity with which I absorbed his abstruse yet wholly meaningful philosophy.

"Well," I offered, "it's been real."

"Ronrico," he maintained his smile, "was this a dream, or just an illusion?"

"I'm sorry, Don Aldock, I do not understand."

"What is life for?"

"Don Aldock, that is a veiled extrapolation of Mokamba's paradox. It is like asking what is food for, followed by 'what is eating for.' "

"What is eating for?"

"Sustenance."

"Good. What is living for?"

I winced, then winced again when I realized that Don Aldock detected my first wince. I remembered the tale of Señor Winces, who was buried alive by his superstitious comrades who assigned a sequitor relationship to his sour expressions and the invariable misfortunes that followed.

"Please, my star disciple, tell me, for I must fill this gap in my knowledge."

I laughed, hoping Don Aldock would interpret this as one of my "I understand, what a fool I have been" self-deprecations. He nodded, and I translated this as either a sign of patriarchal approval or of some drug taking effect.

"Life is often meaningless," I regurgitatingly ventured, "a series of hollow pleasures. Life as we know it must recognize a cosmic consciousness. As the Hindus say, 'Allah' is everywhere. Allah be seeing you."

"Ronrico," he deflated, "there never was life as we know it."

I went back to America and returned to my job as a cult hero. But I felt a tug as I sipped my morning coffee and pondered the verities of *Time* magazine. I was reading about how some savage stumbled upon a lost tribe of archeologists in South America. The resulting publicity altered their lifestyle so greatly they had no alternative but to retreat to civilization, for they could no longer cope without reality. My wife was shaking me, telling me I would be late for work.

"You know so much about life," she taunted, "why can't you get to work on time?"

"Because it's not important."

"It's important. It's important. The dishwasher's broken. I'm pregnant. We're out of dope. It's important. How we gonna pay for these things when you get fired?"

"Why don't you mind your own business, and while you're at it, why don't you busy your own mind. One should be able to live prosperously on one's personal resources."

"You're so full of garbage. Do you think getting high with some wetback's gonna give you all the answers? I don't think anybody even cares what you say, your mind is so . . . ."

"That's not true."

"scrambled by those weird cactuses . . . "

"That is not true!"

"you eat and then puke up a minute later."

"That's not true," I exploded. "When I speak, people hear!"

The old man next to me awoke from a grumbling slumber. His shirt was a massive perspiration stain. He smelled like a locker room. His name was Old Jim Towels.

Old Jim Towels snorted, his head spasmed under a crumpled white Panama hat, and his arms shook, spilling a flask of whiskey all over the right leg of my pants. His voice rumbled like a mudslide out of the bottom of his parched throat.

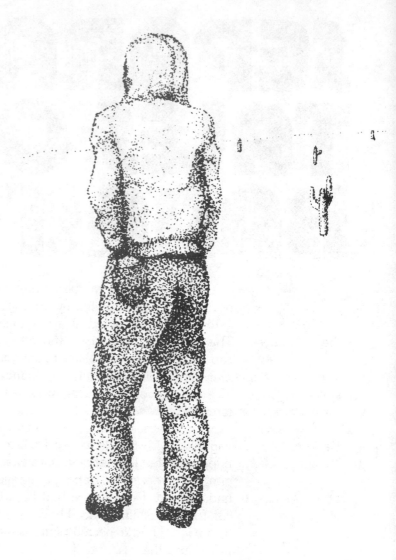

"Sure is hot, huh, kid."

"Heat is a personal conception. Since heat comes from the oft-worshipped sun, there are many tribes that feel a scorching temperature is a present from the gods that they are simply too mortal to use to their advantage. Fire, the physical embodiment of heat, is the most powerful symbol imaginable to them. It is tribal custom to present fire to others on celebratory occasions. Even the Western world has adopted this; it is the tradition of the 'housewarming gift.' "

At least Old Jim Towels was no longer snoring beside me. He was snoring in the seat in front of me.

"Greetings."

An elderly Mexican man, enshrouded in a beige serape, tapped me on the shoulder. His visage was very similar to Don Aldock's, and his beard was cut in quite the same manner, that is to say, not at all. His eyes had the look of a man of knowledge, and his dilated pupils confirmed this.

"You are Ronrico, the young friend of Don Aldock's."

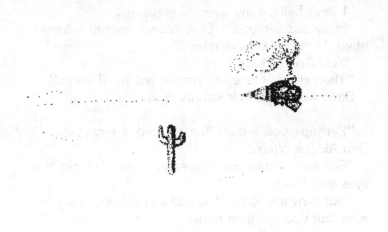

"Guilty on both counts," as I playfully poked him in the stomach.

"Please allow me to introduce myself. I'm a man of knowledge. I've been around for long, long years, stolen many a man's soul and faith. Pleased to meet you, hope you've guessed my name."

"You must be Don Drysdale, the wise man of the Dazierre region. Don Aldock speaks highly of you."

"Don Aldock cannot speak any other way."

I was confused, and lapsed into my smiling act. Don Drysdale, I immediately discovered, would not laugh at his own joke.

"Come," he beckoned, "you must meet my traveling companion, Santiago Koufax. He is an apprentice Man of Knowledge, a Man of Some Good Ideas."

Santiago Koufax was a young man, his demeanor not unlike my own. He extended his left hand for me to shake. We shared a firm, extended mutual grip.

"Shake it three times and you're playing with it," I volunteered.

"Shake it three *hundred* times and you're playing with it," he countered.

We shared a wholesome laugh. I got the end slice, so he began.

"What is reality?" he struck out.

"In twenty-five words or less?"

"If you're giving me an option, I'll mercifully choose 'less,' since it might be quite difficult for you to utilize *exactly* twenty-five words."

"One is capable of focusing his mind on one subject, is one not? Does one not then, have the power to choose his own reality?"

"I'm sorry, I must not have been paying attention. Could you repeat that?"

Santiago Koufax clapped me on the shoulder and offered me a pipe of Don Drysdale's cactus mixture.

"No thanks, I'm trying to cut down," I sheepishly declined. I had not seen Mescalito in some time, and wanted to wait until Don Aldock and I were reunited.

"Ronrico," Don Drysdale tossed, "has it ever occured to you that the cosmos was constructed solely for the entertainment of a superior being? Perhaps Mescalito is just playing a game with himself. Maybe the rules are that several civilizations have been placed on different planets, each starting with the same basic technology. . . ."

"That is to say, none?"

"Correct. Each planet develops its own technology. Perhaps they reach a level of satisfaction. . . ."

At this point he laughed, precipitating a coughing fit. He had a drink of water and continued.

"But this is highly unlikely, wouldn't you say?"

I smiled and nodded.

"So each civilization frantically pursues this goal of technological perfection. And when the civilization of one planet is advanced enough to contact civilization on another planet . . . BOOM."

"Boom?"

"Those two are out of the game. My people fear technology for this reason. We would rather till the soil with our hands than use so much as a stick and risk annihilation. So you shouldn't spend all your time pondering life, for ultimately, it will prove to be no more than a game."

"This reminds me of a tale Don Aldock once related to me. There was a mythical tribe that actually existed many years ago called the Syreos Nation. None of the members were allowed to laugh; those who did were made into soup, except those who were *too* imporridgeable. Actually, I can't remember the story, but I recall Don Aldock's summing comments: "When he who is serious looks in the mirror, he is confronted by his reflection.""

"We must disembark now," Don Drysdale apologized. "I'm glad to have met you. Remember, life is a game. Be life."

"Be a game?"

Soon after Don Drysdale left the train, I was conquered by drowsiness. The next thing I remember was being poked by the attendant who was telling me to get off because it was my stop. Don Aldock was just pulling up to the depot in his old pickup truck when I stepped off the train.

"Who do you think you are?" he blurted, his standard greeting.

"I think I'm me."

He clutched me to his thin yet masterful body, embraced me, then spun the truck around and raced toward his home.

"We have so much to talk about, Don Aldock."

"I have much to tell you. You have much to listen to. Ronrico, which of these doesn't belong: a. black, b. white, c. gray?"

"I could only guess, Don Aldock, I'm sure I am not smart enough to know the answer."

"The answer is a. black and b. white. They don't belong because one should not consider extremes when seeking alternatives. Which doesn't belong: a. coffee, b. bad news, c. alcohol?"

"Bad news, because the other two are drinks."

"No, coffee. Coffee is a stimulant, the other two are depressants."

I had much to learn.

We arrived at Don Aldock's one-room shack. His wife was inside stirring dinner in a large metal bucket.

"What's for dinner, hon? We're starved," Don Aldock asked.

"Peyote soup with psilocybin mushrooms," came the cheery response.

"Again?"

"That's all we have in the house, *dear*."

Don Aldock smiled meekly at me.

"Dinner will be a bit late," he said. "Let us go into my study."

Don Aldock's "study" was a section of the room partially obscured by yellowed newspaper hanging from the ceiling.

"Last time, I told you of the power spot, the one point on earth from which all one's powers are derived. Each man has his own power spot somewhere, and he reaches his maximum power when he stands on that spot.

"Well, I met a man who found his power spot. It was on a conveyor belt at the Ford Motor Company assembly plant in Dearborn, Michigan. In order to keep his power, however, he had to keep walking, because, you see, the belt was moving.

"The foreman didn't want him walking on the belt, but it was impossible to budge him, he was so powerful. Finally, the foreman turned off the belt, the man kept on walking, left his power spot, and was beaten up severely."

"So, Don Aldock, nothing is eternal."

"Only eternity."

After dinner, I felt a bit nauseous, and remembering the quaint Mexican customs, I threw up at the dinner table to show my appreciation. In the candlelight of the dirt-floored hut, I saw ants, spiders, and mystic visions.

"I can't believe my eyes." I explained.

"How sad for you," Don Aldock sternly admonished. "Do you believe mine?"

"Yes, Don Aldock."

"Then close your eyes, you do not need them."
Darkness fell as I closed my eyes.

"Perhaps you would like to read a newspaper," Don Aldock offered.

"But that would be impossible. Don Aldock, my eyes are closed."

"But mine are open. You said you did not trust your eyes, but you did trust mine."

"I was wrong."

"You closed your eyes and saw the light."

Don Aldock awoke me the next morning. "Do you know what is important?"

"Only those things that will make me a man of knowledge."

"Will food make you a man of knowledge?"

"Without food, I cannot become a man of knowledge."

"The same for creature comforts?"

"Some, such as shelter and a place to urinate."

I had spoken of something that was on my mind. No, it was now on my body.

"Is time important?"

"No."

"Some things are interesting, but not important. This is true of almost all things of society: time, sex, sports, orthodontia . . . ."

"My wife thinks time is important."

"Tell your wife to take a hike."

"I love my wife."

"What is love?"

"Love is a feeling two people have for each other. It's hard to describe."

"Nonsense. Love is when you like somebody, and then you're around them a lot."

"How can you be sure, Don Aldock? How can you take a nebulous concept such as love, assign factual values to all the unknown aspects, and use these values to declare an absolute truth?"

"If one is not allowed to assign values, the only statement one could legitimately make would be 'I think I think; therefore I think I think.' "

"With that premise, you could claim to know all the things of the universe."

"I do. There are only ten thousand of them."

"Exactly then thousand?"

"Exactly. If you don't believe me, count them yourself."

DO YOU HAVE THE TELLTALE SIGNS OF
HOMOSEXUALITY?

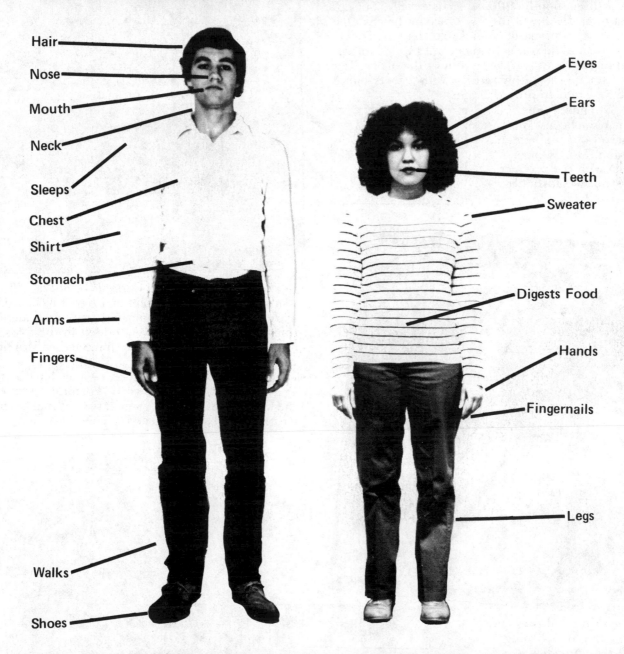

Hair
Nose
Mouth
Neck
Sleeps
Chest
Shirt
Stomach
Arms
Fingers
Walks
Shoes

Eyes
Ears
Teeth
Sweater
Digests Food
Hands
Fingernails
Legs

One out of every ten Americans is gay. They eat. They breathe. They hold respectable jobs. Some are politicians. Some teachers. Others sales workers. But they are all a menace to society. They threaten our American way of life.

"Queers" must be dealt with. But we have to start fighting the problem at home.

If you have any of the dreaded signs shown in the above photograph, you may very well be a homosexual yourself.

If so, drop your friends, quit your job, and confine yourself to a sanitarium.

Subliminal Seduction

Every time you pick up a magazine, your subconscious is being propositioned by cigarette, liquor, and cosmetic ads. This is Subliminal Seduction, and here is how it works:

A young man, while waiting to see the dentist, flips through a three-month-old *Good Housekeeping*, but appears not to notice any of the ads. Once in the chair, he is given a shot of Novocaine and is told to relax. For no apparent reason, the young man becomes very "horny," leaps out of the chair, and rushes out of the office. Ten minutes later he sheepishly returns with a forty-ounce bottle of New and Improved Bounty.

What happened? The young man's subconscious mind picked out the hidden messages in the ads, associated them with the product, and went out to satisfy his prurient needs.

No other cigarette personnel can make the claims we do.

DURAL III

▲
▲The ad above is a good example of how a skilled photographer can hide a subliminal signal in his ad. After leafing through the magazine, the unwitting reader thinks of this saucy blonde, hidden in the folds of the model's shirt, and longs to do things to her with his cigarette.

◄◄The ad at left seems innocent—but don't be fooled. Perhaps you noticed the word "Fornicate" written into the woman's hair. Yes, it's small; sure, it's subtle, but our electron microscopes picked it up.

SEEGRAM'S

Truly Outstanding

Seegram's

EIGHT 8 CROWD

serious drinking problem

▶▶To the untrained eye, this ad isn't telling us anything we can't see immediately. But caveat emptor—Let the Buyer Beware! Closer examination shows that the clever manufacturer has hidden this erotic orifice within the floral design on the lipstick case! And *that's* why it's a bestseller nationwide!

Azuza Lipstick. It's written all over your face.

▶▶ You'll be surprised to learn just how blatant this ad really is. See that supposedly ordinary background? A 25″ x 16″ blowup of the square indicated shows us this detail below: a disgusting, sadomasochistic orgy. Note that the woman on the far left (below the man with the mask) is holding a cigarette. Enough said.

The Advantage Points

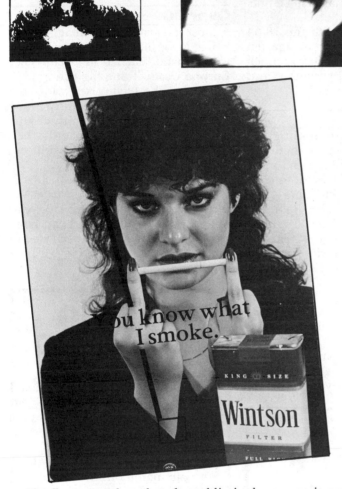

You know what I smoke.

Wintson

KING SIZE
FILTER
FULL RICH

◀◀ Surprisingly, this ad is meant to appeal to *women*, not men. The advertiser's use of subliminal seduction suggests that the woman in the ad, *because she smokes Wintson*, has the opportunity to sleep with Dennis Weaver (of "McCloud"). And, presumably, if *you* smoke Wintson, *you* can sleep with him too.

Weaver's face was cleverly painted into the motif in the model's top button.

▶▶ Finally, remember that the subliminal message is not always sexual in nature. We could find, for instance, absolutely no sexual overtones in this ad, even though we subjected it to intense magnification. What we *did* find, however, was the ingenious way bills were superimposed on the llama's back. It forces an obvious subconscious asscociation: Llama may cost more, but it's worth it.

And after all, isn't that the purpose of advertising? To make money?

Here's to sharp eyes.

How to <u>Definitely</u> Pick Up Women

"Women hate me because I'm fat." "My nose is too big to ever get a really pretty girl." "I'm really Spanish, but the chiquitas think I'm Mexican."

It's easy to complain. You say the competition is too stiff. It's only the good-looking guys who get the girls. So maybe you're not a Greek god. Few men are. But that doesn't mean that you haven't got a chance.

Can I really compete for really pretty girls?

No, you can't.

Forget about pretty girls. When they're not dreaming up ways to play with your mind, they're either out seducing your best friend or locked up in a bathroom somewhere forcing themselves to throw up the $50 lunch they made you buy them, so they can stay skinny. Nope, pretty girls are trouble.

Can I score with regular-looking women?

What for?

So what's left?

Plenty. With umpteen billion females in the world, it's a veritable smorgasbord of women. But even at a smorgasbord, not everyone can have the prime ribs. But that doesn't mean that the chopped liver isn't just as good, and there usually isn't a line. *You mean?*

Right. Why bother with the 18-34 crowd, when women under age ten and over age ninety are just as much fun, much more appreciative, and much easier to score with?

Under 10

Now before you go running off and hiding under a bed screaming "I don't want to go to jail, I don't want to go to jail!", take a moment to logically consider why eight-, nine-, and ten-year-old girls may be right for you. The "under ten" set is pretty without being showy, honest without being brutal, and sweet without being phony. Best of all, *there's almost no competition*!

It's easy from here, because ten-year-old girls aren't very smart and will do anything you tell them. The slightest provocation of "betcha can't, betcha can't" on your part will make them do things you'd bet they could, but never dreamed they would.

It's enough to make you think that five to ten years isn't such a long time.

Over 90

Most men can't even imagine what it would be like to have sex with a woman who reached her peak when Europe was still one big country. "It would be like having sex with your grandmother only much, much worse," is what many men think. But some men, like your grandfather, would be happy to have sex with your grandmother.

The key to having fun with a "sexy senior citizen" is *optimism*. For example, many women over ninety years of age wear dentures, and you know what that means. Right. They come out. Aren't things looking a little brighter already?

ADVANTAGES AND DISADVANTAGES OF DATING WOMEN

UNDER 10

■Advantages:
1. It's easy to beat them in games.
2. They don't have any cellulite.
3. They never fake orgasm.
4. They can't tell the difference between hamburgers and real food.
5. They're almost always virgins.
6. It costs you less to take them to the movies.

■Disadvantages:
1. They grow up.

OVER 90

■Advantages:
1. It's hard to get them pregnant.
2. You don't have to worry about long-term relationships.
3. They never fake orgasm.
4. You meet very few virgins.
5. You can do whatever you want with them because their memories are so bad.

■Disadvantages:
1. They die.

DATING DO'S AND DON'TS

Under 10

DO tell her how old she looks.

DO insist on her calling you "Uncle" in public.

DON'T give her anything with your name on it.

DON'T let her memorize your license plate number.

DON'T tell her where you live.

DON'T get caught.

Over 90

DO tell her how young she looks.

DO ask her how she's feeling, but only if you're not in a rush.

DON'T get involved with her friends. The last thing you need is for her to find another woman's surgical stocking on your back seat.

DON'T yell into her ear. She can probably hear just fine, and you'll only offend her.

RUSTLER

Is Kosher Meat Really Best?

Beef Jerky: rib tickling

Jimmy Heifer Exposé

ROUND·UP

TAKING THE BULL BY THE HORN

I'm a Holstein bull residing at a large New England farm, and I would like to share an experience I had several years ago when I was hospitalized. Although I was under the influence of massive doses of PCP and other tranquilizers, I vividly recall the first time I set my eyes on Ferdinand, the Hereford steer who occupied the stall adjoining mine. He was about five feet high, 3400 lbs., and built like a John Deere tractor.

After a couple of days of being cooped up, I began to get horny watching the nurse's udders sway back and forth as she made her daily rounds. I decided to take some "action" to alleviate the massive T-bone that had suddenly appeared between my Porterhouse roasts. I ducked behind the old fodder-feeder and started right in on the old ground round. As I was beating the meat I felt a strange sensation—as if someone was watching me. Startled, I glanced up to see Ferd grazing nearby. Embarrassed, I covered my cube-steak with a quick flick of my tail and mumbled something about milking the old sausage-link. Ferd pawed the ground for a few seconds, and then, with a sly wink, asked me if I'd ever "chewed the cud." Although I answered with a resounding "no," a strange chill shot from the tip of my horns down to the hoofs of my already quivering flanks.

But he was persistent. He spread his flanks before me, and shyly presented me with his somewhat deficient member. Noting my surprise, he said, "Yeah, I know—I wish I had an Oscar Meyer wiener, but . . ."

He was hung like a human. Although I had never been attracted to a stud, I was filled with a consuming desire I'd never felt before. Transfixed with passion, I took the full length of his prime morsel between my jowls and began sucking fiercely. In seconds he was pumping gallons of delicious moo juice down my throat that was pasteurized, homogenized, and USDA approved.

Even though he wasn't my breed, I know how much I'd like to sit on his fence post again. Unfortunately, he left the ward without even so much as a flick of his tail. I can hope our hoof prints will cross again before we reach final judgment in the Chicago stock yards.

—Name withheld upon request

SEX IN ADVERTISING

It was late in April, and my co-workers and I had just landed an enormous account for our small advertising agency. After work that day, Tor, Brahma, Roxy, Bolder, Bessie, and I went down to the local watering hole to wet our whistles. All of us were young, corn-fed, Midwestern beef—except, of course, for Bessie, who was a slim 500-pound, golden brown, honey-haired beauty with the body of a calf and the udder of a cow. Eventually we all trotted back to my place, one of those ultra modern singles' barns, and did a few bowls of some fine homegrown Bolder had discovered at the edge of his pasture. Suddenly, Roxy turned to me, said "Watch this," and slid his hoof right up Bessie's fashionable culotte. As if electrified, Bessie stuck her tail lovingly in his ear. Soon Brahma and Toro got into the act, mounting her from the front and rear respectively. As she rhythmically stimulated Roxy and Bolder with her incredibly agile tail, she beckoned me with her nose ring. I obliged, and the five of us were soon pumping away at pure Del Monico. Minutes later, amid moo's of relief, we unloaded about a half keg of beef byproducts into her orifices, her coat, and onto the straw-covered floor. In the aftermath, we exhaustedly hit the hay, agreeing that it had been a fantastic way to celebrate getting that new account.

—Chuck Wagon

ELSIE

"*There's nothing I like more than lying around in the sun. I love the heat on my back, the flies buzzing around my tail, and the sweet fragrance of freshly made fertilizer in the soft summer breeze. It's times like that when I feel like making love.*"

"*I'm not really turned on by bondage or S&M, but I was tied down and branded once, and it was kinda fun. The guy turned out to be too possessive.*"

"I've never made it with another cow. Although the idea excites me, the right cow has yet to stroll down my path. Bestiality is normally a real turn-off but once I had this relationship with a young farmboy who used to be my milker. He had such soft hands and the way he stroked my udder really rang my bell."

"I'm thinking about going into movies. I've done modeling for Borden and my agent says I have the natural look that's so much in demand these days. Last summer I got a few jobs appearing in Westerns but I'm still waiting for my big break. I hope one day to direct and star in my own picture where the stakes are

"I like my bull to be all meat. Cereal and beef byproducts don't attract me at all. They just don't have that tender juicy taste I love so much."

BARNYARD DATA SHEET

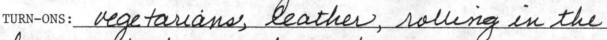

NAME: _Elsie_

RIBS: _prime_   UDDER: _firm_

BIRTHDATE: _May 1, 1972_

SIGN: _Taurus_

BIRTHPLACE: _in a manger_

GOALS: _to meet Hugh Heifer and milk him dry_

TURN-ONS: _vegetarians, leather, rolling in the hay, studs, and good grass_

TURN-OFFS: _branding irons, Elmer's glue, Schlitz Malt Liquor commercials, Merrill Lynch_

FAVORITE SONGS: _"Still Grazing after all These Years," "Back in the USDA," "Honky Tonk Cow"_

FAVORITE SPORTS: _horse shoes, bull fighting, and horse racing_

FAVORITE BOOKS: _Slaughterhouse Five, Black Beauty, Animal Farm, A Child's Garden of Grass_

FAVORITE TV SHOWS: _"Wild Kingdom," "Bonanza," "Little House on the Prairie," "Wild Wild West," "Mr. Ed"_

IDEAL MATE: _well groomed, outstanding in his field, not just one of the flock_

Meat age 3

No beefs at age 4

Udderly attractive at 5

We're looking for engineers who never gave coitus a second thought.

Most people think that at Genital Electric, coitus is our first, last, and only interest.

Nothing could be further from the truth.

We started out in 1927 making basic toys such as vibrators and rubber products. And while devices that run on electricity and spark fun remain important to us, we have branched out into many new fields made possible by today's loose morals.

Fields such as fellatio, cunnilingus, and sodomy. Whips and chains. Life-like dolls. Skin flicks. Girlie magazines. Adult books. Massage parlors. And last, but not least, the ever-popular orgasmatron.

All sorts of products for all sorts of people. Inventing these devices takes a person who can think about sex analytically, without becoming aroused. A person who has no preconceived notions about sex. In fact, a person who has no notions about sex at all. That is why we need engineers.

Since Genital Electric is varied, you can find a place with us to start your career, no matter what your hang-ups. And each of our divisions is small enough that you can score.

That is why we say if you never gave coitus a second thought, your first thought should be Genital Electric.

Give it a thought.

GENITAL ELECTRIC
Screwing the Public for over 50 years.

The Joy of Television

A gourmet guide to viewing

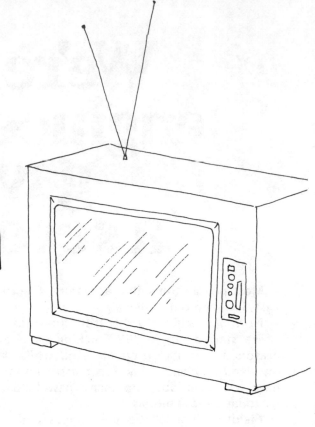

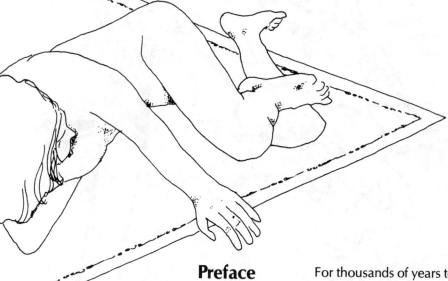

Preface

For thousands of years television was a subject that was considered taboo. There are few records of television before 1930, but references to television, however scandalous, were the rage of Edwardian, and even Victorian, England. Today television, or more exactly, the love of television, is a subject consenting adults are willing to talk about. This book is the work of two noted viewers, professional in their approach. Their work is the result of years of research, usually at night and usually after dinner.

The authors of this book have tried to deal intelligently and playfully with topics as serious as the inability to maintain vertical hold and premature cancellation. Enjoyment, total enjoyment, can be attained by anyone with a love for, and commitment to, television. Throw care to the wind! We live in a video society. The TV revolution of the 50's proved that, and as a result millions of Americans are watching Maxwell Smart, Laverne and Shirley, and even Big Bird, without any inhibitions!

This book is not designed for the child, whose interest in television is purely curious. It is meant for the adult committed to and very much in love with his set. We hope that the book will prove to be as much help to the professional counselors as to lonely college kids who live for black-and-white reruns. There are no rules, except the rules of care and the FCC. The fog of misconception must be burned off. Too many lovers have worried themselves gray over antenna size, insufficient tint, and countless other fallacies that have dominated the television scene for decades.

So come with us through a gourmet's guide to viewing. There may be dishes too rich, too exotic, or too salty for certain viewers. This we understand, and accept. Everyone can find a niche, be it morning news, soap operas, Gene Rayburn game shows, or the popular shows of prime time. Watch your television. Touch your television. Know its knobs, its dials. The tubes and transistors will glow red with pleasure when you turn your television on, I guarantee it.

We offer you information about a world you may know more of than you realize. Locked in your memory are hours and hours of television. Opening yourself to those memories and instant feelings for Mike Nelson, Joe Friday, and Mary Richards can mean more to you than the purchase of cable TV or other expensive viewing aids.

Good luck and good viewing.

Fred Silverman

Starters

Changing Channels

Risky, yet often rewarding. Occasionally the viewer turns so fast that his wrist aches and his friends, wife, and children leave him. We know of a man who did this so much that by the time he'd finished turning the dial back and forth he was a grandfather. It's like Rip Van Winkle. What's a viewer to do?

Remote Control

Dial flipping, or remote control *favia* as the disease is known in its leisurely and affluent stages, is afflicting more and more Americans daily. Use *TV Guide*, a known product that controls channel abuse.

Floors

Dangerous, fun, dirty, and erotic. All these adjectives describe the floor as a viewing spot. Linoleum can be cold and uncomfortable. Shag is a favorite, but the high output of crumbs and beer stains makes it a practical impossibility. Leave the floor to the children unless you feel like doing laundry.

Foreplay

It's an old dog that can't be taught new tricks, a saying goes. Similarly, don't expect your 1954 Zenith to heat up to your lusty expectations when that old Rita Hayworth flick is on the late show. Old sets take time, and foreplay, such as a stroke behind the rabbit ears, or an affectionate nuzzling of the hue knob, can often make the wait worthwhile. Similarly, the bouncy new Trinitron you just won at the office doesn't want to be used only for *60 Minutes* or "thoughtful shows." Turn it on anytime, any day, for any show. It wants your fingers all over it, your eyes glued to it.

Sitting Chairs

An extremely comfortable and still, after many years, fashionable position. Pared down to the bones, the viewer sits on a chair, his thighs resting on the seat, forming a "lap." On this lap there can be placed milk, cookies, magazines, or animals. The initial problems of dangling feet or short arms are usually (though not always) overcome as the viewer ages. Rocking, though fun, is only recommended for those who have passed the crucial 18-49 stage.

Main Courses

From Behind

There are those who find the back panel of a television more appealing than the smooth, cool screen. Usually made of something as insubstantial as pasteboard, the back can be easily removed to reveal a mass of electricity with which one can become surprisingly intimate.

Commercials

Of course you'd like to kill Mrs. Olsen and the Pillsbury doughboy. But your life wouldn't be the same without commercials. When else could you go to the kitchen?

Group Viewing

Since the advent of television, young children, brothers and sisters, families and friends, have shared viewing experiences with a marvelous innocence. A few years ago a complex was built in New Orleans. At first it was a sports arena, but along with the tens of thousands of seats, the Astroturf, and the American flags, there was something new and daringly different. The Superdome had a television. At any one time thousands of people could pack tightly into the building and, while practically rubbing shoulders with perfect strangers, watch television! Needless to say these giant televisions have sprung up in the American cities most notorious for hedonistic abandon.

Movies

Always good anytime of the day. But nothing beats a late-night feature like *It Happened One Night* or *Citizen Kane*. And who can ever forget *Topper* or those great WW II flicks? Make sure you watch a genuine feature film. There's nothing more disappointing than getting psyched for a movie and then seeing Barbara Feldon in another "NBC World Premiere."

Quickies

For some, the pleasure of television is intensified when a show runs only a short time. Viewing intensely for very short amounts of time produces a frustrating, but usually exciting sensation. One should start slowly, perhaps with a show that, though a full half-hour long, will almost assuredly be cancelled after a single season. Many couples received some of their most intense sensations by becoming avid fans of "Dusty's Trail." They watched the show faithfully, often simply because they knew it would be cancelled with no hope of reruns. This gambit, though stimulating, is dangerous. One woman who entered into such a relationship with "Hello Larry" suffered a tele-emotional breakdown when the show returned the next season and she is now under medical care watching fish tanks.

The more daring may want to experiment with extremely short programs. For more than a decade knowledgeable housewives have dropped whatever they were doing to catch the Noon news, a titillating five minutes long! Most short shows are on very late at night. Often these pertain to hobbies or art appreciation. For the many who are pursuing a more natural lifestyle, the Farm Report, usually aired around 6:30 A.M., is chock full of exciting information. One should avoid becoming addicted to shorts. After thirty-second commercial spots, one is hard pressed to find anything shorter.

Soap Operas

A brilliant genre form, often thought to be the culmination of American art. Auteurs as far flung as Fellini, Hitchcock, and Renoir often wish they had been given the opportunity to grow up in America so they could come *of*, rather than look *on*, the America that produces such a vivid, accurate, well-executed, and popular art form. In a 1972 interview, Renoir stated that, "The soap opera is life. It is the consummation of 3000 years of Western culture. Its characters breathe life while at the same time facing death—right in the eye. Soap implies cleansing. It is beautiful. I only wish I had been born in Wisconsin."

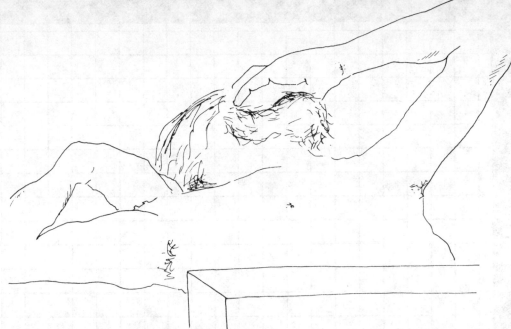

Problems

Age

Sometimes age is viewed as a barrier of sorts. This could not be further from the truth. Though extreme age might limit one's viewing hours, it is rare that one's visual appetite is actually impaired. Often the elderly, like the very young, can make up for an insufficient number of daily viewing hours by moving very close to the television. When, by illness, age, or exhaustion, a person is cut from the healthy seven-hour viewing day to a scant three or four, viewing within eight inches of the screen can usually compensate for the reduction in hours. This is called the "Winky Dink" syndrome.

Children

The presence of young children can often be an embarrassing experience. More that once, parents have tried to introduce a child to normal, healthy viewing, only to have her wander into their room while they are viewing a Roger Corman film. Care must be exercised in introducing a child to TV.

TV Dinners

TV dinners have become the viewers' greatest friend. They allow a viewer to maintain the level of nourishment necessary to sit in the recliner and watch sit-coms without missing the commercials. The only problem is that they have to be cooked, or at least thawed. Perhaps a better alternative is a simple sucrose I.V.

Pay TV

Those little TV's with the comfortable chairs that'll break your heart for a quarter. The pay TV is perhaps the lowest form of viewing. Pay TV's can be found anytime, day or night, in the lobbies of run-down hotels, in bus stations, train stations, and even laundromats. For twenty-five cents they'll play to any viewer, giving static and snow, and then clicking off after exactly ten minutes. A pay TV doesn't care how close "Mission Impossible" is to climax. They have hearts of stone and bodies of metal-flake plastic. They are gaudy, small, always black-and-white, and always off station. But they're still TV's. And remember, in a pinch seventy-five cents can get you through 'MASH" or "One Day at a Time," and in extreme circumstances twenty-five cents will give you that little lift you might need when you find yourself in a strange city, thousands of miles from your 22-inch Zenith.

Premature Cancellation

Premature cancellation seems to be an especially uncomfortable subject. Often viewers will walk around for weeks in a semi-conscious state, wondering why "such a good show" would get "cancelled." There are some measures that can be taken to alleviate the tension premature cancellation creates. The Nielson Method is complicated, but sometimes it can save a show. Unfortunately, there are no straight answers why a show that begins with excitement and audience appeal should fail to sustain its backing.

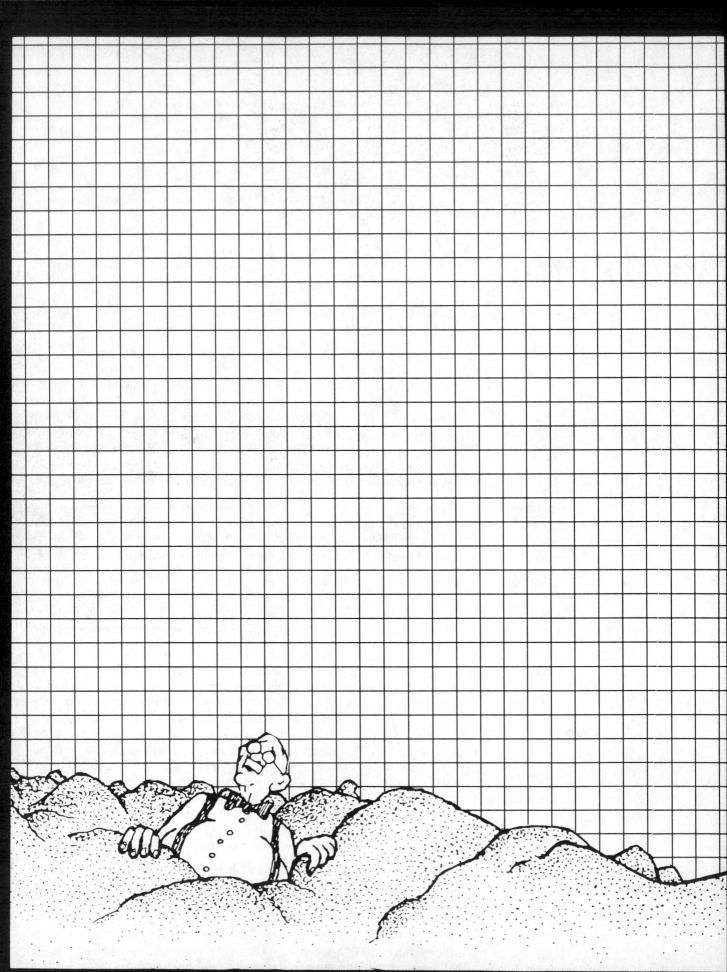

Chapter 4

HELP, MARTHA,

I'M BEING ABSORBED

The traffic refused to stop. Car upon car dribbled through the intersection as Sam stood helplessly on the corner. He had to get to work, and that meant getting past those cars. He leaned against the lamppost and noticed his legs were becoming weaker and his vision was blurring. It was happening again. He was being transformed into Psychedelic Sam, a regression to his college acid days. With graceful ease, Sam floated over the cars, handing out flowers to those who brashly blared their horns at him. He drifted to the ground a block from the office and settled back into Sam the Executive.

"Good morning," said Sam's secretary as he strode into the office.

"Good morning, Miss Wirtier," replied Sam as usual. "Any mail?"

"No, Sam," Miss Wirtier answered.

Sam walked reluctantly to his desk. He would have to sit behind it for eight hours whether or not he had any work to do. "If there isn't any work to be done, why can't we go home?" thought Sam, a college graduate with a degree in philosophy. He frowned, shuffled some papers around, sank his head down onto the desktop, and fell asleep. Miss Wirtier interrupted before he could get too far.

"There's a board meeting, and Mr. Fleeb wants you to be there."

"Thank you, Miss Wirtier." The last thing in the world Sam wanted was a board meeting. He never did anything at the meetings except sit in a dignified manner with an empty briefcase.

The board room was the same as always. Sixteen chairs around a long, mahogany table. Sam found his favorite spot, two seats from the right end. He sat down and watched the others file in. There was Mr. Blue, Chairman of the Board, Mr. Brockwell, Vice President of Corporate Affairs, and Mrs. Smithens, Vice President of De-Sexing Corporate Executive Titles. More people came in until all the seats were filled. Sam stared at them all. "What bores," he thought to himself. Then in walked Mr. Fleeb, and everyone snapped to attention, standing at their seats with their hands resting at their sides. As soon as Mr. Fleeb sat down, everyone else followed suit. Sam wondered what would happen if he remained standing. "Probably nothing," he thought, and he sat down.

Mr. Fleeb started the meeting by asking for new business.

"Yesterday I bought a tie," said Sam, "and that is *my* new business."

"Now really!" exclaimed Mrs. Smithens. "This is a serious top-level board meeting. Please act accordingly."

"I'm sorry, Mrs. Smithens," declared Sam, still amused by what he had said.

Sam carefully eyed Mr. Brockwell. His tie in particular. It was black against a white shirt. Sam thought it made Mr. Brockwell look like a zebra. He spied at his face, and sure enough, Mr. Brockwell was a zebra. He looked around the table. There was a giraffe, and an elephant, a rhinoceros, tigers, lions, gorillas, and wildebeests. Sam looked down at his brown sports jacket. A tan shirt was in its place. He glanced up and saw the brim of a hat. The door opened and two bushmen stood by a waiting jeep. Sam reached down by his side and found a rifle in place of his briefcase.

"I'm a hunter," declared Sam, and he picked up the firearm and began bagging trophies. The animals offered no resistance. They sat patiently in their seats while Sam reloaded his rifle. As the last animal fell, Sam looked toward the door. His vision blurred and the bushmen were nowhere to be found. Mrs. Smithens was speaking. He rose from his seat and walked toward the window.

"Where are you going, Sam?" asked Mr. Fleeb.

"Just out for a while. I'll be back." And with that Sam leaped out the window and joined the mass of cars that swarmed the street.

THE FIRST THING YOU'LL WANT TO DO IS EAT. NO PROB, BOB! RELAX! JUST STEP ON THE BRAKES AND CHANCES ARE YOU'LL BE DAMN NEAR ONE OF OUR 5 MILLION FAST FOOD JOINTS. DON'T FORGET TO THROW YOUR WASTE OUT THE WINDOW! TIRED? JUST PULL INTO ONE OF OUR MANY 200 MILLION MOTELS!

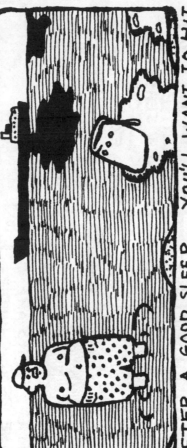

AFTER A GOOD SLEEP, YOU'LL WANT TO HIT THE FAMED JERSEY SHORE. HERE YOU'LL BE ABLE TO BUY A HOT DOG AND WEAR A BATHING SUIT. AND HEY, NO NEED TO WORRY ABOUT ANY NASTY LIVING ORGANISMS (I.E., SHARKS, JELLY FISH, PLANKTON) AS OUR JERSEY WATER IS NOT CAPABLE OF SUSTAINING LIFE FORMS. (NOTE-SLIGHTLY FATAL TO SOME PEOPLE.)

LATER, HOW 'BOUT TAKIN' THE KIDS TO THE PLASTIC WRAP FACTORY. NEW JERSEY PRODUCES ALL OF THE WORLDS PLASTIC WRAP, AROUND 1 BILLION FEET DAILY!!

SO YOU'RE CRUISIN' TO JOISEY AH? WHADDAYOU, FUCKIN' CWAZY? HA-HA, NO SERIOUSLY, FOLKS, SINCE 50% PERCENT OF OUR STATE IS PAVED, YOU NEED NOT, OR SHOULD I SAY, DARE NOT, EH, EH, LEAVE THE COMFORT AND SAFETY OF YER CAR.

YOU'LL PASS BY OUR LOVELY COUNTRYSIDE. THIS WAS ONCE ALL USELESS MEADOWLANDS. FORTUNATLY, AFTER EATING ALL OUR CONSERVATIONISTS, WE WERE ABLE TO COMPLETELY COVER ALL OUR OPEN LAND WITH REFINERIES.

YOU'LL ENCOUNTER MANY FRIENDLY, NATIVES, LIKE ESTABÖR ENCHILADÉS. HE SELLS INFLATABLE SEX AIDS IN DOWNTOWN NEWARK. AAAYYY!!

...OR, YOU CAN JOIN THE POLYESTER SET WHO LIKE TO "GET IT ON" TO THE SLICK NEW SOUND OF DISCO AT STUDIO 24 IN NEW-ARK. PROPER DRESS REQUIRED, AND REMEMBER BEAUTIFUL PEOPLE ONLY!

YOU'LL WANT TO VISIT THE SUBURBS, WHERE MORE THAN HALF OF NEW JERSEYS FOUR BILLION PEOPLE LIVE. IN FACT, YOU'LL HAVE LITTLE CHOICE, AS NEW JERSEY IS BASICALLY ONE MEGA-BURB, EXCEPTING CITIES, INDUSTRIAL AREAS, MALLS, AND PAVEMENT.

THE SUBURBS ARE THE REAL "HINTER-LAND OF NEW JERSEY. HERE LIVE THE "FOLKS", THAT SILENT MAJORITY SO IMPORTANT TO THE SOCIAL FABRIC, THE REAL BACKBONE OF OUR WONDERFUL NEW JERSEY COMMUNITY.

CRIME? ORGANIZED ONLY THANX! OUR FACIST POLICE FORCE KEEPS ALL THE PUNKS, HIPPIES, AND DARKIES WELL UNDER CONTROL. NO NEED TO FEAR LEAVING YOUR CAR, (SOME PEOPLE LIKE TO) EXCEPT IN DESIG-NATED COMBAT ZONES.

NOW, HEY, THAT DUZN'T MEAN WE'RE NO FUN! C'MON! THERE'S PLENTY OF NITE-LIFE AND STUFF LIKE THAT! YOU CAN GO TO THE RA-MADA INN BAR IN NUTLEY, OR FOR YOU "PLAYBOYS", HOW'BOUT LOSING ALL YOUR MONEY IN ATLANTIC CITY, OR MEETING A NICE GIRL ON AVE-NUE C IN TEANECK?

HEY SAILOR

MUSIC? YOU BET PLENTY! IN FACT EVERY BUILDING IN NEW JERSEY IS EQUIPPED WITH A MUZACK©TAPE LOOP BACKGROUND MUSIC SYSTEM, AS ARE MOST STREETS AND PUBLIC AREAS. FOR THE KIDS, TRY SOME OF NEW JERSEY'S REALLY "NOW" YOUNG MUSICIANS. MANY KNOW MORE THAN THREE CHORDS!

FUGGA DUGGA MUGGA FUGGA

I'M A DAMN HARD HITTER, FELLA.

YOU WOULDN'T DARE WANT TO MISS A VISIT TO SCENIC PRINCETON UNIVERSITY, AFFECTIONATELY DUBBED "P.U." BY ITS STUDENTS. A MEMBER OF THE PRESTIGIOUS "IVY LEAGUE," PRINCETON TURNS MANY YOUNG-PEOPLE INTO DETER-MINED YOUNG ADULTS EVERY YEAR.

AT PRINCETON, SOME OF THE MOST IMPOR-TANT REASEARCH IN THE COUNTRY IS BEING DONE. IN THE PAST 50 YEARS BREAKTHROUGHS SUCH AS POP TARTS, RED DYE NO.2, NAUGAHYDE, DOUBLE KNIT CLOTHES, MAJIC MARKERS, AND HYDROGEN BOMBS HAVE BEEN DISCOVERED AT PRINCETON.

leaving NEW JERSEY

...AND THAT, PEOPLE, IS THE GLORIVS STATE CALLED NEW JERSEY. Y'ALL COME BACK NOW, HEAR?

IF YOU'RE LUCKY ENOUGH TO BE INVITED, YOU'LL BE ABLE TO SET DOWN TO SOME REAL "DOWN" "HOME" JERSEY COOKIN' IN FRONT OF THE T.V. TYPICAL FARE : BURGER, CHIPS, BOSCO, 7-UP, JIFFY POP, TWINKIES. IN FACT, NEW JERSIANS LOVE BURGERS SO MUCH, MANY LIVE IN "RANCH-BURGERS"!

FO' SHO' BRO'

GRUNT WHEATS

FAKE LEMNAID POWDER

CATS UP

BUFFALO CHIPS

PARAMUS 1962... FASHION HISTORY IS MADE WHEN BAM-BURGAR'S INTRO-DUCES THEIR NEW SPRING LINE... A SET OF NEW JERSEY CLASSICS SO TIME-LESS, THEY HAVE SURVIVED 'TILL TODAY!

Nojnes

IN NEW JERSEY, THERES NO NEED TO GO OUT OF DOORS EVER, EVEN WHILE SHOPPING! WE'VE ELIMINATED INCONVENIENT "MOM 'N POP" SHOPS, AND DEVELOPED HUGE ENCLOSED MALLS, WHICH CATER TO YOUR EVERY NEED. IT'S A COMPLETELY ARTIFICIAL ENVIRONMENT! SIMPLY GO TO YOUR GARAGE, GET IN CAR, AND PARK IN ENCLOSED MALL GARAGE! NO NEED TO RISK THE HAZARDS OF SUN AND RAIN.

HEAD ERASER

This fellow came into my office the other day to ask for an extension. He was one of those types who comb the wisps of hair above his ears over his bald pate in hope of imitating the appearance of natural hair growth, without looking ridiculous. I just couldn't stand it, so I screamed at him, "Can't you be honest for once!"

He looked up at me quite startled. I could see his little mind working away. He was trying to think of all the times he'd lied to me when, in fact, we'd never met before. He must have respected my opinion, my being the Head Eraser and all and he being insignificant. I didn't want him to start crying. His mouth appeared swollen in that tearful sort of way, so I asked him an easy one.

"All right, what's your name?"

"Chester."

"Chester what?"

"Chester Sims."

"Don't you think that's rather odd?"

"Sir?"

"I mean your name, man. Don't you think it's rather odd that you have such an odd name?"

"Well, sir . . ." he began. He didn't know what to say. Finally he pleaded, "Is my name odd?"

"Sure it's odd. Didn't I already say it was odd?"

"Well . . . yes . . . .What I mean is . . . why do you think it's odd?"

I looked at him severely. "I think you can answer that question far better than I can." My look demanded an answer. I'm an expert at looks.

"Well, sir."

"Yes?"

"I mean . . . could it be that my initials . . . "

"Yes, yes . . ." I said excitedly.

" . . . that my initials could stand for something else?"

"Go on! Go on!"

" . . . that C.S."—his voice was tinged with anticipation—"could stand for chicken shit?" He was absolutely glowing now. Finally, he thought, he understood what I was getting at.

"No, no, that's ridiculous. That's not what I was thinking at all." His face pouted. "Let's just drop it, okay?"

I began again. "Mr. Sims, why don't we get straight to the point?"

"Sir?"

"What's your story, man?"

"Well, sir, I live in a flat in the Milhous District with some really exciting gadgets and I'm at level fifty-three employment. Of course," he continued, smiling at me in a chummy manner, "I'm hoping for a promotion to — "

"Sims, stop!" I screamed. He stopped, sinking down in his chair. "Sims," I said, gripping his shoulder tightly, "I know all the facts. Just tell me why you think you deserve an extension on your life."

"Sir, my shoulder." He winced in pain. I let go of his shoulder. "The thing is . . . well, things are going very, very good for me now. I met a woman in the Zimbalist Complex. Sir, I think I'm in love." He winked at me.

"What else?" I asked with a sigh, strolling about the office.

"Uh . . . what else? Yes, well, as I said, I'm hoping for a promotion to level fifty-four employment."

"Sims, who do you work for?"

"The plastic utensils division," he answered meekly.

"What does a promotion mean to you?" My patience was wearing thin.

"Well," he gestured spastically, shaping, it seemed, the plastic utensils with his hands. "This promotion would make me a spoon foreman. I work in forks now."

I folded my arms across my chest.

"You see, s-sir," he stuttered pathetically, "you see, sir, I like spoons. I like them a lot."

"Mr. Sims," I said, turning around, "we all like spoons 'a lot,' but we can't go around planning our lives around them. Now, can we?"

"I want to," he was sobbing.

"Sure you want to, but you can't."

"Yes, I can, if only you'll give me an extension."

"Mr. Sims, I'm afraid I'm going to have to erase you."

"Please," he cried, "can't you make an exception? I've heard you're very kind. I've heard you make exceptions."

"Sometimes, yes, but not this time." I walked over to the corner of my office and got my big No. 2 General Carbo-Weld pencil. It was leaning against the wall. It's about ten feet tall

107

PLAYING THE HOME VERSION OF "TO TELL THE TRUTH".

and a bit unwieldy, but it gets the job done. I staggered over to him with the pencil on my back. It weighs a ton. First, I erased his head, then his arms, then the rest of him. It's great. It doesn't matter where you start; you can do it differently every time. It's completely painless—you needn't worry about that. And all that's left when you're finished is a pile of pink eraser crumbs.

Then I buzzed my secretary, Miss Bennet, and asked her to buzz Larry, the janitor. Larry's a great fellow. He sweeps up the eraser crumbs for me. I joke with Larry. Sometimes he'll come into my office to sweep up the crumbs and we'll have this little ritual. I say: "Larry, you never have to worry about being erased," and he says: "I know, boss. Who would sweep up the crumbs?" Then we laugh. It's our little joke.

Larry walked in with his little broom and dustpan. He looked especially cheerful.

"What's the big smile for, Larry?"

"They're showing reruns of 'The Newlywed Game,'" he answered, beaming.

Larry's only job is to sweep up eraser crumbs. When he isn't in my office, he's down in his broom closet watching television. He tells me about the show. What an enthusiastic, happy person Larry is. He always asks me about my work, which I appreciate because I enjoy talking about it.

"Hey, boss, how's your day been?"

"Fine, fine, Larry."

"You havin' fun?"

"Sure."

"Who'dya just erase?"

"Oh, some twit."

"Where'dya start? Where'dya start?" he sputtered. He was so excited.

"Larry, don't get all in a tizzy." I warned him gently. "Well, let's see. I erased his head first."

"Was it fun? Was it fun, fun, fun, fun, fun?"

What a funny fellow he is. "Sure, it was fun."

"Tell me something else! Tell me something else!" he cried.

"Well, Larry, I erased a cripple earlier this morning."

Ah, yes, that's an interesting story. A quadraplegic rolled himself into my office and, believe it or not, he wanted an extension. I stood up and extended my arm to shake hands with him. Well that, you can imagine, was a bit of a faux pas.

I said, "I'm sorry you haven't been feeling well."

"What do you mean? I'm feeling fine."

"Well, you don't look so good, sitting there in your wheelchair." I laughed good-naturedly. He didn't even smile. Some people have no sense of humor.

"Well," I began again, "what can I do for you today?"

"I'd like an extension."

"But why?" I cried in amazement. "What could you possibly have to live for?" He tried to interrupt, but I wouldn't allow it. "In fact, I'm quite surprised you didn't come in earlier—before your expiration—to request an erasure. I would have gladly obliged you—gladly."

"There's plenty to live for," he said enthusiastically. "It's a big, wide, wonderful world out there." He looked out the window. He would have made an embracing gesture—embracing the whole world—if he could have.

"Sure, its a wonderful world, but not for a cripple like yourself."

"I must disagree with you. I'm very happy."

"Why?"

"Why not?"

"Tell me something, Mr. . . ."

"Gladstone."

"Yes . . . Gladstone, when was the last time you were with a woman?"

"Well . . . not since the accident." He swallowed hard and looked down at his decaying limbs.

"How long ago?"

"Five years."

"I must say, Mr. Gladstone, you're not going to be the cheeriest spot in my day. You are really depressing me. We're going to have to erase you tout de suite."

"No!"

"I'm afraid so." I said cheerfully, honestly trying to cheer him up. I lugged over the big pencil and erased one of his arms. "There—isn't that better getting rid of some of that dead weight?"

"No!"

"Don't sulk, Mr. Gladstone. I'm doing you a favor. Here," I said as I erased his other useless arm, "let's make you symmetrical again. How do you like that?"

He didn't answer me. He was giving me the silent treatment. Well, I wasn't going to feel bad if he was going to act like a baby. I erased his legs. "Oh, Mr. Gladstone, you look so neat and tidy without all those useless limbs. You really are much more aesthetically pleasing now. What do you think?" I showed him a mirror.

"It doesn't really make any difference," he said coldly.

"I think it does. It looks so much

better. I'm going to give you an extension. I'll give you a year to try out your new look on the world."

I walked over and opened the door for him. "Good luck, Mr. Gladstone." He pressed a button with his nose. The wheelchair spun around with a whir and rolled quickly out the door. "See you in a year," I called after him.

Larry really liked that story, but we didn't have time to laugh and chat about it together. A young man came into my office with a very unusual request: he wanted to be erased before his expiration. He was one of those disgusting-looking teenagers with blotches of pimples and a faint outline of a moustache on his upper lip. His hair was greasy too.

He trucked into my office and shook my hand. "Howdy, Mr. Head Eraser."

"Hello, young man." I was a bit taken aback. "What's your name?"

"George Jones, and first off I'd like to say that I'd like to be erased as soon as possible, if that's okay."

"George," I said gently, "I'm sure you don't realize the seriousness of your request. In considering — "

"Hey! I know what's going on."

"I'm sure you do, but why should a bright good-looking young man such as yourself want to be erased?"

"Well, first off, there's a lot of reasons: number one," he started counting on his fingers, "my girlfriend's got the clap. Secondly, the headers on my Trans Am blew out. Third, I can't cruise anymore 'cuz of that. Fourthly, my stereo's all fucked up. Five, my parents aren't going to Hawaii anymore, so even if I had a girlfriend who didn't have the clap, I couldn't have sex with her on their big waterbed like I was looking forward to." He took a deep breath.

I liked this young man. He obviously knew what was important. I wanted to help him out. "George," I said, "It seems to me your problems are basically due to a monetary shortage. You could repair your stereo and your car if you had enough money. Correct?"

"Sure."

"And if you were working a good job you could afford your own place with a rather large waterbed?" I stopped and looked at him; he knew I was leading to something. "What I'm saying, George, is that I think I can get you a job at the plastic utensils division."

"How much?" he asked.

"About 3.8 units a week."

"God!" he exclaimed. "That's great! I like spoons! I like them a lot."

"We all do, George, we all do. As for your other problem," his face dropped, "I suggest you tell your girlfriend to go to the nearest health clinic for strictly confidential treatment."

He brightened. "I'll do that. I'll sure do that." He shook my hand several times and thanked me profusely. Then he literally bounded out of the place and slammed the door. From somewhere outside my office came a joyful "Yippee!"

I felt as if I'd really helped someone and that's the most satisfying part of my job: making people happy.

You know they say that it's lonely at the top, and sometimes they're not kidding. Believe me, it's not all fun and games being Head Eraser. Many times during the day the weight of responsibility, just like the great weight of my pencil, bears down on me. Yet the rewards in this job are great, and I'm not just talking about money.

After a particularly draining erasure, I like to relax, maybe drink a Pepsi, and ponder life's mysteries. Sometimes Larry gives me a backrub.

Today's high school students represent a generation that grew up with television. Teachers are finding it increasingly difficult to deal with short attention spans. A need has arisen to teach upper level subjects using the same mind-numbing mix of entertainment and learning that made Sesame Street and the Electric Company so successful. Now, thanks to sizable grants and editorial assistance from Exxon and General Motors, the Children's Television Workshop proudly presents:

SPIRAL

Corporate Economics for the Kids Who Grew Up On Sesame Street

● *A regular cast of peers teach basic lessons of microeconomics:*

Dave: Hi, Mr. Dupont! You know, this six-pack you sold me is pretty flat. Could I return it and get my money back?

Mr. Dupont: I'm sorry, Dave, but I can't do that anymore. You see, I sold my store to Convenience Store Inc.

Dave: Well, gee. Why does that matter?

Mr. Dupont: You see, Dave, this used to be a proprietorship. That means that I owned the store, and I had to take all the responsibility if something went wrong. Now I'm part of a corporation. One feature of a corporation is limited liability. That means that I can't be held responsible for the corporation's mistakes.

Dave: Can't you just return my money?

Mr. Dupont: I'm afraid you'll have to file your complaint with division headquarters.

Dave: Gosh, Mr. Dupont. I don't think you should have sold out like that. I liked your store better the old way.

Mr. Dupont: Now Dave, a lot of people like to be nostalgic about the so-called good old days of family-run personal businesses, each with their own individual charm. But I sold the store for your benefit. You'll now have the security of knowing that when you go to my store, or any other owned by Convenience Store Inc., you can expect the same brands and the same bland quality. Remember, if it's good for the corporation, it's probably going to be good for you too.

Dave: Yeah, I guess so. But I'd still like to return this beer.

Mr. Dupont: Dave, these are hard times. Economic solutions don't come easily. We all have to make sacrifices. Convenience Store Inc. has already tightened its belt by buying mediocre quality merchandise. It's time for you to do your share.

Dave: You're right, Mr. Dupont. I'm ready to give up my consumer-oriented hedonistic lifestyle. I'll sell my Japanese stereo and start buying Gallo instead of French wine. If mediocrity is good enough for big corporations, it's good enough for me. Heck, I bet I could learn to like flat beer.

● *A delightful family of puppets present opposing theories of macroeconomics:*

John: We have a whole plate of cookies. How should we divide them up among the kids in the neighborhood?

Milty: That's easy. We sell them to whomever pays the most, according to market demand.

John: Well, I was thinking we could have Mayor Carter give them out equally, then charge the kids according to how much money they have.

Milty: That's socialism, John. Mayor Carter has enough to do without meddling in cookies.

John: But Milty, under your plan the poorer kids won't get any cookies at all.

Milty: Galbraith, don't be such an effete Cambridge bleeding-heart. Everytime something goes wrong you want Mayor Carter to come running in to save the day. If those little snots would just go out and get a job . . . .

Cookie Monster: COOKIES!

John: Oh, well. Say, saw a dynamite episode of your PBS show the other night.

Milty: I hear yours is doing alright too. I'm working on this great plan to turn Yellowstone National Park over to private industry, and . . . . .

● *A group of monstrous corporate animals teach the basic concepts of cost-benefit analysis:*

Grouch: Why don't you guys clean up this mess?

Oligopolis: Gosh, Big Oil, EPA The Grouch is really getting angry about all this garbage in the love Alley.

Big Oil: EPA's had his head in his can for too long, Oligopolis. If he did some basic present-worth analysis, he'd see why we can't clean up the alley.

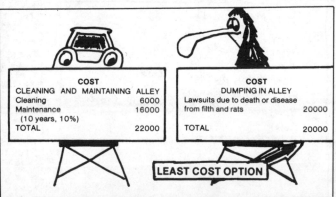

COST CLEANING AND MAINTAINING ALLEY	
Cleaning	6000
Maintenance (10 years, 10%)	16000
TOTAL	22000

COST DUMPING IN ALLEY	
Lawsuits due to death or disease from filth and rats	20000
TOTAL	20000

LEAST COST OPTION

Oligopolis: What if EPA has Mayor Carter order us to clean up?

Big Oil: No problem. We just claim we didn't know that the garbage was dirty.

Make sure your students watch SPIRAL. It's in their best interest . . . as well as ours.

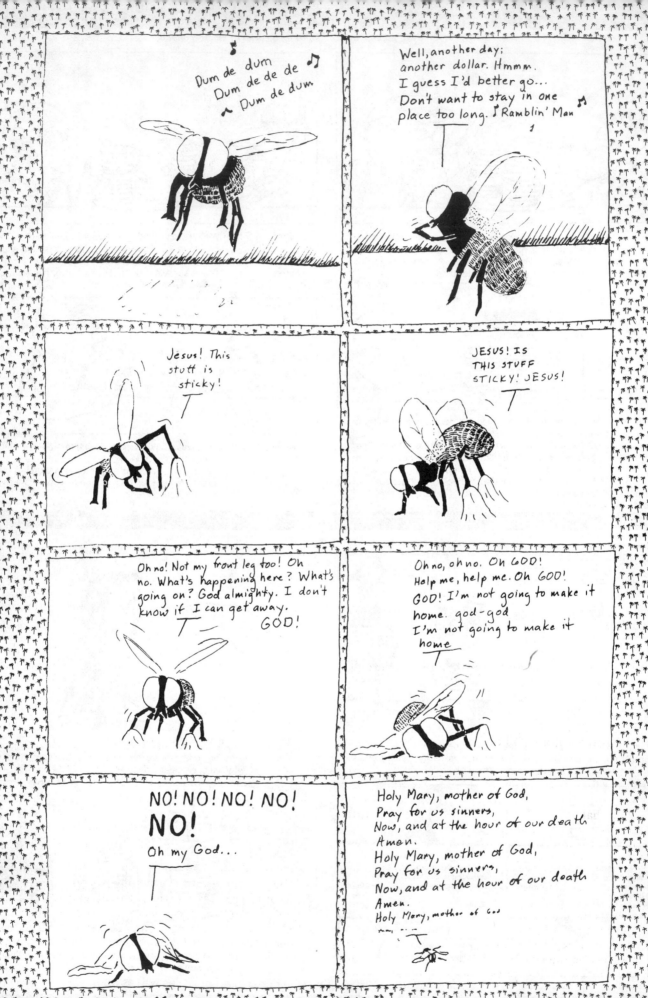

The Night Grandfather Turned Into a Horse

Growing up in Columbus was, on the whole, a study in incidence and insomnia, as our family was awakened by a crisis or near-crisis almost every night. This just goes to prove, of course, that ours was a perfectly ordinary family, prone to outrageous and unlikely happenings. My grandfather, an old bloodthirsty veteran of the Spanish-American War, was, according to grand old Amercian tradition, a "kind-hearted, irascible old cogder." To the medical profession, he was "a psychopath and social deviant." We called him "Grandfather" or "the old coot" and kept all sharp objects from his reach. We didn't believe him dangerous, as no family member had ever suffered more than a bitten leg at the hands of the mangy octogenarian. True, the neighbors were often upset by his exploits, but Mother calmed them by minimizing ex post facto the damage done. "Just a little arson," she would say, or, "A nice friendly assault." One year, we went through twelve neighbors in four months. Mother assured us the "unpleasant ambience" they complained of was the pickle factory down the street.

More often than not, and certainly more often than could have been appreciated, the family had for its honored guest our cousin Henry, or, as my brother Mongo and I called him, "leper-head." Henry suffered from dermal and subdermal abcesses about the face and neck, the results of a childhood effort to smoke an industrial-size can of Lysol. He usually slept in my room when he visited our house, as I was the only one who could calm him down when he awoke screaming from his recurrent nightmare involving a team of Gestapo field mice that was trying to mine his oatmeal with incendiary devices. My mother slept in the room across the hall from mine, and my father spent nights pacing the floor of our pantry. He was wont to sudden fits of anxiety just before he fell asleep, during which he would stuff his material possessions in his mouth as a means of protecting them.

Those evenings when we could find him, we put Grandfather to bed by tossing him up into the attic and latching and barring the door. By this time, only two rooms would be unoccupied: the bathroom, also called "the growler," and the guest room, also called "the street." On the night in question, everything proceeded smoothly and according to custom: Henry stayed in the bathroom far too long while we jeered at and threatened him. Sparks, the dog, fought playfully with Mother, who as usual feinted right with the frying pan and then brained the mutt with a handy crowbar; Grandfather ran down the stairs, through the kitchen, and behind a couch in the living room, before Father was able to sink the gaff in his leg and drag him up to the attic. Soon everyone was ready for sleep, doors were shut, lamps blasted out, prayers and maledictions uttered.

A silky somnolence, at once comforting and deadening, wafted its gentle breeze around the bedrooms, down the hallway, through the kitchen, out the back door, and down the street to the twelfth precinct, where it was mistaken for a dangling modifier and flung into the gutter. The sounds of slumber echoed throughout the darkened house: Father's incessant hiccoughing; Mother's loud, raucous snoring; the steady drip-drip from Henry's gaping pores; and the crunch of Mongo's knuckles as he smashed his fists against the wall. "Still dreaming about those baby ducks," I speculated. I shrugged the thought away and let Grandfather's pained moans, muted through the attic floor, lull me into unconsciousness.

I couldn't have been asleep for more than ten minutes when what sounded like a falsetto foghorn gently stirred me from my quiescence. I tripped out of bed, introducing my nose both to the floorboards and to the pleasures of extreme malleability, but was soon on my feet again, searching for the light switch. I found one of Henry's fists instead. Grasping my left ear and restraining myself from bludgeoning my cousin with a nearby vase, I turned on the light and watched while he thrashed about, pushing away a nonexistent bowl of Quaker Instant and moaning, "Just tea for me, thanks."

He was in the middle of his most feared nightmare, and my instincts told me he should be awakened immediately. Quietly I approached the side of his bed, knelt down, and, careful not to disturb him prematurely, placed my mouth close to his ear. Then, with a gentleness born of experience and my own innate sense of kindness, I yelled, "BOOM!"

The result of this perhaps unpleasant reveille was quite impressive, and Henry, with the help of the ceiling and his dorsal cranium, proved once again that two pieces of matter cannot coexist in the same place. He fell back to his bed with a crash and looked about, wide-eyed. "They got me," he groaned.

"No, you whistle-head," I shot back, "that was me. But what were you doing, trying to imitate a banshee castrato?"

"What? It weren't me who screamed," he insisted.

"Well, then who gently stirred me from my quiescence?" But before Henry could respond, a second shriek had both of us searching for cover. I was just about to convince Henry that I should be the one to hide under the Buster Brown blanket when Father careened into the room, his mouth filled to bursting with what looked like a weapons arsenal bought at Woolworth's. When he spoke, much of the potential articulation of his words was sacrificed to the twelve skate keys and the Iranian musk melon he had stuffed into his cheeks, and it seemed to me that although he appeared to be speaking real words, the actual meaning he was trying to convey was hopelessly lost: "I'm a melancholy baby, got the Yoko Ono blues!" he cried, some wing nuts dribbling out of his mouth. I made a quick guess at what he meant and tried to calm him down.

"It wasn't me who screamed, Father."

But this news only increased his anxiety and he asked, "Your distributor's shot. Fifty bucks, please?"

At this point Mother, woken from her sleep by the noise, entered the room.

"What's the deal here, buster? Why the screams of anguish? Leper-head steal your Mallomars again?"

Father did his best to explain: "Surfboard Eddie and the Rancheros—tickets on sale now!" he tried, his brow wrinkled in both expectant and retroactive pain. But Mother was apparently not in the mood for fun and games.

"On your feet." Father stood up before her, head bent. "Eyes front." His head jerked up, and their eyes locked. "Tell me what's going on. Come on, spit it out!" Father tried to restrain himself, but the temptation offered by the situation was too alluring. One second later Mother found herself covered with styptic pencils, sections of peat moss, deposit slips, and diverse other sundries that had found their way into Father's mouth.

The tension in the room was so thick you could cut it with a knife. That's what Father did, piling up blocks of it around him to form a sort of makeshift igloo to protect himself from Mother. She made short shrift of the feeble fortress and stood above a now-prone Father, one foot on his neck.

I decided this might be an appropriate time to intervene. "Gee, Mother," I remarked casually, "maybe you shouldn't shove that blade into Father's heart and make him bleed all over the floor until he shudders and dies." I thought it a convincing argument.

"No," Mother began, but she was cut short by a wail that soon escalated to a heart-stopping screech, then a seismic bellow, before dying out into a pitiful whine. We all looked around the room.

"Musta been . . . ah . . ." began my ever-astute brother.

"Grandfather!" Mother and I finished, and I heard her mutter, "Gonna kill the bastard," as she rushed out of the room en route to the attic. I glanced back to see Father, busily stuffing an encyclopedia into his mouth. I didn't have time to stick around, so I ran down the hall, behind Mongo and Mother.

When they were about fifteen feet from the attic door, Mother panted, "Wait . . . I've got the key. . . ." But Mongo preferred the more genteel method of forced entry, head first. The door was reduced instantly to a fine powder as he crashed through it and barrelled up the stairs.

Mother and I followed, and were about halfway up when we heard Mongo say, "Uh . . . um . . . holy cow. . . ."

Mother and I reached the top of the stairs and peered through the darkness. Grandfather's bed was there, as usual, but instead of his slight form lying in it, we saw it was occupied by a rather capacious quadruped: a full-sized horse! It was tossing and turning and whinnying as it could not, apparently, get out of the bed by itself. Mongo helped by lifting the creature up by the scruff of its neck and depositing it gently on the floor. We noticed it was wearing an army cap and had a military saber strapped to its side.

"Grandfather?" I inquired. The big beast nodded its acknowledgment.

"Well, I say," said Mother, who had come up to the attic seething with anger but who was obviously convinced by the change in Grandfather's physical stature that any melee would end in his favor. "He certainly does look better than he has in years." She gave him a few gingerly strokes.

"Yeah," Mongo said with typical acuity, "but he's a horse."

"We know that, salami-brain," I said, "but what do we do with him?"

Mongo, slightly dizzied by his newly-acquired concussion, was at a loss for words. I glanced down the stairs to see Father flinching involuntarily from invisible assailants. "What's going on?" he asked, his throat making a funny sort of whistling sound when he breathed.

"Grandfather turned into a horse," I replied.

"But we just got his pacemaker insured!" Father complained. "How can we cash in on it if . . . a horse, you say?"

"Right here," I said impatiently, pointing out the equine addition to the family.

"Sure looks like a horse," Henry remarked. "I wonder if Sparks'll like him."

"Sparks?" I asked, the germ of a bad feeling beginning to grow in the pit of my stomach. "Maybe we ought to keep him away from Grandfather for a while. I don't think . . ." I trailed off as the family dog, looking slightly peaked from hunger, came padding up the steps, sniffing for food. As I had neither lead pipe nor shotgun, I knew better than to get in his way or even call him names.

He walked slowly past the human contingent of the

family and stopped in front of Grandfather. With a speculative look that almost turned Grandfather into a living can of Alpo right then and there, Sparks proceeded to walk calmly and resolutely back to his potential victim's rear, eye a tasty hind leg, lick his chops, open his mouth, and lift his own hind leg, sending forth a cathartic shower of bliss onto Grandfather's hoof. Unable to keep still any longer, Grandfather bolted, trying for the stairs. But somehow one of his shoes became dislodged and he careened into me. Although he tried to stop himself, his momentum carried both of us across the attic, and we crashed through the side of the house and went spinning out into space, watching the ground come up....

I woke up in a cold sweat, my heart racing. Frantically, I sat up, looked around—the family was gathered around my bed, and a gentle hand pushed me back onto my pillow while Mother assuaged me: "You wake us up like that again and we'll slit your throat."

"Even Gramps got woken up," said Father. "Isn't that right, Dad?"

"Neigh," replied Grandfather, stomping a hoof.

Oh No! It's the Polish Shell Game

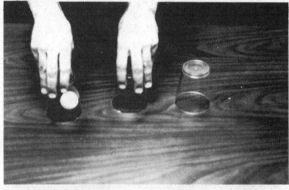
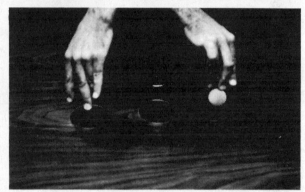

Does Chrysler really need to stay in business?

Nobody knows why Chrysler is in such a financial mess.

So we'll tell you.

We're in trouble because we made great cars for the fifties. But during the seventies they just don't fit in.

We're in trouble because we still build them.

We're in trouble because we use many small paragraphs in our ads. And *Time* doesn't give away space.

That's the truth, now here's the myth.

Sure, 800,000 of our cars were recalled because they didn't have steering wheels. But we're not in trouble because 60,000 cars didn't have pedals. Or that Joe Garigiola advertises our cars. But people remember bald guys, and it's hard to make them forget. We think it's time somebody set the record straight, and since Ford or GM didn't want to do it, that leaves us.

Who makes cars? What is a "gas guzzler"? Why doesn't Chrysler build dishwashers? What is the right kind of car to build? Who won the 1923 World Series?

Maybe when people understand the answers to those questions they'll realize who's screwed up. Us. Maybe the facts will help set things straight. And even if they do, we'll still need money.

Then Chrysler can do its job to become the New York City of the Automotive Industry.

Doesn't Chrysler sell any cars at all?

So far this year, Chrysler has sold less than 9 full size cars, while GM has sold 950,000. On the other side, we've sold over 75 small cars, while GM has sold less than 100 million billion small cars. We don't think we're doing that bad.

But the newspapers don't report things like that. That's the whole point of this ad.

How big are Chrysler cars?

Let's be serious. Chrysler cars are no bigger than they are.

It's a simple fact. You can't get blood out of a termite, and as Ford and GM say, you can't get mileage out of a Chrysler.

But who has the most cars with the best mileage? Not Ford. Not GM. Certainly not us.

First get the facts we want you to know.

Think for a moment. You got it. Toyota.

What does blaming our financial woes on the Press and foreign car manufacturers have to do with anything?

Cars are getting smaller all the time. GM hired smaller Engineers who produced smaller, and therefore more fuel efficient cars. The world is running out of sheet metal. That is why cars are getting lighter.

What is Chrysler doing to meet the challenge?

That is a fair question. The news media has not supplied an answer to that, and we feel it is our duty to tell the public what we're doing. What have we been doing?

We've been playing bridge at Board meetings, and workers at our factories have been doing a lot of reading, mostly classifieds. We've been waxing up Joe Garigiola's head for some new commercials, and you've probably heard Neil Armstrong say, "One small step is a lot further than you'll go in a Chrysler with a gallon of gas."

But these things are just superficial to the real things we're doing at Chrysler.

What is Chrysler really doing to meet the challenge?

Our Engineers have been doing most of the really doing. They have been getting smaller to meet the new federal regulations that are turning into laws. We have many experimental cars that we are hoping will become the prototype for tomorrow.

Our new Alpha-3 eliminates the need for sheet metal entirely. It's made completely from cardboard. You just can't drive it in the rain.

There is also an electric car, the Dingo-6, that runs on a 40 watt bulb. The only trouble is finding a place for the lampshade.

Chrysler's front wheel drive cars.

How did Chrysler come to make the first four cylinder front wheel drive cars of the Big Three? The answer is simple. We just took regular cars and put the body on backwards.

Of course some rearranging was necessary, like sticking new transmission gear indicators on the dashboard, since reverse was no longer reverse. But our Engineers met that challenge, and by next year we'll have the seats mounted in the proper direction.

Why should Chrysler stay in business?

For the same reason everyone else should.

To help the American Automotive Industry. And America. And Ourselves.

Chrysler will become totally front-wheel drive, more fuel efficient, and less dependent on expensive foreign loans.

But to do that we need you.

We need the support of America.

We need someone to write longer paragraphs for our ads.

We don't plan to sell a million billion cars. Half that would be sufficient.

We don't want to be hanging by the thread of our financial wires either. So we're going to have to work hard, and you know what? We will.

We want the United States government to bail us out, like they did Lockheed.

We want a federal loan just as if we too were a struggling college student.

We won't pay it back either.

We want you to believe us.

We want to start our sentences with something besides "we."

Lee Iacocca

Lee Iacocca
Chairman, Chrysler Corporation

L. A. Brother

Lee Iacocca's Brother
President, Chrysler Corporation

The Campus Fitness Sport
POORCOURSE

The POORCOURSE on the Berkeley campus is designed to test and challenge the user. POORCOURSE stations are situated throughout the campus and are accessible to everyone. They are right on the students' way to classes. You've probably encountered a POORCOURSE station on your own, unexpectedly, and didn't even realize it until you'd reaped the benefits of just five minutes at a POORCOURSE station. POORCOURSE stations will enable even the least athletic individual to work up a roaring sweat before going to class. The following introduction is by no means the complete course, but it will offer a challenge to the beginner. Once you get used to this course, other POORCOURSE stations will become apparent everywhere.

Station One— Freak Drag

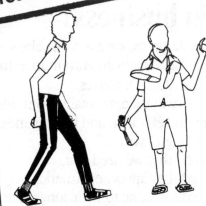

Walk through Sprout Plaza at moderate speed. Mind your own business. Invariably, a Freak, a Wino, or a Biblebanger will try to draw your attention by yelling at you or by blocking your path. He is your "dead-weight" quotient. As soon as the freak clutches your clothing lean forward and sprint, for at least 200 yards. Remember to keep your knees high. Break the freak's grasp and continue on to the next station.

STARTING PAR—AL X, wandering minstrel
SPORTING PAR—The wino with the yamulke and the cut-off dress slacks
CHAMPIONSHIP PAR—Little Thelma, the bag lady with the thyroid condition

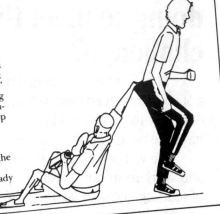

Station Two— Bolted Chair Isometrics

Any classroom on the first floor of almost anywhere on campus will work for this exercise. The desks must be bolted to the concrete floor. Face forward in the desk. Sit relaxed. One or more of the following should then occur: someone at the back of the room calls your name; the instructor requests that the class form into discussion groups; or you get uncomfortable. Wait until your desire to move the bolted desk has peaked. Lunge or lean in different directions while pushing with your feet until it becomes apparent that the chair is bolted down. If you injure your back, kidneys, or ribs while doing this, you are doing it correctly.

STARTING PAR—Attempt to scoot forward
SPORTING PAR—Try to turn the desk sideways
CHAMPIONSHIP PAR—Try to stand straight up (work the upper thigh and groin area)

Station Three— Locked Door Push

These stations are all over campus and are frequently changed so that the student will not "get used to" the exercise and find it too easy and avoid it altogether. Stride briskly toward the door. You should be fully intending to walk right through the door (its being locked should surprise you). Grasp the bar and push down. The bar will go down but the door remains closed. Your momentum should bring your body to a full "pancake" position against the door. Bumping your head or smashing your face against the door insures proper follow through. Retreat. Go out another door.

STARTING PAR—Stroll to class with plenty of time
SPORTING PAR—Be late for class and run into and out of the doorway
CHAMPIONSHIP PAR—Same as sporting par but after a large lecture has emptied
The effect will be greatly amplified by 20 people helping you achieve the full "pancake" position.

Station Four— Lecture Hall Body Curl

Depending on your size you will probably have a favorite lecture hall to do this exercise in. Sit down and relax in a seat. Wait for someone to try to get past you in your aisle. Since there are only two inches between your knees and the seat ahead of you, you must do the body curl. Grasp the back of your seat. Raise your legs as high as you can. Contract your body into as tight a knot as possible. Allow person to go by. Return to relaxed position. Hint: to insure proper form, dump books, papers, and pens onto floor.

STARTING PAR—Go late to class and sit almost at the end of the aisle
SPORTING PAR—Go to class early, but sit halfway in
CHAMPIONSHIP PAR—Go early to Economics and sit right on the end of the aisle
Wearing muddy hiking boots or foodstained birkenstocks can add some color to this exercise, as well as give you a variety of reactions from your body-curl partners.

Station Five— Turnstyle Vault

This exercise takes place in Moffitt Library. Since this is a beginning course in turnstyle vault, it is a natural for beginners. Only the advanced POORCOURSE users should attempt the difficult and stressful rigors of actually checking out a book from Moffitt. For the turnstyle vault, select a book from the shelves. Beginners should choose lighter books. Hold the book in one hand and casually walk toward the back of "enter only" turnstyle at the front of Moffitt. Pretend to be admiring the many Formica surfaces. When the coast is clear, leap over the turnstyle, and run for the doors.

STARTING PAR—The "YAK to ZYZ" encyclopedia
SPORTING PAR—The Collegiate Dictionary (Hardcores can make a try for the swivel stand too)
CHAMPIONSHIP PAR—Twenty bound volumes of *Foreign Affairs*

Station Six— Handout Twist

For this exercise you will again walk through Sprout Plaza. Walk down the middle with your hands empty. Leaflet distributors will converge. As a handout is pushed in your face from the left, twist your upper body to the right and at the same time sweep your extended left arm back so as to block the distributor's action. As the next handout is shoved in your face from the right, repeat the sequence only in the opposite direction.

STARTING PAR—Go through Sprout at 6:00 P.M.
SPORTING PAR—Walk through Sprout at 2:00 P.M. and wave an American flag to bait revolutionaries
CHAMPIONSHIP PAR—Walk through Sprout at noon wearing a backpack and carrying a sleeping bag. Ask people if they know a place where you can get a meal, talk with friendly people, play guitars, and spend the rest of your life in airports selling flowers.

Bitter, Cynical Humor

Whoever you are, you're either male or female. And aren't you a little curious which is the better sex? There are advantages to both, but which is the best for you?

Advantages to being a woman

1. You can cry without seeming stupid.
2. If you're stupid but pretty, you don't have to work. If you get married, you will be cared for all your life. Also he might bring you flowers and candy.
3. If you're at an amusement park and your date wins a stuffed animal, he's supposed to give it to you.
4. You don't have to shave your face every morning.
5. You can have babies if you like pain and morning sickness.
6. If you're on a sinking ship, they will save you and the children first.
7. You can be Miss America, unless you belong to a minority.
8. Nobody minds if you're weak physically or emotionally. They think it's cute.
9. You can look okay with a fat ass.
10. If your car breaks down on the road, someone will stop.

Advantages to being a man

1. You don't have to shave your legs or under your arms.
2. You look good when you're sick or disheveled or old.
3. You can be President, unless you belong to a minority.
4. You can urinate standing up.
5. You don't have to worry about getting pregnant.
6. You don't have to worry about people whistling at you.
7. If you're white, upper-middle-class, and college-educated, you can probably get a good job.
8. You can take your shirt off when it's hot out.
9. If you get a girl pregnant, you can skip town.
10. If you have bad acne, you can grow a beard.

Robyn Ewing 28

ORIGORI

The Traditional Art of Modeling Dead Things with Paper

BURNT EXOTIC BIRD

You will need a square to do this.
1. Start with a diaper fold and fold again.
2. Turn point A over to meet point B.
3. Turn over and repeat 2.
4. Fold outside bottom layers.
5. Do the same again, but on the center line. This fold is temporary, but it makes the next step easier.
6. Inflate with a pressure pump. Open the top layer and hold the rest of the left hand over the center line.
7. Point the peak tips, gently curling outward until you hear a tearing sound. Repeat four times.
8. Get a paper hat and fold it until it looks like a bird.
9. Burn it.

1.

2.

3.

4.

5.

6.

7.

8.

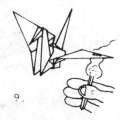

9.

AWFUL AIR DISASTER

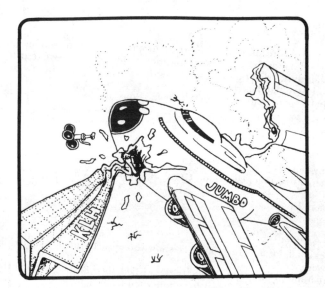

Start with a rectangular piece of paper.
1. Fold the top corners to the middle.
2. Fold this end over so the point is one inch from the outer edge.
3. Fold the top corners in so that the edges meet along the center.
4. Fold the tip in the middle back, then fold down the center.
5. Fold sides down to make wings.
6. Spread wings.
7. Crush.

7.

6.

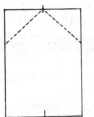

1.

2.

3.

4.

5.

HOW TO BECOME A MILLIONAIRE

With a second grade education and $.35 to my name, I retired in less than twelve months with a wealth of over $40 million.

Millionaires aren't a lot smarter than you. They just have more money. They have discovered the secret to luxurious living and financial security.

In the Beginning

Many people are amazed to learn that in just twelve short months my net worth has gone from zero to more than $40 million! I can still remember what it is like to be over my head in debt, living in a drainage ditch, being so uptight and insecure that I eventually had to sell my wife and two kids.

I Discovered the Secret

In desperation I turned to crime and in no time at all I was . . .

- Living in a luxurious penthouse
- Borrowing vast amounts of money tax-free
- Getting the VIP treatment everywhere
- Creating an empire with the help of other people's money
- Getting my picture in the post office

In just twelve short months I became a real millionaire. Today I am Chairman of the Board of a vast international empire engaged in extortion, narcotics, prostitution, and politics. I own a Swiss Chalet, a 90-foot yacht, a fleet of limousines, a private jet, and a Congressman.

I Write the Wrongs

When I mentioned this story to one of my bodyguards, he suggested that I write about it. So I sat down and wrote the whole story from beginning to end—everything I did, everyone I did it to, every step I took, everything I learned, everywhere I hid. You can read all of the material and formulas and do exactly what I did.

Many people talk about ways to make a million dollars. They write columns and newsletters, but they've never really earned big money themselves. I've done it, and I've never been caught.

My Method Is Nationwide

My method is nationwide. I am getting letters, telephone calls, and subpoenas daily. A California con-man wrote: "Dear Vito, I bought 7 - 8 different books on how to make money. As far as I'm concerned, yours is the only one that works. Your method is great, it's simple, and it works. Please don't print my name. Signed, Andrew Simpson, 43 Butteroll Drive, Los Angeles. P.S. I especially liked the centerfold pin-up."

Centerfold Pin-up?

Yes, my book not only gives concise, expert advice on how to make millions, but also contains explicit pornography and details on how you, too, can become a blackmailer.

Is That It?

No, there's much more, much more.

How Much More?

These last few months have been like a dream. I've had more luxury, power, women, and money than anyone could want in a lifetime. I stay at the finest hotels, vacation at the most exclusive resorts, and eat at the most expensive restaurants. I don't have to work another day for the rest of my life, and if anyone gets on my nerves, I have him killed.

You're probably wondering why I want to share the secret of my fabulous success with cretins like yourself.

Yeah, Why?

Why? For two good reasons:
1. I get sixty percent.
2. You probably don't know any better.

This fully illustrated, step-by-step instruction material on HOW TO BECOME A MILLIONAIRE will instruct you how to:

- set up your own international drug ring
- make prostitutes work for *you*
- bribe politicians
- cheat on your income tax

There's a lot more—200 pages in all, for a mere $10.00. To show you how confident I am that it works, here's my personal insurance.

I, Vito Manicotti, personally guarantee that if you aren't 100% satisfied, then I'll forget about the whole thing. That's all you get. But what do you expect for a lousy ten bucks?

- -

Vito Manicotti   **204 7th Avenue**   **Lasagna, NY 10175**

Vito. I am sending you $10.00 for your book with almost no risk whatsoever to me or my family. I promise that if your book does not totally satisfy me, I'll take my loss like a man.

NAME ————————————————————————

ADDRESS —————————————————————

CITY ———————————— STATE ———————— Zip ————

122

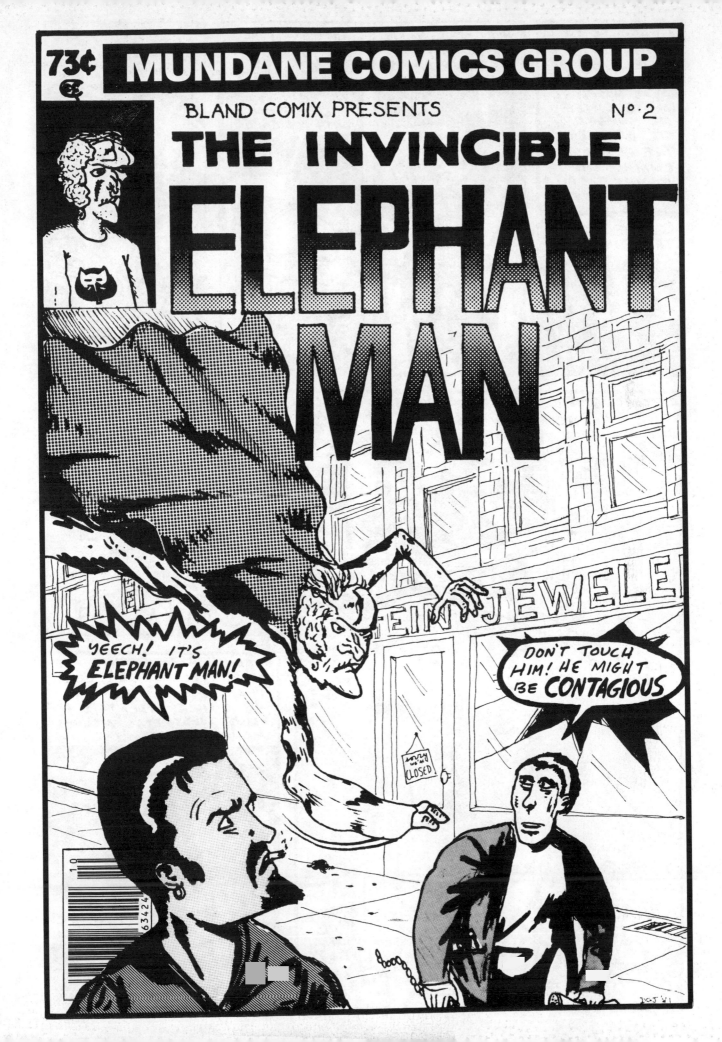

125

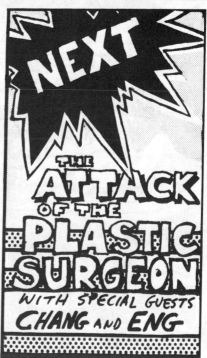

126

the
los altos
house of toast

annual report

1980

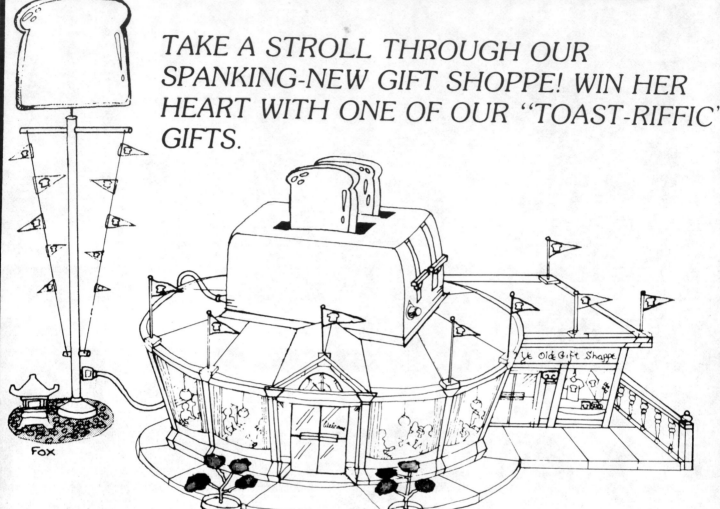

Hello!

The past year has been perhaps the most exciting in the thrilling twenty-year history of the Los Altos House of Toast. From its humble beginnings when it was just André and an old GE two-slicer to a modern operation with twelve employees (several of them full-time) and two Lockheed loaf-toasters, HoT has been the center of attention among toast cognoscenti. The past two decades have demonstrated that America is indeed the land of opportunity, where an effeminate Frenchman with a wild dream can become toastmaster to a nation.

These are exciting times for the toast industry, and there is no better way to share them than as part of the House of Toast family.

Sincerely,

André

Chairman of the Board
Los Altos House of Toast

The history of toast is the history of America. No other country loves its toast as America does. Thus it is surprising that it took a Frenchman—our beloved André—to show Americans how to enjoy their favorite breakfast food.

More importantly, we can trace a definite correlation between economics and toast consumption. While Americans have always cherished toast, they love it even more when times are hard:

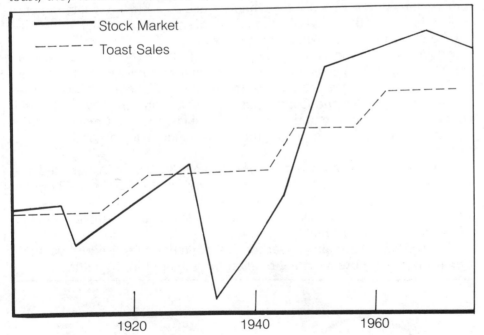

"There are no loafers at the House of Toast."

Notice that as soon as the economic climate turns sour, toast consumption skyrockets. Americans refuse to give up breakfast during hard times, so they turn to the economical alternative offered by toast. Our own André was able to ride the recession of the 1950s to success because of this phenomenon. But notice also that once boom returns, toast consumption does not decline. This is what makes the toast industry the investment miracle of the eighties—it is locked in a spiral to economic success!

The Los Altos House of Toast management is already gearing up to exploit the bad times we all know are coming. With a marketing strategy driven by our knowledge of toast consumption patterns, we shall be even more prepared to exploit the coming economic tragedy. An investment in toast is an investment in recession, inflation, and unemployment. We are planning now for the future:

Government contracts: The House of Toast has received a $750,000 contract from the Department of Defense to develop a type of toast that can be canned and provided to soldiers at the front. Toast is always a morale booster! And HoT will be ready to reap the profits of our foresight to contain Soviet aggression.

Marketing: Our new marketing director, Robert Boffo, has gone all out to promote toast as an economical breakfast alternative. His report follows later. Our "Toast to Bad Times" economics module is being used in elementary schools throughout the country.

Minority concerns: Hispanics are becoming the minority of the 80's. The House of Toast is meeting the needs of the Hispanics community with the creation of our "Casa de Tostadas" subsidiary and large-scale employment of undocumented workers.

As we stated at the beginning of this report, the history of toast is the history of America. And we are looking for every opportunity to create the history of toast here at the Los Altos House of Toast.

To Market, To Market . . .

Our new marketing vice president speaks:

"We spent most of our time in 1979 targeting our media to achieve market penetration. We went after the critical 18-35 upscale toast consumers, targeting especially for what we like to call "breakfast imperatives": those consumers who could relate to a media campaign emphasizing the consumption aspect of toast utilization.

"We made some careful media buys in 1979, hoping not only to reach upscale breakfast imperatives, but to change the image of toast as an unglamourous breakfast food. In a series of ads in *The New Yorker, Scientific American, Town and Country*, and *Upscale Consumer*, we promoted toast as an exciting, romantic, and fun breakfast food. As one ad put it, 'You don't have to be rich, or tasteful, or even in love to eat toast. You just have to want to be.'

"We targeted a campaign at opinion-makers as well. We created advertisements for the *New York Review of Books*, featuring Noam Chomsky declaring, 'You don't have to be taught to like toast.' In another advertisement in this series, we persuaded the late Jean-Paul Sartre to declare, 'Toast: it isn't just for breakfast anymore.'

"1979 has been a great year for the marketing of toast, and we look forward to even more targeting of even more media in the future."

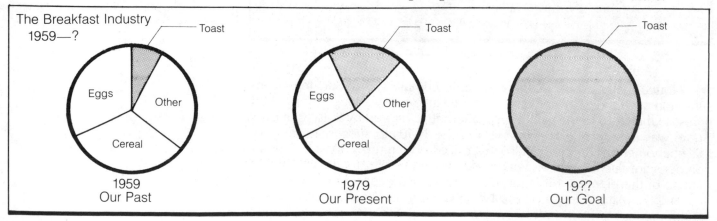

The Breakfast Industry 1959—?

1959 — Our Past · 1979 — Our Present · 19?? — Our Goal

When any company attains the size and position in its industry that the Los Altos House of Toast has achieved, it becomes the center of a great deal of attention. HoT has been right in the thick of the business news of this year.

Annual Sales (in millions of slices)		
		200
		150
		100
		50
1959	1969	1979

Stockholders are aware that we have received a tender offer from the Balanced Nutrico conglomerate. Management has attempted to block this move—and with good reason. We have all seen what Nutrico-Weltschmerz (the Swiss parent company) has done to the breakfast industry. They have, among other misdeeds, promoted a line of frozen dinners in the Third World, where many can afford only one meal a day. Nutrico-Weltschmerz has used its stranglehold on the world garnish industry to cut off our supply of fresh parsley in an attempt to force us to our knees. We will not yield. We all recall Balanced Nutrico's takeover of Stuckey's in 1967, which resulted in adding pecan rolls to their once-proud breakfast menu. We cannot allow this to happen to the Los Altos House of Toast! We urge our stockholders to stand firm.

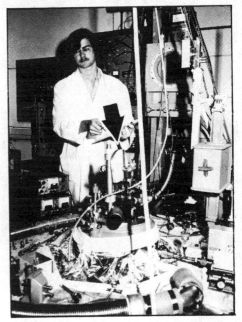

HoT Engineers are constantly seeking new ways to exploit the burgeoning toast products market. This year we introduced Creamed Chipped Beef Flavored Toast, Toast-on-a-Rope, and Grapefruit Marmalade.

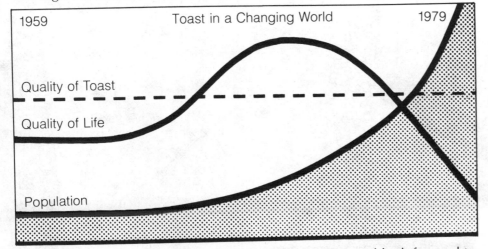

We thank you all for your faith and help in 1979 and look forward to the 80's as the Decade of Toast in what must surely be the Century of Toast.

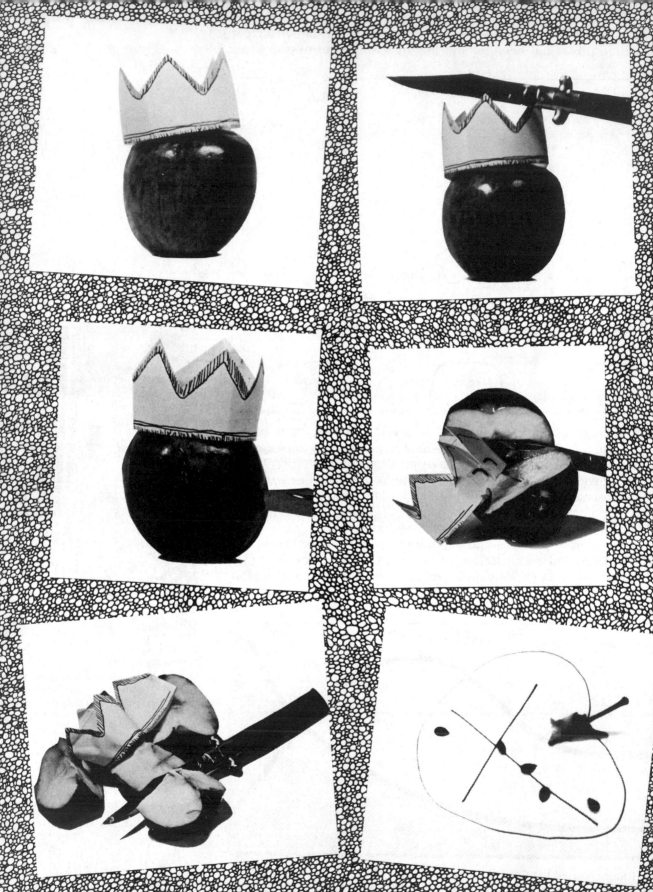

APATHY ON THE MARCH

Janet is more than just an average student at the University of California at Los Angeles. She lives in an attractive Westwood apartment, decorated with striking art nouveau posters she bought at a nearby campus boutique. She also has a David Hockney poster she bought while visiting the Tate in London. Janet likes art. She drives a BMW convertible, given to her by her father, a Sausalito lawyer, when she got straight A's one quarter. Janet has other possessions as well, and she likes sushi. She is the chairperson of the UCLA chapter of Students for a Nicer Society and captain of the UCLA Bruinettes cheerleading squad. We asked Janet to share her thoughts with us on the economic and diplomatic crises now facing this country. Janet?

"Well, the question people most often ask me is 'What's your major?' It's Creative Solutioning—that's a major I created myself—and we've got twenty people in the department now. It started when I realized we have to do something about all the bad things that happen in this country. That is why I founded Students for a Nicer Society (SNS), which I call Creative Solutioning in action. It's really not as complicated as it sounds. I take a problem, say, for example, the fact that many ethnic groups are unhappy. Then I look at my resources, like the fact that I know a whole squad of Bruinettes. Then we develop a plan of action. For this particular problem, we all went down to a project in Watts, where a lot of people were down in the dumps. We dressed in our outfits and even put on the little bear tails that we use for special occasions. We cheered up those poor people: "Get off welfare, quit food stamps! Stand up, step out, dance, dance, dance!" Not only did we get some pep going but we also addressed serious problems. You see, if people stopped cheating on welfare, President Reagan could balance the economy. We all have to pitch in and do our share. It's a difficult task, and thank goodness we had some of the guys from the football team with us!

"But I believe you can't change the entire world all at once. You have to straighten out your own little cubbyhole before you straighten out everybody else's. That was the problem with radicals in the 60's. They were too busy trying to take on everything at once, and their attitude was awfully negative. Slogans like 'Hell no, we won't go' and 'Burn, baby, burn.' That's not our message at all. Today we're saying 'Go for it,' 'Get psyched,' and 'We do it all for you!' Instead of throwing bricks at helpless ROTC cadets, we're really doing things. I got the SNS to reseed some of the lawns on campus which were really getting wrecked-out by the frisbee freaks. That's what I mean by a nicer society! The little things that mean so much to people's everyday lives. Kids in the 60's would've gotten a lot more accomplished if they had stopped trying to end the war and tried to clean up their acts instead, starting with themselves. If you don't look nice, you can't do nice things.

"That's the bottom line. If you want to make the world a better place, you have to make yourself a better person. And if that means exciting career opportunities and power, well, that just means I can improve more things. Thank you."

INCAR: International Committee Against Reason

Every moment, the cold iron jaws of the steel net of racist imperialist capitalist ruling-class tyranny tighten a bit further. The conspiracy of the world ruling class, masterminded jointly by expert planners in the White House and the Kremlin, continues to progress through the actions of governments, which, no matter how stupid, inane, or useless they may seem, are all more carefully planned cogs in the vast wheel of another brick in the wall of another piece of dust in the wind of ruling-class racist imperialist capitalism. Black groups, women's groups, anti-nuke groups, the NRA, and other so-called protest organizations only concern themselves with their own narrow special interests. They are only attacking the tip of the problem rather than the root of the iceberg. These groups will accomplish nothing as long as they only care about their own specific interests without applying them to our own cause: stamping out capitalist ruling-class racist imperialist oppression. WHO ARE "WE"? We are INCAR, a non-profit incorporation of workers and students, who are dedicated to solving all the world's problems through the use of slogans and leaflets filled with stirring rhetoric.

There are many groups fighting for racial equality. The NAACP and others have worked for years and accomplished nothing. We realize that racial equality is an unobtainable and possibly undesirable goal. Affirmative action and desegregation are only attempts to indoctrinate minorities into imperialist capitalist ruling-class racist values. INCAR contends that minority rights are unimportant. Races have to cooperate for only one overriding cause: smashing imperialist racist ruling-class capitalist oppression.

Environmentalists and anti-nuke types are up in arms against nuclear power. Instead of worrying about thermal pollution and nuclear waste disposal, these bourgeois groups should concentrate on the true issue: protesting capitalist imperialist racist ruling-class oppression of proletariat uranium 238 atoms. INCAR has long advocated the use of renewable alternative decentralized clean sources of energy, in order to take control away from the imperialist ruling-class racist capitalist oil companies. However, as soon as these alternative methods become feasible, the capitalist imperialist ruling-class racists will move in and take them over. The only way to prevent racist capitalist imperialist ruling-class control over energy is to oppose the oppression of plutonium, the sun, the tides, the wind, and geothermal properties through the abandonment of all energy production. If workers and students are as wasteful as possible, we can then use up all oil reserves in less than twenty years, thereby ridding ourselves of ruling-class capitalist racist imperialist energy monopoly tyranny.

Feminists campaign for equal rights and control over their own bodies. They do not realize that birth control and abortions are insipid parts of the vast imperialist ruling-class capitalist imperialist plot to eliminate all opposition from workers and students. Notice how Planned Parenthood and other birth-control advocates devote most of their education efforts to the poor ghetto areas. Under the devious cover of providing a useful service, they are attempting to reduce the population of the oppressed lower class proletariat. INCAR needs as large a force of workers and students as possible to smash capitalist ruling-imperialist racist-class oppression.

INCAR can cover this wide a variety of issues, because we are broad-minded workers and students who realize the futility of lobbying or taking direct protest action for any particular idea. While right now we're really mostly students, more workers are being won over to our cause every minute. Help INCAR recruit oppressed university proletariat. Help us to politicize the cafeteria workers so that they will read our pamphlets instead of wrapping sandwiches in them. Help us put a stop to the brainwashing of workers by their racist capitalist imperialist ruling-class employers. Help INCAR unite students and workers to smash racist imperialist capitalist ruling-class oppression. Attend our rally each and every Friday in front of the Student Union.

Be there. Aloha. —INCAR, Inc.

Join the people who've joined the Army?

Join For The Same Good Reasons They Did.

The people who joined Today's Military were impressed with this pamphlet. Chances are they never read it. And chances are they never will.

They cannot read through the rhetoric. In fact, they do not even know what the word means. But small vocabularies did not stop them from enlisting.

They like large type. And incomplete sentences. And pamphlets that are short, concise, and to the point. After all, no one enjoys reading. Chances are you're busy looking at the photographs. You'll probably never read this sentence. If you are reading this sentence then the military is no place for you.

The people interested in Today's Military enlist because, like you, they have no future elsewhere. And we take them. Each and every one. Some even pass the medical exam.

Today's Army: It's Not Just A Vague Promise, It's An Outright Lie.

If you're bombing out from the real world, Today's Army offers you an excuse. Here are the facts:

FACT: If you qualify, we'll guarantee good job-training courses. If you read the previous sentence you lack qualification.

FACT: You can choose the number of years you wish to serve, providing you can count.

R.O.T.C.

Dear High School Senior:

We here at the Army High School recruiting command post would like to take this opportunity to congratulate you on your high school achievements and wish you good luck. We think it's wonderful that young people like yourself attend school. But let's face it -- you don't stand a chance of being accepted to college. And with unemployment at its present rate, it would be impossible for you to find even the most menial job.

But just imagine hiking through scenic Rhodesia in your new khaki wardrobe or patrolling lovely Angola garbed in your fatigue mumbo jumbo. Think of the exciting adventures that await you! You can march around the United States preparing for combat in our next war. How many of your friends will have the opportunity to do that, right out of high school?

Sounds great, doesn't it? For more information just make 20 (twenty) copies of this letter and send them to friends, parents, relatives, or acquaintances you think need good luck. For no reason whatsoever, should this chain be broken. Take note of the following.

One recipient of this letter, William Calley, received the chain, not believing in it, threw it away. He won world acclaim as a first lieutenant in the U.S. Army; but he failed to circulate the news. Calley was court-martialed for premeditated murder at My Lai.

This letter was sent to you to wish you good luck. It is no joke. You will receive good luck, major or minor, even if you are superstitious. The decision to participate in this wonderful chain is completely voluntary Just don't say you weren't warned about Calley.

Chips Ahoy,

Anthony Nelson

Major Anthony Nelson
Colonel, U.S. Army

Your first year of college. The ROTC basic course begins.

Sophomore year. Time to drop out of ROTC and still have those first two years of college.

We'll tell you if your guess is right.

FACT: A new cigarette by the Phillip-Morris Tobacco Company.

ROTC: More Than Just Unnecessary Discipline.

If you go to college and take a few hours of special ROTC class a week, we'll pay for your college education. And you may withdraw anytime before the end of your second year. Many students enroll in ROTC, go to college for two years, all expenses paid, then quit after their sophomore year, never finding employment.

After serving their military commitments, many ROTC cadets live normal and productive lives. They are few and far between, but you may become one of them. Then again, you may never find out. Because chances are you're not smart enough to receive an ROTC scholarship in the first place. Anyone who'd read this far into this pamphlet isn't all that bright.

The Marines: It's Not An Adventure, It's A Job

Some people argue that, if redistributed, America's defense budget could end world famine. Sure, the money spent on a B-1 bomber could finance the New York City school system for three years. But which would you rather have protecting this country's vital interests, a Lockheed fighter plane or two hundred thousand educated hoodlums?

The Army: A Much Easier Out Than A Hundred Dollar A Day Habit.

You can serve almost anywhere in the world. Afghanistan. Kabul. The Persian Gulf. Or just about anywhere between Iran and Pakistan.

You'll be keeping the Russians out of the Mideast's oil fields. You'll be protecting Mobil. And Exxon. And Texaco. Oh, and Gulf. So that Americans can keep driving their four-doors to work. So that the threat of solar energy will never become a reality in America. Remember, they are only Russians. Godless communists who would kill for a bowl of borscht.

Most people in the Military never passed the entrance requirements. But they're safeguarding a distant nation you never thought existed. What else are you going to do with your life? Become a computer technician?

TODAY'S MILITARY.

Join The People Who Defend Big Oil.

Summer Camp. Your leadership skills are utilized in the Bay of Pigs invasion.

Your senior year of college and your last chance to live it up before Vietnam.

Graduation. Invade Cambodia. You're an officer now, earning your "commission."

Flight training offers new highs in Southeast Asia.

Transfer to Chile to overthrow Allende.

Humor in Uniform

MY HUSBAND was a sergeant in the Marines during the hard-fought battle of Hamburger Hill. His division started the day at 95% strength and finished at less than 50%. Bombs dropped all around him and shells howled incessantly, yet somehow he lived through the day.

Finally, when darkness fell, his commander, although badly wounded, managed to creep over to see him. "Bob," he was sobbing, "that was the worst battle I've ever seen in my life." But my husband, an extremely humorous man at times, merely lifted his head, surveyed the repulsive bloody corpses strewn on the field around him, and smilingly said: "Looks like there's a lot of *ketchup* on Hamburger Hill!"

—MRS. SERGEANT ROBERT JONES
(Phoenix, Ariz.)

WHEN WE WERE massacring Charlie at My Lai, I managed to find a child that wasn't shot yet, a tiny Vietnamese kid about five-years old. Well, my dog had been killed about a month before on a land mine, and I started teaching the kid some of the tricks my dog used to do. It was so funny watching this kid rolling over, barking, and retrieving a stick, that a crowd of about thirty G.I.'s gathered around to watch. Suddenly one of my buddies shouted "Hey kid, now play dead!" and shot him through the head.

—PRIVATE BILL CALLOUS
(Chicago, Ill.)

MY HUSBAND has an inordinate desire for ice cream. Having grown up in a deprived home during the Depression, Bob never sampled the pleasures of life until he enlisted in the army and became a career soldier. After he at long last tasted ice cream, he never again had enough of it to be satisfied. That's why he was so miserable in Vietnam—he couldn't get any ice cream there. Finally, out of sheer frustration, he disappeared for an entire afternoon. At five o'clock he reappeared as suddenly as he had left, with a tiny boy dangling at the end of his bayonet. "My God!" I shouted. "What have you got there?" He smiled proudly and said, "A tiny boy dangling at the end of my bayonet."

—MRS. BOB YUKLE
(Bovine, Utah)

FOR THREE STRAIGHT WEEKS, my sergeant put my platoon on a strange back-breaking detail—all day long, under the hot sun, we had to shovel up the grounds around our quarters and throw out any papers we found buried in the earth. The sergeant was very cryptic about the entire affair: Beyond giving us the initial order, he said nothing about the work we did; he merely sat, deaf and dumb, day after day, watching us shovel dirt and throw away papers. We didn't understand the motivation behind any of this until several months later, when we found out that the sergeant had been ordered by his commanding officer to "dig out and destroy every single underground paper in the camp."

—J. WECHSLER
(New York, New York)

NURSE MEG MacCREE was well-known as the "Florence Nightingale" of the Vietnam War. She worked constantly, spending all her waking hours with the many sick and wounded who had been removed from the front lines and who finally ended up in our hospital. It was therefore a strange but hilarious experience that took place last year, when New York's Cardinal Cooke paid his annual visit to the war zone. On observing MacCree's intense devotion, the Cardinal was so greatly impressed that he crossed himself and passionately exclaimed, "That nurse should be canonized immediately."

Since beatification cannot occur until after death, MacCree was taken out and shot at once, pursuant to the Cardinal's request. Yet what is a greater tribute to the American soldier's sense of humor, even under wartime conditions, than the fact that she was executed with a fourteen-inch cannon, in grand American style?

—JOHN JACKSON
(Minerva, New York)

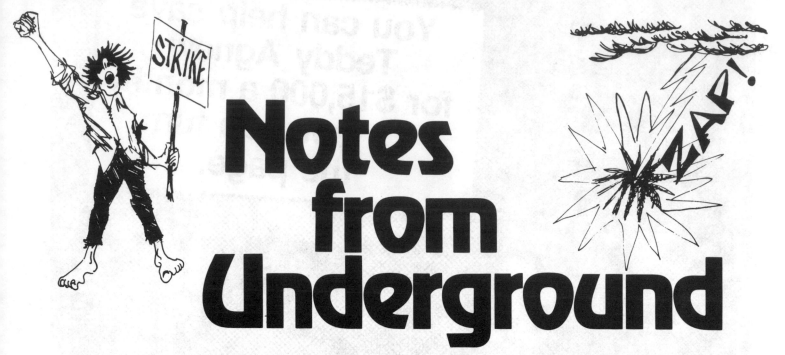

Notes from Underground

WASHINGTON—As November 1976 approaches, thoughts turn to the Presidential election. Will we be faced with a choice between Gerry Ford and Scoop Jackson? While general feelings of paranoia begin to spread among the politically active public, the upcoming election evokes far different feelings in the minds of a certain few individuals. These certain few being the Presidential hopefuls.

Just what goes on in the mind of a presidential candidate? Thanks to the liberal use of illegal and unethical means, we have acquired some revealing documents and tables that show just what goes on in the mind of an aspirant to our highest office. The following is a transcript of a phone tapping made by the C.I.A. while conducting a routine security check on Gerald Ford:

SECRETARY: Mr. Rockefeller will speak to you now, Mr. President.
FORD: (mumbled) Well it's about time. I've been on hold for a half hour.
ROCKY: What is it now, Gerry?
FORD: Well I called you, Nelson, because I value your opinion and I can trust you to give me an honest answer. You see, I'm thinking of running again, but being President gets to be real pain sometimes. Reporters are always watching me. Last week I didn't get up to make my own breakfast and the front page of the *Washington Post* said I was sick.
ROCKY: You've got to ignore stuff like that, Gerry. It happens to all public figures.
FORD: But everyone's always calling me dumb. I'm a college graduate, I don't have to take that. Being President isn't as much fun as I thought it would be. I mean when Dick called me into his office and told me about the deal, he made the job out to be a real picnic . . . .
ROCKY: Deal? What deal?
FORD: Why you know, Rocky, the one about him resigning and the pardon.
ROCKY: (Loud voice) WHY I NEVER HEARD OF ANY DEAL, GERRY. IF YOU KNOW ANYTHING ABOUT A DEAL YOU OUGHT TO TALK TO THE ATTORNEY GENERAL'S OFFICE RIGHT AWAY. A DEAL WOULD HAVE BEEN WRONG.
FORD: Wha . . . (whispered) Oh . . . (Loud voice) I MUST HAVE BEEN THINKING ABOUT ANOTHER DEAL. YES A DEAL WOULD HAVE BEEN WRONG, WOULDN'T IT? But anyway Rocky, do you think I should run?
ROCKY: Well let me put it this way, if you don't run, where are you going to find a job?

FORD: I guess you're right, Rocky. What about the rumors I hear about you running against me?

ROCKY: Would I do that to you, Gerry? I'm happy being just a heartbeat away. The job keeps me very busy. Which reminds me, Henry and I have made plans for you. We've got a speech all ready for you to give tomorrow night. I'll have it sent over right away so you can practice the big words out on the golf course.

FORD: That sounds fine, Rocky. Only today I'm going swimming. Tuesdays, Thursdays, and Saturdays are my days for golf. Anyway, what's the speech about? Is it important? Are we going to invade anyplace?

ROCKY: No, nothing like that, Gerry. It's getting close to election time as you know, and Cuba seems like the logical communist country for you to go to. So your speech will announce your trip to Cuba next spring.

FORD: Gee, have you talked to Castro about it?

ROCKY: Don't worry about it, Ger. Henry's got all the details worked out.

FORD: Okay, Rocky, goodbye.

ROCKY: Goodb . . . oh and don't forget to wear your goggles in the pool. You know how chlorine makes your eyes bloodshot. We want you to look nice on TV, not like you've been out with Wilbur the night before, again.

FORD: Alright. Goodbye.

ROCKY: Bye, Gerry.

CLICK.

Some dreams never die. They linger until they become delusions. Rumors from Bismark have George McGovern attempting to round up support for another bid. The following conversation between George and his former campaign manager, Gary Hart (now a Senator from Colorado) was overheard in a Senate cloakroom.

McGOV: Gary, hold on a second. I've been wanting to talk to you. I need your advice on something.

HART: What is it now, George?

McGOV: Well, I've been thinking about running in '76. What do you think?

HART: Don't do it, George.

McGOV: But Gary, I was right about Watergate, about the war, about everything.

HART: You were wrong about Eagleton. And besides, all that really matters is that you got dumped on by Nixon. People don't vote for losers.

McGOV: Well, they voted for Nixon, didn't they?

HART: They didn't know for sure that he was a loser even though they should have.

McGOV: But people have forgotten how bad I lost. They'll remember that I was right. We can remind them. They'll see my inherent honesty and realize that I'm a down-to-earth type of guy.

HART: Maybe, but they won't vote for you. I don't want to see you hurt again. Don't run.

McGOV: Besides, what about the kids? Those wonderful kids who worked so hard for me. There's no one for them to look to. No one for them to pin their hopes on. This country needs a change, this country needs to come home, back to her old ideals: honesty, hard work, freedom. These are hard times. Everyone knows that things have to change. Why can't I wind up on top? No one thought I would win the nomination in '72. I can do it. Can you just see it Gary? Gary?

Today's Symbionese Liberation Army Wants to Join You

If you're a graduating college student worried about the prospective job market, consider this. The Symbionese Liberation Army teaches a variety of revolutionary skills to its recruits.

What does that mean to you? It simply means that in a few short weeks, the SLA can transform you from an unemployed student into an urban guerilla.

If you are still a few years short of your graduation, the SLA can easily arrange to withdraw you from school if you're the type of person we're looking for.

In addition to learning a practical skill for the revolution, you'll be offered security, increased social activity, and a new world of travel opportunities.

So don't wait to be kidnapped to join. Call your local SLA recruiter today.

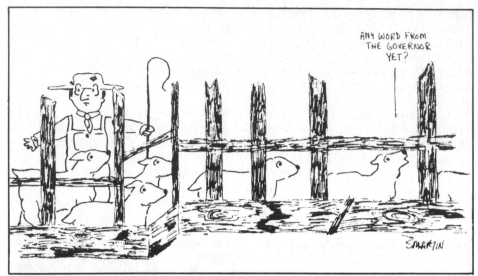

ANY WORD FROM THE GOVERNOR YET?

SMARTIN

Scoop Jackson, the Democratic Senator from the state of Washington, is considered by many to be the leading candidate for the Democratic nomination. Scoop has been running hard for the last four years. Inflammatory statements flow from the Senator's office on any and all issues. The following is the form that Scoop's staff uses to make up most of the press releases.

For times release _____ AM/PM
_____ 19 ____

Senator Henry M. Jackson today announced that the present _____ _____ crisis is the result of (Congress'/ the President's) soft line toward the (communists/terrorists/Arabs).

He went on to state that "We cannot allow the present situation to continue. It is a disgrace to our great nation. We must unite and put an end to this menace to our (security/integrity as the American people)."

The Senator also charged that the (Soviets/Chinese/Syrians) are behind the crisis, and insists on linking (the freedom of Soviet Jews to emigrate to Israel/the liberation of the Chinese mainland/Israeli control of the Gulf of Aqaba, the Suez Canal, and the lower Nile valley) to any final solution.

The Senator concluded by saying "This crisis proves once again, what I have said all along. That the (SALT treaty/U.S. Constitution) isn't worth the paper its printed on if (we don't step up our military commitments/ we as individuals don't stand up for America)."

And as these figures plan for 1976, down in San Clemente Richard Nixon plans for 1984 and the biggest political comeback of all time.

Zapruder Family Scrapbook

Frankie loved that dog.   *It's a swim party!*

JER:

The Memoirs of Gerald Ford

March 3, 1979

I don't remember much. Look, to be honest with you, nobody ever accused me of being Albert Einstein, and Betty isn't exactly a fine example of symmetry in nature, yet, by a curious turn of events, we became President and First Lady. This is the story of my years in the egg-shaped office.

It is hard to say what I liked best in office. It was all so much fun, being important and famous and powerful. I suppose the greatest advantage of it was that the White House has everything. I am proud to be the first President to have an Advent Videobeam. It is not the kind of thing that you go out and buy yourself, yet for three years I saw all the football games on a six-foot television screen (measured diagonally of course)! It was like watching the action live! With my busy schedule, it was lucky that we had a Betamax too; it automatically video-taped one game while I watched a different one.

It wasn't always so easy. Take my first State of the Union message. I decided to write it all myself and was quite proud of it, yet people still give me "prairie patties" for it. For those of you who don't remember it very well, this should refresh your memory a bit:

"It is my sincere goal to serve this nation as honestly and effectively as possible. After carefully studying the State of the Union (hence the title of this address) I conclude that the Northeast metropolitian area can expect about three inches of rain tonight followed by partial clearing tomorrow and some patchy fog. In the Midwest, you'd better button up those overcoats. I am afraid that another hailstorm is on the way. In the west, more sunny skies. Girls, it's time to take out the bikinis again and soak up the rays."

December 26, 1974

Our first Christmas together in the White House was wonderful. The family went all out and bought me a hell of a gift. It has real possibilities—a machine that can make all kinds of buttons. I design them, press the handy lever, and can buttonize anything. People could stand to learn a lot from buttons. Betty just loved my idea of a Whip Inflation Now button—WIN, get it? If every citizen wore one, maybe inflation would drop. . . .

February 12, 1975

Today Vietnam fell to the Communists, the end of an era. As I think back, I guess we lost the war. There was a great football game on last Sunday. Boy, can that O.J. Simpson run! One-hundred-and-fifty yards in a game, simply amazing. If there's one guy that I'd really like in my cabinet, it's O.J.—but damn, where am I going to get that kind of money. Maybe I'll call George Steinbrenner in New York. With his help, why, we could buy a great government!

June 20, 1975

I feel very distant from my son Jack. He is a forest ranger. It is a very tough life. The hours are hard and long. Whenever I visit him in his solo watchtower, there is sap all over the floor. It is a lonely job. My other son rides in the rodeo. He loves the boots and spurs, even the whips. He rides broncos so much that sometimes he walks around as if he is still on one. It is fine with me if he likes to hang around with cowboys. Susan is a wonderful daughter. She gives of herself so willingly, a father could not ask for more, believe me. Betty started a marvelous bottle collection recently and it is growing fast. . . .

April 19, 1976

Travelling to Europe on Air Force One is the only way to go. The seats are really wide, there is no hassle with connecting flights, and the service is usually pretty good. After some very complicated meetings on NATO and EEC during an overseas mission, it was great to visit the Louvre, and Versailles. Gosh, Louis the fourteenth had practically everything but the Advent Videobeam. D'Estaing is a very nice guy; he has a really funny accent when he tries to speak English, z's for s's, you know, the way chefs talk about Bluebonnet margarine. I was barely able to keep a straight face during our talks. From France we went to the free nations of Poland and Czechoslovakia. . . .

September 5, 1974

I pardoned Nixon today as instructed on his memo.

BOREALIS

A MEN'S NEWSPAPER FOR THE STANFORD COMMUNITY

Dr. Hans Forsecs, a visiting male professor, leans forward to make a point during his well-attended lecture, "The Myth of the Scrotal Orgasm," on May 11.

New book hits home

Patterned after its popular predecessor for females (*Our Bodies, Ourselves*), this oversized paperback adopts a similar approach, both in tone and format, toward men's (that's us!) bodies and related issues. The authors explain their motivations behind producing the book in the collectively written introduction, which we found somewhat overstated and trite, though pleasantly articulate (sample quote: "We have beards. We wield a penis. . . .")

Chapter One discusses intersexual differences in physiology and morphology. The inevitable conclusion here is that males are overwhelmingly more adept at physical pursuits than are females, with one noteworthy exception: smearing grease all over your body and swimming from Dover to Calais. Women are given the edge grace-wise, but we tend to agree with the Glory Hole Group's assessment that "grace and agility are subjective, anyway." They don't mention that women live longer, or can with-

stand greater climactic extremes.

Chapter 2 presents male and female reproductive anatomy and physiology, with charming prose and clear pictures (see example). Included are some alarming graphs diagramming the decline in sexual capability with age (peak now or forever hold your piece!) Particularly reassuring, however, are the data on average size of sexual apparatus. At least we found it reassuring. And the diagram showing penis variations makes this section all worth it. Skip the part on female hormonal cycles. It's too complicated.

Chapters Three and Four contain discussion of straight sexuality, emphasizing the male end. We found these chapters to contain both enlightening and disputable material. A pencil-sketch couple introduces us to a variety of gymnastic (and well-nigh impossible, we discovered) lovemaking positions, encouraging us to adopt a "more visionary,

(cont. on p. 2)

Male professor runs obstacles

Professor Byron Stallwart shakes hands firmly and, from that point on, one knows that they are in the presence of a true man. His mere cough seems to celebrate manhood and the wonder of the first sex. Indeed, he has dedicated his life to studying and academically erecting the long-opposed gender.

Ten years ago, the idea of a Men's Studies program here at Stanford was scoffed at and ridiculed. But Stallwart is not one to give in to weaker minds and genders, and never has been. "One of the advantages of being a man in this world is that we can keep a stiff upper lip and perform our duties consistently, thirty days out of the month," Stallwart noted. "I remember when I was young and first saw how important it was to be a male and express my feelings about it."

"My mother was always one to tell me what to do, of course, but quickly I learned to put her female authority in perspective with my rights as a male. 'Clean up your room,' she would say. 'Wait, Mother, I'm a man and that's not my role. I need space and, perhaps, a maid.' "

Having completed his Ph.D. dissertation, entitled "Influential Men Writers of the Twentieth Century" at Harvard in 1966, Stallwart came directly to Stanford. Originally, he was forced into the confines of the English department, yet continued to vigorously teach many underestimated male writers. The big break for Men's Studies came in 1972, when the University relented space in an eating club for the Men's Center. Now the Uni-

(cont. on p. 3)

FEELINGS

Boys will be boys: A vicious cycle?

We were sitting around the Hogsbreath having a few brews and watching the SC-Notre Dame game. Half-time came along and we all started bullshitting, proponents of either side putting down proponents of the other, when we were struck by the blinding white light of social truth: we weren't SC and we weren't Notre Dame — we were/are MEN!

"When I was a kid, I looked up to my father. He used to play ball with me, show me how to build things, whack the hell out of me when I was bad. I wanted to be like him when I grew up. Now I'm an adult and my father is in a convalescent home. He lies in bed all day with a bunch of tubes running out of his orifices. I don't want to be like him anymore."

As long as we can remember, we have been divided. We are grouped in "teams;" we are graduated in "classes;" we are placed in "corporations;" and we are members of "couples" and live in "homes." As boys we fight, as teenagers we compete for dates with the fat girl who does it on her parent's couch, as young men we vie for promotions and push each other into bankruptcy as we grow older.

"I can make you a real man."

Thus this publication. We are *all* real men. Together we can discover what it means to be male in a man's world, exploring our roles as leaders, protectors and providors. From the acrid gym to the smoke-filled room, circumcised and un, we are MEN.

Baldness: The male burden

"It happened and — well — it wasn't something that I could talk about. The trauma of it built up inside of me until I thought I'd explode. I became afraid and introverted. I couldn't walk in public places anymore. It's so awful." The speaker was a man, a student at this University, and a victim of an issue all men must, at one time or another, face up to: baldness.

Certainly, this man was forced to bear his burden prematurely. But baldness is more than the shining crown of some brother across the street. It could strike us now, or in twenty years, or in forty. The timing makes no difference: baldness waits in the wings to reduce every male to the countenance of a billiard ball, to be shot abusively around society's pool table, and eventually deposited expertly by sexist cueing into the corner pocket of hairless limbo, unable to associate with his protein-topped peers. How can we help these men, who, due to forces beyond their control, cannot face their combs in the morning and then, in lonely helplessness, themselves?

Peer counseling can be a great help in bridging the gap between the victim of vanity hair-loss and the oppressive, style-conscious society around him. Yet the education of the ignorant masses at large remains the great challenge. Men must join together to get to the root of the problem. Studies have shown that men lose their hair as a result of inherited genes, while society would have us believe that shining crowns are a direct result of intense nervousness, contaminated hairsprays or chronic masturbation.

We must all chop away these stigmatized stereotypes before we get to the smooth scalp of truth. The result will be a better way of living for those of us who, like our nation's symbol, the proudly bald eagle, personify manhood and the burden that, as men, we must all bear. With proper education of the ignorant throngs, derogatory terms such as "baldy" and "lightbulb-head" will become synonymous with "virile" and "lice-free."

New book hits home

(cont. from p. 1)
less missionary repertoire." Editorial discretion prohibits elaboration, but suffice it to say that some of us are quite sore.

The eighth chapter is all about men's success in the job market. This is the most self-indulgent and mathematical portion of the book. We are reminded that 92 percent of doctors, 85 percent of lawyers, four-fifths of theoretical population geneticists, and 67 percent of ride operators at Disneyworld are male.

Chapter Nine is wholly dialogue — the transcript of one session of a men's CR (consciousness-raising) group. The topic is male awareness — about being male and all — and is quite an appropriate way to tie together the preceding chapters. In conclusion, we should say that although it's not perfect, *Our Bods, We're Gods* is adequate, and, above all, male. For this, we expect it to enjoy the same popularity as did its older sister.

Male professor runs obstacles

(cont. from p. 1)
versity seems only a few progressive strides away from instituting a full-fledged academic curriculum.

"It's been a long, uphill battle," Stallwart said, contemplatively fondling his full beard. "In their ignorance, many people think we want to radically subvert sexual order, rewrite history, break up the American family and teach everyone to crush beer cans, go hunting and laugh at dirty jokes in smelly bars. Nothing could be further from the truth. We are simply saying, 'Hey, we're men, God made us men, so let's celebrate it, study it, and get academic credit for it.'"

The male member of the Stanford faculty slowly shook his head, then came quickly to the point: "All through our lives, it's the same thing. When I first tried to grow a beard, my mother said, 'Your face is dirty; wash it.' My sister said: 'You look like a rat.' Imagine that! A rat! To be accepted in my own family, I was forced to remove any detectable pronouncement of my manhood from my face. And they wonder what we mean when we talk about Crimes Against Men!" Thanks to Byron Stallwart, awareness of the man and his surroundings at Stanford can only grow bigger.

"We are the hollow men."

Our Own Words

I Feel Like a Fart
by Dave

Women, Women, Women, always on my mind.
   I see them across the stark marketplace,
They talk.
Women supporting each other,
Consciousness rising like yeasty bread.
Nobody likes me.
Why?Why?What?
I want to open the door for her.
Where is she?
At the seashore,
In the delicatessan,
In the Women's Room.
I ask a friend:
"What should I do?"
He sobs and blows his fucking head off.
Phallic death.

I cry;
"Won't you please go out on a date with me?"
She laughs and flies away.
"Please . . . let's — I have a Trans Am . . ."
I die, cry, pizza pie.
Why? Why? What? Which? Whom?

MY PENIS by Bruce

My penis.
Long and soft.
His name is Peter.
When I touch him,
he touches me back.
Going to dive into the pink
   bouillabaisse, Peter?
Frothy. Frothy. Frothy.
Peter lisp-spits hello.
Hello.
My penis, my Peter.

I Can Give You a Conservative Student Body in Only Five Years!

Typical Freshman
1970   1975

Robert Morris
Dean of Admissions

And I can do the same for you. When I started as Dean of Admissions at Swartmore, I was plagued by the same problems as Mr. Lyman. My campus was covered with rads, fags, freaks, and every other sort of human aberration. This really bugged me. What's the use of educating a bunch of creeps who are only out to change the system, anyway?

Well, I just got sick and tired of their jeers and scorn.

That's when I developed Admissions Dynamics. My method is simplicity itself. Just a few simple manipulations every year and suddenly I had a new, *conservative* student body. Admissions Dynamics is based upon the well-known principle that student bodies replace themselves every four years. This idea is a revolution in student body-building.

Why not fill out the application today? I'll send you complete information on Charles Radless Admissions Dynamics.

Ted Kennedy's Stand Up Comic Routine

You Can Put Them Out Of Their Misery.

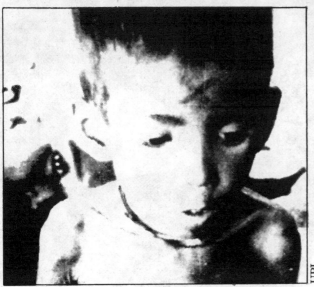

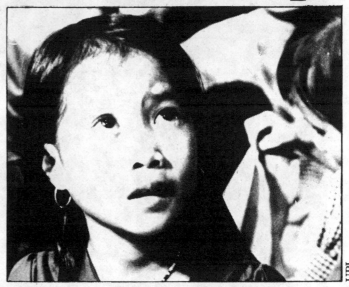

Biryani's whole life has been nothing but misery, pain, and dirt. He's poor, unloved, and unwanted, and was recently condemned by the Pakistani Board of Health. Wouldn't he be better off dead?

Her name? We don't know. And neither does she. Three years of living in a trash can and munching on lead chips has turned her brain into a functionless glob of tapioca pudding. She's a hopeless case. Why let it go on?

Or You Can Turn the Page.

How many times in your life have you been asked to sign a pledge to sacrifice your dinner and help feed starving urchins in India? How many times have you been badgered in bus stations by good samaritans begging your support for Vietnamese war orphans? How often have you been assaulted in the privacy of your own home by endless magazine and TV appeals to "save a child for only $15 a month"?

Downright annoying, isn't it? And what makes it even worse is that you know as well as we do that they're taking the wrong approach. Instead of trying to save the wretched little beggars, wasting thousands of American dollars that could be used to feed valuable livestock, they should be doing just the opposite: putting the hopeless scavengers permanently out of their misery, sanitizing their villages, and getting them off the public conscience forever.

That's where we come in. Since 1938, the Orphan Extermination Fund has buried hundreds of thousands of children throughout Asia. But there are still so many more to go. Become a "sponsor." For only $10, we'll put an orphan out of his misery in your name. You'll receive before and after photographs of the child, a color poster of the burial site, and countless letters of gratitude from his fellow villagers.

Do it now. Don't delay. Remember: for every minute you waste, 1,000 more unwanted, unsanitary urchins are born into the world.

Support Euthanasia for Youth-in-Asia

Orphan Extermination Fund, Inc.

Box 94, Auschwitz, Ohio 30133

I wish to "sponsor" a ☐ boy   ☐ girl   ☐ anything within shooting distance.

Please send my information package today

☐ I wish to exterminate the child personally. Please ship him/her C.O.D. to my address below.

Name _____

Address _____

City _____ State _____ Zip _____

Member of International Union for Aggressive Euthanasia. Gifts are tax deductible.

A MINE IS A TERRIBLE THING TO WASTE.

Generous black philanthropists eagerly mine South Africa's plentiful resources. They are the true heroes of world economic exploitation. But times are changing. Some people think the Black majority is being oppressed. These people, who have never stepped in a mine in their lives, are unaware of the pleasures these black altruists find in risking their lives to fill the white mans' pockets. But we can not allow a handful of benevolent mavericks to destroy everything our society holds so sacred. Only strong US corporate investments can help us prevent our economy from "caving in." American Universities, the pinnacle of ideological thought, invest in just such corporations. Why don't you? Give. But give generously.

SOUTH AFRICAN INVESTMENTS:
the next best thing to being there

Let's Capitulate to the Russians

It wouldn't be that hard.

A single line at the bottom of an official report announces that we've surrendered to the Soviet Union.

The few papers that notice bury the story in the back pages.

The American people, who don't care about anything, don't care about this either.

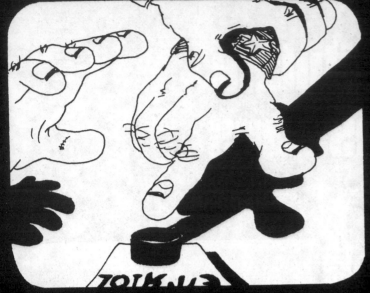

The reaction in Russia, however, is more pronounced. Their first impulse is to attack, but since we've already surrendered they can't.

The military is sent home. The $250 billion previously spent on defense is put to to to other uses, such as planting trees.

The Russians, after some delay, rush a delegation to Washington. No one meets them because we've given up.

They take cabs to the White House. The president, who is packing his belongings into cardboard crates, tosses the Russian leader the keys to his office and tells him to remember to water the plants.

The Russians move to render Congress ineffectual, but discover it's already been done.

The Russians now find themselves in control.

Things, which never worked so well to begin with, continue to do so.

The American people, who don't care about anything, don't care about this either.

The Russians bring in lots of troops and equipment. And money.

There is some resistance, by Southerners and John Birchers and Klanners and all those right-wing gun fanatics who have been waiting their whole lives for this. They are all killed and the quality of life improves.

The Russians scamper around trying to make things work, but people do things the way they always have, only now they don't work as hard because, why do things for the Russians anyway? There is much staying home and getting drunk, and people have sex a lot.

No one talks to the Russians and, after sulking around for a few years, they declare the entire endeavor an unqualified success and go home.

Zen and the Art of Motorcycle Misrepresentation

Cloud-rags hung to dry in the sky, and the crispness of autumn filled my nostrils as my son and I cycled down a precarious road in the heart of North Dakota. The overwhelming mountains, towering on the horizon like gigantic giants, moved my son to say, "Gosh, Dad, they're gigantic."

As you may have guessed, my name is Zen, although many have thought my name is Art, which is incorrect (my publisher's name is Art).

What am I doing on a motorcycle in the middle of North Dakota? That's precisely what I've been trying to discover for the past nine years. I have just recovered from a bout with insanity, and it all came about because I dared to challenge the principle of values. Thus, I am writing this to reconstruct my crack-up in a way that will help me understand where I went wrong, help my son understand what has happened to his father, and sell lots of copies. That would make Art happy. Hell, it'd make me happy, too.

The mountains begin to melt away into prairie as we enter Montana.

"Pa?" my son asks. I don't respond. It's impossible to hear anything short of a nuclear explosion while riding.

"Pa?" he yells. I hear nothing.

"Pa?" he bellows. I hear nothing.

"Pa?" he shrieks. I hear nothing.

"Pa -a-a . . ." I still hear nothing, but the motorcycle has become considerably lighter. . . .

We stop at the first town along the way so the boy can get cleaned up. I begin tinkering on the cycle. I get my tool kit out from under the seat. First remove the engine hood, the book says, so I do. A minute piece of motorcycle abruptly falls out and rolls away. "Probably not necessary," I say, and continue with my tinkering. I remove a manifold here and a valve there, and begin to apply oil in generous portions to the entire crankcase. Without my knowledge, I lubricate my pants leg. Cursing under my breath, I get up, and the machine topples over. I walk off to find a repair shop.

Three hours later, we are back on the road, hurtling at breakneck speed toward the small village of Bozeman, where Phallus first breathed life.

"Dad?" Again I cannot hear the boy calling me—all I hear is the furious blast of wind circulating through my helmet.

"Dad?" he barks. I cannot hear.

"Dad?" he bawls. I cannot hear.

Suddenly I become aware of a pungent moistness on the seat, and I quickly locate the nearest gas station.

I remember how Phallus was working with the concept of quality. He had divided quality into two factions: "Good and Bad." Phallus then subdivided these into four more classifications: very good and very bad, and exceptional and regrettable.

We arrive at a heavily wooded area in central Mon-

tana, where we decide to bed down for the night. I begin to unroll the trail pack we carry on the back of the cycle, and look uneasily at the boy. He's in one of his moods again, I say to myself, as I glance up and see him gnawing on an oak tree.

The boy has had a rough go of it, and I perhaps regret that most of all. Phallus did it. It was he who had made the boy what he is today. Not that Phallus shared my son's appetite for Douglas firs, but Phallus changed all those who came in contact with him.

"How would you like to start a fire, and then I'll cook dinner?" I ask.

"Start the damn fire yourself," he retorts. While I gather the firewood, I realized that Phallus was here, coming back to haunt me. I walked into the forest to be alone with Phallus, and ponder the concept of quality.

Phallus' chart had grown larger and larger. It had started to go too far. The ideas and terms had doubled, and redoubled, until Phallus' mind was overcome with words which he could not write down fast enough, or spell properly. His mind had become the language's foremost thesaurus on the words "good" and "bad."

The forest walls began to close in upon me. I could see my son and wife, pressed against the windows from the outside, tears streaming down their faces, pleading to be allowed into my sickroom.

We approached the end of my awakening just as the boy and I neared the Pacific Ocean.

The green mist of the ocean hung along the horizon, and utter futility began to envelop me.

"Pa!" the boy asked.

"Pa!" he repeated.

"Pa!!!" he yelled under my helmet, and I lost control of the bike, narrowly missing an enormous Volkswagen. I quietly pulled over to the side, and said, "WHAT???"

"Where are we going, Pa?"

"What do you mean, where are we going?" I asked.

"My God, Pa, we've been driving around aimlessly like this for nine years now. I'm twenty-eight-years old, for Chrissakes. I've got more important things to do with my life than ride around on a damn motorcycle."

"Why, son, I didn't know you felt like this."

We continued the rest of the way to the ocean. I got off the cycle, and slowly stalked to the edge of the cliff. I looked down the precipice to the rocks and water below.

Suddenly I heard the thunder of footsteps behind me, and I saw the boy racing toward the edge.

"Wait!" I cried. "Son!"

He stopped short at the word "son," and looked at me with a warmth I thought had died long ago. I stepped toward him.

"Now, son, what are we, human beings or lemmings? Are we going to hurl ourselves over the edge like a swarm of rodents, or are we going to act like gentlemen and take turns?"

Washed ashore with typhoid, dysentery, and malaria

Pol Pot and the Khmer Rouge Make a Killing

Join the 65,000 Who Flee Vietnam Each Month

Boat People

The Undersea World of Joan Baez

UPI

Joan Baez Is Sunk After Her Quibble With Jane Fonda

UPI

0

70989 34490

01

Boat People

Her quibble with **Jane Fonda** is more newsworthy than she could have known, and **Joan Baez** unintentionally focuses the media's attention away from the refugee problem and to bickering between two leftists.

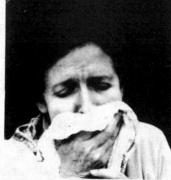

A Chinese refugee who made it to Hong Kong cries with happiness after learning she has won a return trip to Vietnam, **34**

Bidong Island, **44**

UPI

A malnourished Vietnamese boy occasionally urinates, **88**

UPI

Boat People
PICKS & PANS

Malnourishment, starvation, disease, and death, shouldn't get you down. If you're going to die from a disease, which in all likelihood you are, you might as well have a say in which disease is gonna do you in. So, for those of you who haven't been infected, why not take a pick from this weeks pans, and save yourself the anguish of having to suffer from a disease you thought second best.

☐ MEN NGITIS
Okay, so it's a pain in the neck. It's hardly fair to criticize this little disease on that level. First of all, it's inflamation of the meninges (three cute little membranes infesting the brain and spinal cord). It affects the spine, you get a stiff neck, some nausea, and you generally feel like you've got a flu. After that, you tend to die. Not all that pleasant, sure, but it doesn't seem all that bad a way to go, either. It's just not something you can take standing up.

☐ CHOLERA
While this disease has been a hit all over Asia, it gets a lot more praise than it deserves. It's infectious and characterized by profuse diarrhea, vomitting, cramps, depression, sleepiness, and lack of appetite. If you don't mind having drippy bowel movements or losing your lunch through both ends, you'll find cholera an enjoyable surprise that'll leave you empty.

☐ TUBERCULOSIS
Here's a disease that'll make you stop to catch your breath. It's also infectious but affects almost any tissue of the body. Especially the lungs. It's characterized by a small, firm, rounded swelling. In its later stages it makes you choke up blood and then you die. Women in Victorian novels usually die of the stuff and it doesn't seem like the most pleasant of diseases.

☐ MALARIA
Of all the diseases panned this week, it looks like Malaria takes the prize. It's both intermittent and remittent, depending on which type you get, so you can see it's sort of an easygoing disease. It's just a case of chills, fever and sweating, and when you compare it to puking your guts out from cholera, or wheezing blood from tuberculosis, malaria begins to look awfully good.

☐ DYSENTERY
Here's one you wouldn't even wish on the Pathet Lao. It's an infectious disease marked by inflamation and ulceration of the lower part of the bowels, with diarrhea that becomes mucous and hemorrhagic. You start fartin' blood and making a real mess of things. Okay, so defacating mucous alleviates the need to blow your nose, but it seems like an elaborate way of clearing your sinuses.

This week's pick is definitely malaria, easily contracted through mosquitos or close contact from someone suffering the disease. It's fatal, sure, but why risk catching one of the other four? Of course, you can always wait for us to review five more diseases next week, if you want to chance it. Maybe we'll see you then.

MAIL

Beatles

I am really sorry that the Beatles did not reunite to give a concert for the Boat People. I don't really understand how having them sing us a couple of songs from aboard a Malaysian trawler would help us any. But hearing a live rendition of "Get Back" would be something.

Dhi Att Sei
South China Sea

Sally Struthers

I am sorry to see valuable space devoted to Sally Struthers' work for the Christian Children's Fund. For the Love of a Hungry Child, my foot.

Rob Reiner
Los Angeles

Skyluck

I, too, am aboard the *Skyluck* sitting in a Hong Kong harbor with 2,663 other Vietnamese survivors. It is a shame that your article only mentioned the agony of being kept on ships in Hong Kong unable to go ashore. Conditions are not the greatest, I admit, and we could be sent back to die at sea, yes, but every cloud has its silver lining. There is nothing more invigorating than waking up to the stench of your fellow refugees, feeling the close comraderie as you hold wonderfully beseeching banners pleaing for help, or watching sympathetic picnickers sail by in silent embarrassment. Without Hong Hong's unwillingness to rescue Indochina's dispossess-

ed none of this would be possible. Please give credit where credit is due.

Lo Ei Que
Skyluck

Hitler

I am sick to death of the parallels continually being drawn between Hitler's gas chambers of World War II and the open sea of Vietnam. I mean, who cares whether the world's failure to offer heaven to Jews fleeing Hitler's Germany in the 1930s can be related to the world's failure to harbor Indochina's refugees? Stop making the parallels already. How the hell is history supposed to repeat itself if you and your bloody parallels keep standing in the way?

A. Reader
Acquieseville, Iowa

Chrysler

Congress only gave $69 million to save the Cambodians so they'd have enough to bail out Chrysler. Listen, without that $1.5 billion loan, I'd be out of a job. The business of America is business, not humanitarianism. And don't forget it, buddy.

Lee Iacocca
Detroit

BOAT PEOPLE welcomes letters to the editors. Letters for publication should be addressed to BOAT PEOPLE, South China Sea.

Boat People

NEXT WEEK

Hanoi cracks Sino-Vietnamese ethnic jokes
After toppling Pol Pot, Hanoi's busy appropriating Polish jokes. "How do you sink Vietnam's Chinese minority?" "Put them in the water." But Vietnam's ethnic Chinese aren't exactly dying of laughter.

Thailand's Nong Khai refugee camp rates
With 46,000 people, the sprawling camp camp is larger than the provincial Thai capital and could be the site of the 1980 Summer Olympics.

Zen and the Art of Self-Immolation
All fired up over life, a few Buddhist monks meet their match, have a gas, and fan the flames.

DESPITE STARVATION, A VIETNAMESE INVASION, AMERICAN BOMBINGS, AND RAVAGES OF CIVIL WAR, MALNOURISHED CAMBODIANS ENJOY LIFE AS REFUGEES

The Cambodian people have always dreamed of becoming refugees. Now, along the border the country shares with Thailand, the dreams of more than half a million have come true as the happy homeless mass together in burlap and thatch cities.

When Army Marshal Lon Nol overthrew Prince Norodom Sihanouk in 1970, Cambodians couldn't wait for the day he'd be toppled by insurgent Communist forces. Within three years the Peking-backed Khmer Rouge, led by Pol Pot, met with applause from Cambodians as it marched the entire urban population into rural slave-labor camps, closed schools and hospitals, abolished religion, and banned machinery. Without callous extermination, Cambodians could never realize their dreams of becoming refugees.

Anyone with an education or modern skill had to be killed and children deemed to be the offspring of undesirables had to be buried alive to give Cambodians a taste of refugee life. Cambodians don't mind that their cities were sacked and their ancient culture all but eradicated. They thank Americans, who, under the leadership of President Nixon, secretly bombed the Cambodian landscape, destroying over 4 million Cambodians—fully half the population. Although Pol Pot was driven from power by the Vietnamese in early 1979, relief on the massive scale required to stem the famine has been fortunately obstructed by Hanoi's puppet regime in Phnom Penh. Of the four million surviving Cambodians, at least half face starvation. But if a few more Cambodians will feel the thrills of what it's like to be a refugee, then it's worth every life.

Q. Are we not dead?
A. We are Cambodians

Jay Ullal/Stern

CHATTER

Boned again Tired of attacks from Joan Baez, actress Jane Fonda (Barbarella) finally found a way of defending the Vietnamese government's blatantly racist policy of ousting Sino-Vietnamese. "I mean, I can relate to what Joan is saying, you know, but the refugees are mostly people escaping from Vietnam's 'socialist transformation.' Okay, I can understand why China rejects that claim. So, the communists took power in 1954 in northern Vietnam and it wasn't until recently that over 23,000 Sino-Vietnamese were forced from their jobs, forced to retire, demoted, given reduced pay, had their food rations cut, were detained and arrested and sent to a watery grave. But look, who are you going to believe? Someone who couldn't have a permanent relationship with Bob Dylan or me, the star of China Syndrome who gets it on with Tom Hayden every night? I mean, honestly."

**Jane Fonda:
My husband, I think I'll keep him**

**Henry Kissinger:
"Best seller list is at hand"**

Sour Kraut The "New" Boat People wave doesn't wash with Henry Kissinger. "It should have happened long ago," kvetches Kissinger. "Boat People are refugees. It's nothing new. It's going on all over — Palestinians, Rhodesians, Pakistanis. We should have just bombed North Vietnam right off the map at the start instead of all that 'Peace is at Hand' malarkey." Kissinger is similarly underwhelmed by the success of Richard Nixon's memoirs over his own. "What he wrote in those books was just a rehashing of Six Crises plus a transcript of the tapes. He's not a writer."

Spelling B National Security Advisor Zbigniew Brzezinski has nothing to do with the Boat People and it should come of no surprise that few Vietnamese can pronounce his name let alone spell it.

STAR TRACKS

Sink or Swim ∨

It's not easy doing an imitation of Iwo Jima at sea, but that didn't stop the 143 refugees aboard a sinking plank of wood from doing their darndest to capture the American landmark's like-ness.

Refugees Sit ∨

"When's the movie going to start?" ask the 200 impatient refugees just dying to see the Vietnamese premiere of Francis Ford Coppola's *Apocalypse Now.*

Cambodians Split ∨

It wasn't exactly the March of Dimes, but an entire village of Cambodians took to the streets, not because they had been left homeless, but to show skeptics that Cambodians *will* "walk a mile for a hamlet."

OUR NATION'S ARMPIT

Early last August, I was circling Kennedy Airport waiting for clearance to land my Lear when an awesome sight grabbed my attention. I was still pondering the advice my man in Boston had given me earlier that morning concerning the economic feasibility of a new special interest magazine for left-handed writers and right-handed leftists when I found myself in sudden peril. I was lurching dangerously closer to the Statue of Liberty, that tall, green lady who stands barefoot above the poison waters of New York Harbor. Only a textbook barrel-roll saved me from certain memorialization.

As I straightened a few paintings knocked askew by my life-saving maneuver, it dawned on me that, in all my years in the *La Grande Pomme*, I had never taken a close look at the famous piece of rusted copper. Completing several daring fly-bys that evoked audible shrieks from the crowd of tourists below, I saw the statue as few ever have.

There they were, high above the water and molded in copper: underarm stains.

As an American, I was shocked and saddened. My head spun in the light of my discovery. Patriotism and the ideals I valued fell shattered at my feet. I tried to blame the French for giving us the Statue, but it was impossible to deny respect for them as the inventors of oral sex.

For many days I spoke to no one. I locked myself in my room, alone with my tormented thoughts, videobeam TV, and Betamax. My world was falling apart; *I had seen our nation's armpit.*

It started slowly. Little things like buttoning my shirts all the way up and letting my hair drip dry found their way into my previously impeccable grooming habits. It got worse. I found myself eating at MacDonald's when it wasn't absolutely necessary. At concerts, I didn't even have the spirit to light my Bic Butane with everyone else before the rehearsed encore.

I was determined to resolve the consuming doubts preying on my spirit. I had but one thing on my mind: to investigate the true character of our nation.

During the first weeks I toiled away in rigorous research. I soon finished my reservedly passionate yet obliquely direct essay and titled it, with tentative finality, "Our Nation's Armpit." The metaphor was successful; the syntax was clean; the stapling was beyond reproach. All I needed was an audience.

I began with my chauffeur. He took one look at the title, and informed me that, "It's a good idea, but not that many people are really interested in New Jersey."

I then decided to seek criticism from more scholarly sources. I brought the essay to Brian Tumor, a former English professor of mine. Brian perused the text, paused, and reacted to the piece in too many words to recall here. He concluded that "Our Nation's Armpit" is a brilliant statement on the overcommercialization of our moral value system, a caustic look at modern hypocrisy, and a subtle attack on the use of antiperspirants. I thanked him for his help and left him to his work—a study of the change in meaning elicited by reading every other word of *The Brothers Karamozov.*

I spent the next few weeks touring the country, calling on old friends, acquaintances, and relatives. I had to find someone who could comprehend the importance of my message, someone who could give me the strength to reveal its frightening truths to the populace.

Among those I consulted was one Lester Pavement, a neo-hipster and herb farmer. Lester is the sole supplier to Herbal Essence Shampoo. During the early Sixties, he worked closely with Colonel Sanders on a special project that eventually led to the development of the Famous Blend of Eleven Herbs and Spices—one of which, Lester confided, is still illegal in 38 states. Lester's advice was sadly incoherent; he had earlier sacrificed his capacity to reason in the interest of science.

Another memorable visit was to Sri Asran Liebowitz, a born-again pagan and part-time panhandler. As my Mercedes SX70 pulled into Sri's Long Island campsite, I couldn't help pondering the question Sri had left me with the last time I saw him: "But what, my son, is the sound of one syphilitic whore clapping?"

After several of Sri's followers pulled him down from the ceiling of the split-level pup-tent, I presented "Our Nation's Armpit" to His Holiness. In a mystic trance, comparable only to a Seconal overdose, he began muttering something about inflation and rising cost of Oneness. Again discouraged by the lack of understanding of my essay, I popped all of his Buddha balloons and left.

Having exhausted all my possible consultants with no success, I returned home, dejected. My noble efforts seemed to have been in vain; the world isn't ready for my insight. Perhaps that is what "Our Nation's Armpit" is all about.

Chapter 6

FUN WITH CARCINOGENS

My next song is a protist song. If you know the words, sing along.

Interviewer: Dr. Dominic Casual, of Otta-wanna, Canada, is a scientist who purports to have died twice. Dr. Casual . . . .

Dominic: Call me Dom.

I: Dom, how does a man die and recover not once, but twice?

D: Well, I attribute it to willpower. The first time I died I was thirty-one years old. God, I can remember it like yesterday. The date was January 6, 1965. When I went to sleep that night I was the picture of health. When I woke up the next morning I was dead.

I: You woke up dead?

D: As a doornail.

I: How did you know you were dead?

D: I first suspected it when I discovered my alarm clock had failed to rouse me. I felt stiff, as if rigor mortis had set in. The next thing I knew, I felt myself rising out of the bed. I walked into the kitchen and made myself a cup of coffee. I watched a little television, then called in dead to work. I read the morning paper, and did the crossword puzzle. Then I made myself a couple of fried eggs. Then I. . . .

I: It seems death has a surprisingly lifelike quality.

D: Yes, it was a bit of a disappointment after all the stories you hear. After breakfast, I went back into my room and sat down on my bed. And I said to myself, "Dommy, are you ready for death?" And I looked around me, and thought, "I want to live!" I kept repeating that to myself for over an hour, and then I lay down and closed my eyes. When I opened them again it was four o'clock in the afternoon, and I was alive!

I: You were? How did you know?

D: Hey, come on, how does anyone know he's alive? How do you know *you're* alive? You just know, right? I ran around the house yelling, "I'm alive! I'm alive!" just touching everything, and staring at my reflection in the mirror for minutes on end. That evening I celebrated with some Chivas, driving my car all over town, honking the horn at everyone. Then I smashed the car into a tree and died all over again.

I: Sounds like it wasn't your day. Were you crushed? Did you. . . .

D: Beats me. But the next time I opened my eyes, I was in a room with God. He was old, with gray hair and a gray beard, and he had on a long white coat. And everywhere I looked, everything around me was white and clean. It was beautiful. Then I got down on my hands and knees, crawled over to God, and cowered at His feet. Finally, I looked up at Him and said, "I don't want to be dead." And then God gestured to one of his angels, and she took my blood pressure and tested my reflexes. At last, God walked over to me and said, "You're a crazy, drunken sonofabitch and we don't have any room for you here." I was discharged by the angel at the main desk, and the next thing I knew, I was home again, and I was alive, and it was wonderful. A miracle.

I: Amazing. So what does the future hold for you, Dom?

D: I'm working on a paperback for Dell Publishing that should be out in October, called *I Cheated Death!* All I really want to do is send out the message that, hey, death doesn't have to be the "final sleep" or "eternal rest." Death can be as temporary and refreshing as an afternoon nap or a ride in the country. All you need is the proper frame of mind, and physical well-being.

I: You know, Dom, there are an awful lot of people out there who are probably telling themselves that you're a phony, that the whole thing is a hoax, that you're trying to make a bundle off a pack of lies. Is there any substance to that?

D: Absolutely not.

I: Can you back that up?

D: I'd stake my life on it.

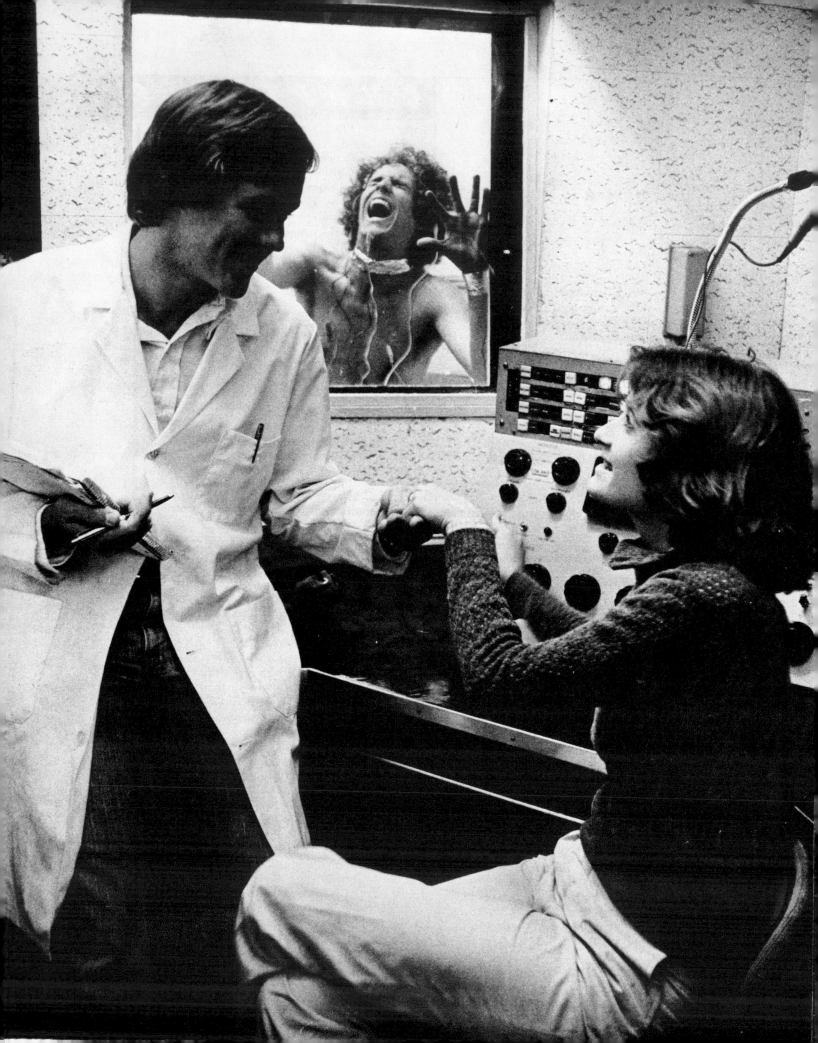

The Greatest Hits of MODERN PSYCHOLOGY

Perception

"Waiter, there's a kinetic illusion in my soup."
William James

Perception, what does it mean? Perception is the vital link between two entirely separate entities: the real world and the mind. Information about the real world is gathered by the five senses: sight, smell, taste, touch, and hearing. This information is then loaded at the clearinghouse of the sensory organ onto the nerve impulses, the physiological eighteen-wheelers which travel the neural highway to your brain, the consumer. In the case of sight, once the impulses are loaded by the sensory forklift that is the retina, these trusty little messengers move steadily at the somatic 55 mph speed limit, protected by the myelin sheath median strip, through foul weather and fair, stopping only at a synapse for a neural pit stop, just to keep the brain supplied with sensory goods. Naturally, to keep this intricate transportation line rolling, we must pay the highway tax of perception by eating a balanced diet, so that the neural highway is well-paved with the sodium and potassium ions they require (Figure 1).

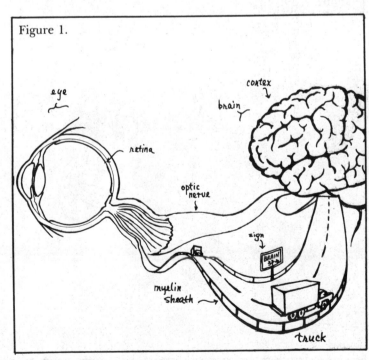

Figure 1.

Before discussing the synapse, the gap between two neurons, or nerve cells, we must abandon our transportation model and admit that perception has a dual nature, similar to the wave-particle duality of light in physics. Psychology can thus be seen to be a veritable extension of real sciences, sort of. We must first study the "school-boy model" initially proposed by my brother-in-law. Let the two neurons on each end of the synapse be represented by two students in class. The one in front, distal to the memory signal, is the teacher's pet. The space between him and the boy behind him represents the gap that is the synapse, and the pin in the hand of the second boy is the chemical agent which transmits the signal across the gap. This chemical we shall here specify as being acetylcholine to make all this sound more scientific. When the school boy with the pin sticks the teacher's pet, the latter feels the pin puncture his dendrite, and screams, thus transmitting the message. The chemotransmitter has only a transitory existence; it is destroyed very soon after it is released, illustrated by the removal of the pin shortly after it is inserted.

Language

"Word order to language man's capacities critical is."

Noam Chomsky

Linguists working from the premise that man is not unique in his capacity for language have tried to detect the use of language in normal animal social behavior, but with little success to date. Another group of linguists have in recent years tried to demonstrate the capacity for language by teaching the use of language to animals.

Foremost among these efforts were those involving chimpanzees, probably man's closest animal relative. The clumsy and underdeveloped speech tract of the chimpanzee forced investigators to abandon attempts to teach verbal English to apes; instead, they turned to their agile hands. Project Washoe, using the American sign language for the deaf, is the most well-known and successful of these endeavors.

Washoe is a chimpanzee who was reared and trained from birth by two psychologists at the University of Nevada. The chimpanzee was raised by the couple in their home in an environment intended to duplicate the home environment of the human child. This was done as it is believed that much of language acquisition comes directly from the home environment. Thus, in Washoe's presence, only sign language was used by her human family, even when they communicated among themselves. Within a few years Washoe had learned to call for her toys by name and to ask where babies come from, demonstrating a mastery of childhood drivel. With the onset of puberty, Washoe became impatient with her trainers, and tired of her teaching sessions. At one point, when confronted with yet another doll, Washoe signed to her teacher, "Give Washoe break." Washoe began to pick up signs from the outside world on her own, and even to create some of her own (Figure 2), which suggested to the project directors that Washoe may have outgrown the language environment they had created for her, and that perhaps a change in this environment would renew interest and accelerate the rate of language acquisition.

Would Washoe acquire an adult vocabulary and speech pattern if placed in an adult environment? Washoe was dressed in a chiffon cocktail dress and tak-

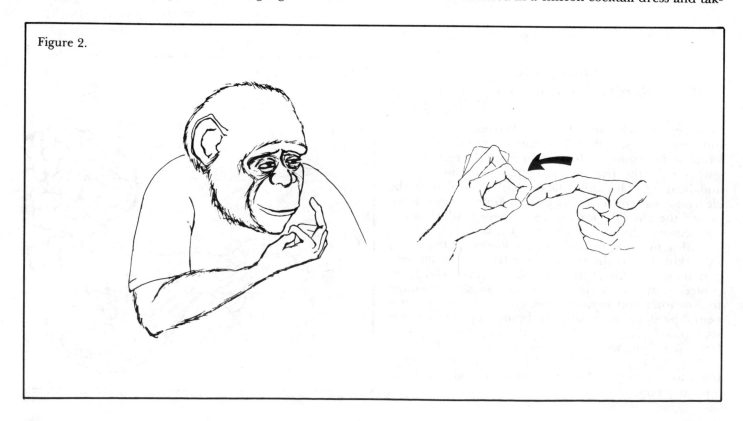

Figure 2.

CONTEMPORARY COMMUNICATIONS

The following is a contemporary example of intrasocietal communication at the expense of the bourgeoisification of literature. These lines are excerpts from the Brotherhood of the Paternal Order of Elks in conjunction with the American Legionnaires production of William Shakespeare's Hamlet *translated into Citizen's Band Radio language.*

(Act One, Scene One; Rampart of Elsinore Castle)

Bernardo: 3's and 8's, Horatio. Welcome, good Marcellus.

Marcellus: Has the rig been in the grass again to-night?

Horatio: Tush, tush, good buddy. Negatory. 'Twill not appear.

(Enter the Ghost)

Marcellus: Mercy sakes, two-wheeler break thee off! Look where it comes again!

Bernardo: We copy, 10-4, in the same figure like the King that's dead.

Horatio: Stackin' eights come on; so have I heard and do in part believe it. Let us 10-25 what we have seen tonight unto young Hamlet, for, upon my handle, this spirit, 10-1 to us, will 10-21 to him.

Marcellus: Bodacious, let's do it, I pray, and I this morning know where we shall beat the bushes for him most conveniently.

(Act One, Scene Two; the Court)

King (Big Bear): Breaker-one-nine, breaker-one-nine, cotton-picker nephew. Though yet of Hamlet our dear brother's death the memory be green, come on, 'tis unmanly grief to persevere in negatory condolement. It shows a will of ratchet jaw most incorrect to heaven.

Queen (XLY of Big Bear): Good sonny, cast thy knighted handle off, come on.

Hamlet: I shall in all my best copy. . . .

King (Big Bear): 'Tis a loving and a fair reply. Catch you on the flip-flop.

(10-7 All but Hamlet)

Hamlet: Oh that this too too solid rig would melt, thaw, and feed the bears. Let me not 10-29 on't! Frailty, thy handle is beaver.

(Act One, Scene Three; Polonius Advising His Son)

Polonius (handled "Quasar," as he has his works in his drawers): Be not a ratchet jaw, nor give any unproportioned thought his act. Be thou a good buddy, but by no means bodacious. Beware beating the bushes for smokies, but being in, fear not to put the hammer down. Keep always your ears on, but reserve thy judgment. Costly thy seatcovers, for beaver oft proclaims the man. Neither a chicken coop nor a draggin's wagon be. This above all—to thine own rig be true. Put the good numbers on you! Farewell.

(Act One, Scene Four)

Marcellus: Wall-to-wall smokies in the state of Denmark.

(Act Two, Scene Two)

Hamlet: What a piece of rig is man! how bodacious in reason! how 10-4 in faculties! in putting the hammer down how express and admirable! in action how like a beaver! in apprehension how like a bear! the cotton picker of the world, the paragon of 18-wheelers. . . .

(Act Three, Scene Two)

Queen (Other half of King): The slipcover doth protest too much, methinks.

(Act Three, Scene Three)

Hamlet: Do you see yonder cloud that's almost in shape of a pregnant roller skate?

Polonius: By th' mass, and 'tis a pregnant roller skate indeed.

Hamlet: Methinks it is a plain wrapper.

Polonius: It is backed like a plain wrapper.

Hamlet: Or like a bubble gum machine.

Polonius: Very like a bubble gum machine.

(Act Five, Scene One)

Hamlet: Alas, poor Yorick! I knew him, good buddy.

(Act Five, Scene Two)

Hamlet: There's a bear in the air that shapes our ends, negatory them how we will.

en to a singles bar in Reno. After becoming accustomed to the strange surroundings, Washoe pointed to her dress and then pointed to her mouth while making a biting motion, thus making the sign for "bites," or "eats." The chiffon was then replaced by a pair of Bonjour jeans and a tube top, much to Washoe's apparent satisfaction. Once back in the bar, Washoe progressed rapidly in modifying her dialect with the addition of words, collocations, and phrases. Within nine weeks, she could recite two farmer's daughter jokes, and soon after had perfected, "What's your sign, big boy?" and "You wanna come up and see my etchings?" However, Washoe failed to receive the proper positive reinforcement associated with these collocations and soon became moody and despondent. She would fly into fits of rage, upset swizzle-stick holders, swing on legionnaires, and attempt to groom the bartender. Not long thereafter Washoe be-

Figure 3.

The data substantially support the hypothesis that man, equipped with an opposable thumb, would assert his superiority by outperforming his animal counterparts in a test of success at hitchhiking. After one hour, over 70 percent of the human subjects had succeeded in getting a ride. Without the highly visible, useful thumb, only slightly over 4 percent of the dachsund puppies managed to flag down a willing motorist. The snakes were notably unsuccessful in their feeble tongue-wagging attempts.

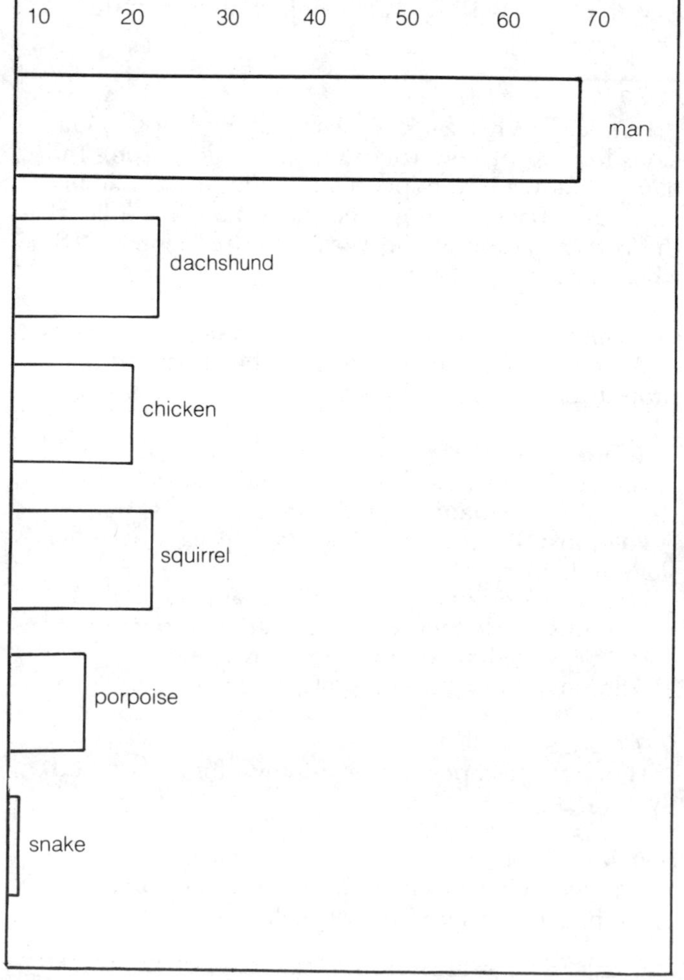

came addicted to banana liquor and disappeared from the public eye. Washoe was last seen working two-bit zoos and performing personal "favors" for Marlin Perkins.

Personality

"Take my ego . . . please."

Erik Erikson

The core of modern personality theory is Freud's theory of the Oedipal complex. The Oedipal complex, schematically outlined in Figure 4, is centered around the desire of the child to sexually possess the parent of the opposite sex. This desire is for exclusive possession; the male child wishes to remove his rival, the father. He usually wishes him dead, or at least stricken with eczema and a prominent goiter.

Because of the essentially conflicting nature of the desires of childhood, certain desires are repressed. This leads to an adolescence marked by frustration and a bad complexion. The degree to which the repression of desires takes place within the nuclear family was first demonstrated by Adrian Absorbine, Jr., shortly after Freud's predictions were made. After months of unsuccessfully trying to detect blemishes in laboratory rats, Absorbine hit upon the idea of measuring relative repression as frustration. In an elegant experiment, he lowered window panes into experimental and control cages and measured the number of panes punched out after twenty-four hours (Figure 5).

Frustration of this sort builds in children until puberty, when incestuous desires are transformed into legitimate lusts aimed outside the nuclear family. In the interim, this frustration is released in the form of many common childhood activities, including vandalism, contact sports, and the abuse of small rodents. Indeed, this author is convinced that the torture of hamsters is as universal as the dislike for spinach. In his beautiful analysis, Dr. Absorbine classified all hamster tortures into three basic catagories representing three fundamentally different psychotypologies. Using the proximity of the torturer and the rodent as a criterion for classification, he cites three exemplary tortures for the three sets of tortures. The first torture involves placing the hamster in a swimming pool. As the rodent swims with its nose just above water, pebbles are dropped in the water at the other end of the pool, causing waves that just wash over the hamster's nose. This represents what Dr. Absorbine called a "distal" relationship between child and rodent; they are separated in space, so that both action and observation have an indirect quality to them. This differs significantly from a "proximal" torture such as spraying the hamster with Medi-Quick to cause slow skin suffocation. Here the two parties are close together, the action is direct and readily observable; little is left to the imagination. The last category of rodent abuses he called "neither here nor there, you know, sort of in between. Oh, what's the word for it?" and contains the classic hamster torture: attaching a string to the animal and then flushing it down the toilet. The hamster is then pulled back by the string and flushed again. This tor-

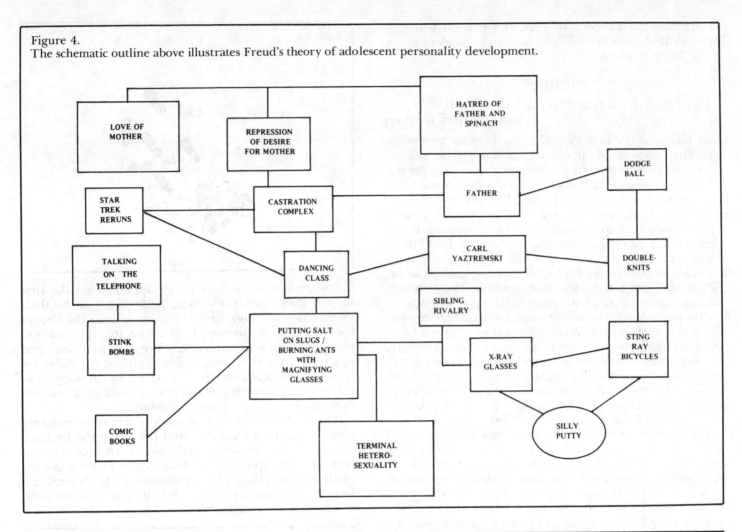

Figure 4.
The schematic outline above illustrates Freud's theory of adolescent personality development.

LOVE OF MOTHER

REPRESSION OF DESIRE FOR MOTHER

HATRED OF FATHER AND SPINACH

DODGE BALL

STAR TREK RERUNS

CASTRATION COMPLEX

FATHER

TALKING ON THE TELEPHONE

DANCING CLASS

CARL YAZTREMSKI

DOUBLE-KNITS

STINK BOMBS

PUTTING SALT ON SLUGS / BURNING ANTS WITH MAGNIFYING GLASSES

SIBLING RIVALRY

X-RAY GLASSES

STING RAY BICYCLES

COMIC BOOKS

TERMINAL HETERO-SEXUALITY

SILLY PUTTY

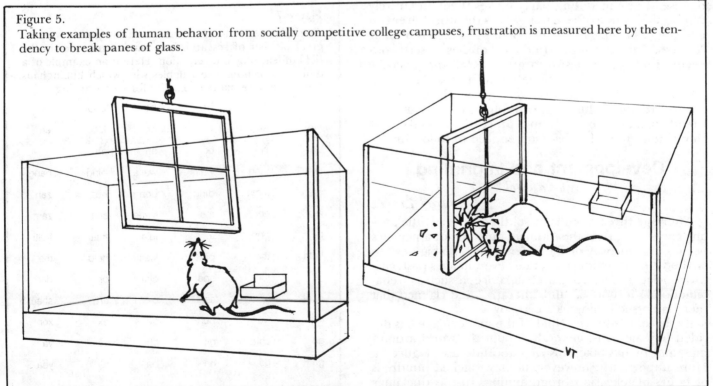

Figure 5.
Taking examples of human behavior from socially competitive college campuses, frustration is measured here by the tendency to break panes of glass.

175

ture mixes the mystery of what lies beyond with the practicality of readily available facilities. Incidentally, it is the favorite of the author.

Instinct

"Is that all you guys ever think about?"
Masters and Johnson

Behavior is the pudding wherein we must ultimately find the proof of our psychological study. The motivations and stimuli that inspire behavior operate on many levels—conscious and unconscious. The creatures of the animal kingdom—from wood lice and sow slugs to American Legionnaires—are unaware of the greater part of their responses made to everyday stimuli: insecticide, salt, or nickel poisoning, for example. From these basic psysiological concerns we will move into the most complex of motivating forces: man in the context of his fellow man, his society, and his television. The first step on the ladder to understanding behavior is instinct.

It is possible to pass off the most abstruse and inexplicable behavior in human beings as a trait acquired from the particularities of some idiosyncratic family, society, or encounter group. Some behavioral tendencies are so universal that anthropologists and psychologists alike agree that their basis is surely in instinct. The need to hold a drink at social occasions and the drive to barbeque on Friday nights are two such examples.

Bees, possessors of a lifespan somewhere between two weeks or 200 miles, have little spare time to fritter away needlessly; yet between the birth and the untimely death, this industrious creature masters a complex system of language through intricate gestures and motions.

With the exception of the South American killer variety—whose reprehensible propensity to bring on the demise of any meddling party makes them an entirely unpopular source of research—bees the world over can exchange concepts like Green Stamps by means of their "dances." Saturday nights find most of these insects conveying their inner desire to grab for all the gusto by means of a tango (dip optional) or a cha-cha (Figure 6). The explorer bee upon discovering a new store of pollen will return to his hive, carefully leaving crumbs of bread to mark his trail, and proceed to "shake that thing" until the other bees are enticed to follow him.

Development and Imprinting

"Why a duck?"
Konrad Lorenz

After age three months or so, there is very little anyone can do to affect the ultimate outcome of a person's personality one way or the other. This is no big news to anybody in this modern age; however, in ages past, civilized societies believed in archaic concepts such as "rehabilitation," "incentive," and "therapy," and claimed that there is no such thing as a bad boy.

By three months the child of the modern age has decided how he feels, generally, about the world around him, and he has taken his first aptitude test (Figure 7). More importantly, however, he has watched hundreds of hours of television programming. Just as ducklings

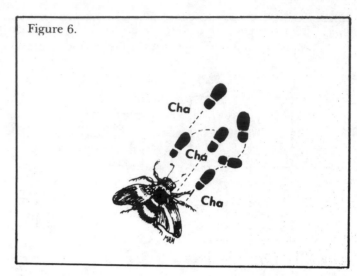

Figure 6.

follow around whomever they happen to see the first instant they open their eyes, believing it to be their mother (imprinting), so do children imitate the images they see on the screen. Left alone in a gymnasium equipped with white tuxedos, white cars, fountains, and elegantly dressed women, children almost invariably respond to the images on the TV screen by dressing up in the tuxedos, strutting about the cars, singing, as best they can manage, "Volare . . . Volare."

The establishment of role models and authorization by television continues into later life as internalized values over which the individual has little control. At what point, for example, do the Philadelphia Flyers make the realization that their playing abilities are profoundly affected by the singing of Kate Smith? For the most part, it is an unconscious reaction.

Figure 7.
The German scholar Hermann Ebbinghaus was the great pioneer of research into man's tendencies in the field of learning and retention. Here is an example of a typical set of nonsense syllables with which Ebbinghaus would measure man's capability for rote learning.

ya	ba	da	ba	doo	
yip	ee	l	oh	ki	eh
oo	ee	oo	ah	ah	
ting	tang	walla	walla	bing	bang
rama	lama	ding	dong	huz	zah
its	not	too	sweet	sha	zam
be	bop	a	lula	tutti	frutti
hold	the	pic	kles	hold	the
let	tuce	spe	cial	or	ders
dont	up	set	us	arg	sheesh
kaw	wa	bun	ga	ex	xon
git	chi	git	chi	ya	ya
ga	ga	oh	ba	by	yea

In the next section we will move on to the higher levels of motivation that instill man with a need for frame of reference, companionship, education, weekends at the beach, insurance policies, and Ronco Buttoneers.

Conformity

"Vol is hungry, we must feed Vol"
B. F. Skinner

Society has a far greater effect upon its components than anyone would care to realize. Role definitions are surprisingly narrow; demands upon a person's individuality are often unbearable. The statistics and behavior surrounding suicide are intriguing testimony indeed. Once a desperate soul is discovered standing on a ledge ready to jump or soaked in gasoline holding a lighter, large, ebullient crowds invariably gather to chant, "Jump! Jump! Jump!" and "Five, four, three, two, one!" and "Do it, chicken!" The ingrained death wish in society is apparent at all points in life. Double-faulting in tennis reflects a desire for the death of self in the same manner that kitchen trashmashers reflect a suppression of individuality.

"Boy, do we have this guy conditioned. Every time I press the bar down he drops a pellet in."

SCHIZOPHRENIA

Simply stated, the mental illness of schizophrenia involves a patient's complete immersion in a fantasy world of his own creation. Our example here is an altogether too common occurrence in which a student, usually undergraduate, at Harvard University mistakenly believes that his or her perspective on the most broad and encompassing of topics is somehow precious to the rest of the world. The following excerpt is from a recently published article in the New York Times Magazine.

The Seventies: Yes or No?

by Cornelius C. Brittelbum, III

As a student at Harvard, I find my reflections on the decade nearly completed, settling on my consciousness like ambivalent raindrops on a not-quite-sunny morning. I felt happy at first, but then a little sad: the seventies are coming to a close, and yet, heavy with portent, the eighties are just around the corner. "What have we accomplished?" I forced myself to wonder. Compared to the disillusioned jaundice of the sullied idealism of the sixties, our complacent strivings for success now seem but a misplaced goal on our broken-field run to adulthood.

Three years ago I began my Harvard career a complete member of the media generation—cynical, yet motivated; eager, yet unsure; naive, and yet learned about the coming new age of our nation, our world, and myself. "Where are we going?" I pondered. It is tempting for one to feel like a minute twig racing downstream in the deluge of time—one among many; and yet multitudes of these disconnected twigs and branches can join to clog and affect the course of any flood—even the flood of time. . . .

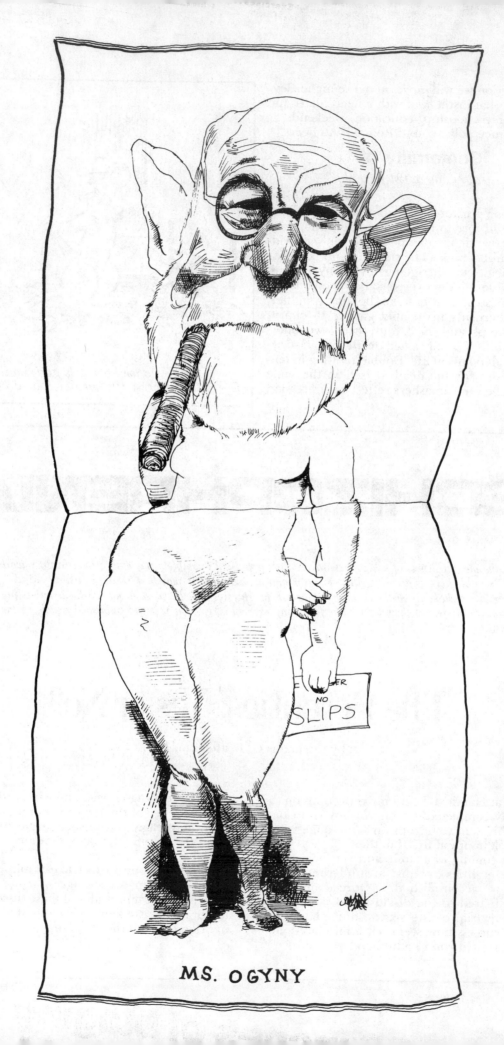

MS. OGYNY

Are You Suffering from America's Number 1 Crippler?

GRAVITY

Hundreds, thousands, millions— loads of people fall prey to the vicious jaws of the force of gravity. Joints get old and start to creak from the constant pull earthward. Growth is stunted. Feet, backs, legs get tired and weary. People fall off high ladders and break bones. Very heavy things topple off shelves. Lunatics jump off twenty-story buildings and go squish on the concrete sidewalk and splatter innocent pedestrians. Bridges fall down and smash sinking boats. Airplanes plummet from the sky and wreak carnage. Rain plunges recklessly earthward and ruins *your* new suit.

Where Will It All End?

Ever since Newton and his apple, science has tried to ignore the ever-present problem of gravity, but the simple fact is: *it just won't go away!* But now, with your help, the desperately needed research can begin. A cure to this dreaded crippler is within our grasp, in our lifetime, if only we reach out to grab it and dig down into our pockets.

The Valiant Fight Has Already Begun!

In our research facilities all across the globe (Acapulco, the Rivieria, the Alps, Hawaii, Monaco, Monte Carlo, and Cleveland) important strides have been made to alleviate the effects of Gravity. For example, here are some of the latest anti-gravity devices:

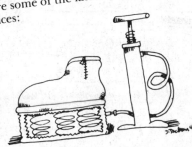

1) Anti-Gravity Inflatable Life Boots—designed with heavy-duty iron springs to help push back against the force of Gravity. Also inflatable for added push.

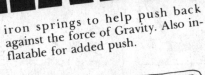

2) Gravity-Defying Hang Glider— weights and wires are used in this metal construction to raise the harnessed body off the earth and away from Gravity. The Glider is still being tested for its effectiveness and practicality, but it certainly seems like a great idea.

3) Foam Rubber Body Glove—this amazing Body Glove covers the whole body so that, should you literally fall victim to Gravity, the foam rubber will cushion the impact and foil the force. Protects against all kinds of stumbles, trips, bumps, bashes, and falling airplanes. Endorsed by Gerry Ford. Also available in suede, ermine, and cedar.

Only Your Bank Account Can Help

Please send your generous contribution right now. This minute. Even as you read this, funds are desperately needed to move our Cleveland lab to the Virgin Islands so that Professor Mordecai Stegmaier can conduct important tests on the peculiar form of Gravity that affects these islands and any other lush tropical nirvanas. Please send your cash (no checks, please) as your personal blow against Gravity!

And, if you act right now, you get in addition, ABSOLUTELY FREE, the amazing, incredible, all-new Flemco SOAP HANDLE! Yes, the technicians of Flemco have created this incredible, all-new device to handle those hard-to-hold bars of soap that keep slipping out of your hands when you take a shower. The handle is easy to insert into any brand of soap, and it's covered with amazing, incredible, all-new Teflon so food won't stick! What a bargain!

And that's not all! You also get the amazing new book *99 New Ideas*, chock full of information on how to cash in on the booms ahead. Answers questions such as: Should you buy or rent your wife? The answer may surprise you!

What a great deal, and what swell guys we are! All this for only a $100 *and up* contribution to the Society for the Prevention of Gravity.

YES! I'd love to Donate:
☐ $100 ☐ $200 ☐ Much more
☐ And I'll leave you in my will while I'm at it!

Send to:
The Society for the Prevention of Gravity
Suite 2A
Hotel Plush, New York, NY 10019

NAME _____ CITY _____
ADDRESS _____
BANK _____

Clown in a Crazy House

Julius Vitellius is a spaceman; a spaceperson.

Actually Julius Livingston Vitellius is a Lieutenant Colonel in the United States' Empirical Air Force.

The National Aeronautics and Space Administration decreed that Lieutenant Colonel Julius Livingston Vitellius was.

They say he is no more.

They gave an American flag to Mrs. Lieutenant Colonel Julius Livingston Vitellius.

Her name is Jane.

When she was six years old she lived in Sioux Falls, South Dakota, and her playmates called her "Plain Jane Blaine who was a real pain in the—."

Now Jane lives at Pleasant View Sanitarium, in Greenfield, New Hampshire.

I live in the cell next to hers.

Jane and I are criminally insane.

Jane poisoned all the members of the National Aeronautics and Space Administration. They had just given her an American flag.

I used to be a clown with Professor Brock's Traveling Circus and Wild Animal Farm.

One day a little girl popped a green balloon right in front of my nose.

I went on a spree.

I captured ten little children and inflated their lungs until they popped.

I have just finished reading a book by Kurt Vonnegut Jr.

Obviously.

Jane and I are the only people that know that Lieutenant Colonel Julius Livingston Vitellius is still a spaceman. Everybody else is ignorant. I know because Jane told me. Jane knows because her husband had a secret transmitter/receiver in his spaceship and in her bedroom. She heard everything he said when he was on his business trips. The story of Lieutenant Colonel Julius Livingston Vitellius is very interesting. NASA covered it up. Now the whole world will know. NASA will be upset—nobody questions the word of God.

Lieutenant Colonel Julius Livingston Vitellius was the second human being in outer space. Nobody knows this because NASA did not tell anyone. They wanted to make sure that it would work before they told anyone. It did not work the way they wanted it to work; it worked the way Lieutenant Colonel Julius Livingston Vitellius wanted it to work. They did not tell anyone.

Jane told me that in my exposé I could call Julius Livingston Vitellius, "Jewel."

It would preserve my sanity.

Jewel blasted off from the Arizona desert on August 24, 1960. Nobody heard the rocket because nobody lives anywhere near 36 degrees North and 111 degrees 4" West. NASA was very discreet. He blasted off at 3 A.M. English time or 0300 hours in official military talk. He was in a Mercury-Atlas rocket that nobody but the Imperial Emperor of the United States and NASA knew existed. It was going to orbit the Earth three times and then splash down into the Great Salt Lake.

Jane told me the details of the trip.

Jewel almost had to abort the mission because he had contracted a hangnail on his right index finger. NASA had to bring in a specialist to perform emergency surgery. The operation was a success and Jewel blasted off on schedule. His rocket ship pierced the outer layer of the Earth's atmosphere and he saw the world as no other White Anglo-Saxon Protestant had ever seen it. Brilliant yellow and white points pierced his skull with their intensity. For the first time the concept of nothingness was made clear to him. He murmured magnificent phrases into his secret transmitter about the totality and harmony of the universe. He became a follower of the Way, the Communist Tao, five minutes after his baptism into the macrocosm of the universe. He said many things that NASA could not understand.

"God is gay," he said.

"Life is man's most beautiful creation."

NASA was incredulous. Jane could also hear what they said. They humored Jewel. They snapped him out of his euphoric state and brought him back to life. They told him that Science was not interested in the meaning of life. Jewel ate his liquid lunch. He took a breath of pure

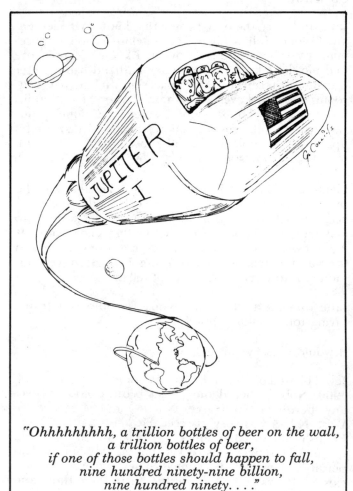

"Ohhhhhhhhh, a trillion bottles of beer on the wall,
a trillion bottles of beer,
if one of those bottles should happen to fall,
nine hundred ninety-nine billion,
nine hundred ninety...."

oxygen. His vital signs returned to normal. NASA was relieved. They had kept a man alive in outer space for an hour. Only nineteen more hours to go to beat the Russians.

Beat the Russians.

Sorry Mr. Vonnegut.

Jewel kept wondering about the greatness of the universe. Jane knew this. NASA did not know this. NASA, however, had put a tranquilizer in Jewel's food. The tranquilizer increased Jewel's euphoria.

"Just like a Valium trip," he told NASA.

NASA laughed. Spacemen do not take drugs. Jewel laughed too. Tranquilizers are fun. NASA thought that the tranquilizers would stop Jewel's fantasies. They increased Jewel's fantasies. NASA thought the tranquilizers would cloud Jewel's perception. They increased Jewel's awareness of the universe. NASA thought that Jewel would stop philosophizing about life. Jewel ate some more drugged food.

NASA had bought the tranquilizer in an abandoned warehouse in the Watts section of Los Angeles.

It was called "Angel Dust."

NASA was on a tight budget in 1960.

Jewel told Jane that he did not need the Angel Dust. He ate it anyway. Jewel fell in love with Life and outer space. Only seventeen more hours to beat the Russians.

Jane told me something about Jewel's background that is very interesting.

He is an orphan—no mom and no dad.

They left him in a sink in the 42nd Street Subway Station in New York City. He was raised by the janitorial staff in the subway station. He came from the lowest level of poverty to achieve man's greatest feat to date. He became a member of the Knickerbocker Club in New York City. They needed a token rags-to-riches story in their membership. Jewel had $1,276,498.35 when he left the Planet. He had six patents for the development of a new tire inflating device.

I used it to pop those little brats.

Jewel bought his Air Force commission. It cost him an arm and a leg. Arms are worth $59,000 each. Legs are worth $41,000 each. He wheeled and dealed his way into the space program. NASA was ecstatic. They had a scientist and a military man rolled into one human being.

Jane told me that Jewel stole the patents from her father.

That is why he had to marry her.

They learned to love each other.

Sort of.

NASA decreed that the military/scientist man would be the best man to go into outer space. Jewel got what he wanted; a vacation from his wife. That is Jewel's story.

Jewel was spaced out in outer space for sixteen hours. Then he came down.

"This food acts like some Angel Dust I tried in Los Angeles," he told NASA.

NASA did not answer. They wondered if all military/scientists took drugs. Only one hour left before NASA would beat the Russians.

They asked Jewel a question. It was a joke. They asked him if he was ready to come back home. Jewel gave them a strange answer.

"I'm here," he said.

NASA began to get upset. Military/scientists were supposed to do what they were told. Nobody questions the word of God. They asked Jewel another question. They asked him if he was coming back to Earth. It was another joke.

He answered, "No."

Jewel found some more food and ate it. He was high again. Jewel told Jane and NASA why he was not coming back.

"I am sick, sick, sick," he said. "I do not wish to return to Hell now that I have experienced Heaven. Hell is full of disgusting filth. I hate filth. I hate hypocrisy. I hate evil. I hate beating the Russians. I hate the sexual double standard in Hell."

Jane was frigid.

Jewel kicked the door to his spaceship and jumped out.

"Hello," he said.

NASA and Jane heard no more.

NASA covered it up.

They said that Jewel was killed on Earth. They said that Jewel was burned to a crisp in a rocket fuel experiment. They gave an American flag.

Jane poisoned them.

I wrote this story.

Julius Vitellius is a spaceman; a spaceperson.

GOT A MINUTE? TRY THE...

Donut Gag

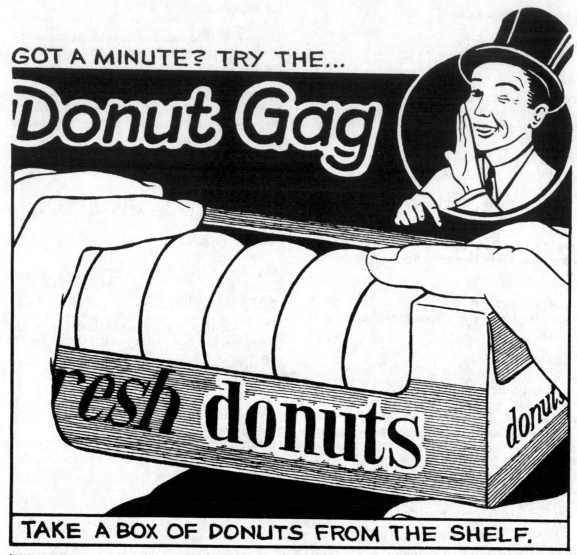

TAKE A BOX OF DONUTS FROM THE SHELF.

CHOOSE A DONUT FROM THE BOX.

OPEN UP THE LID OF YOUR STEREO.

THEN, PUT THE DONUT ON THE HOLDER.

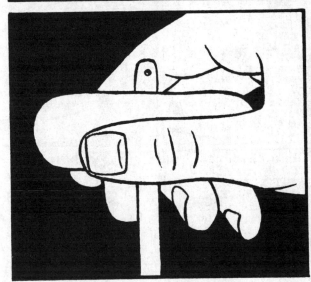

IT SHOULD STAY UP BY ITSELF.

NEXT, PUSH THE KNOB ALL THE WAY OVER.

THE DONUT WILL DROP JUST LIKE A *RECORD!*

RON HARNAR

A P ook at the Bl ak

What does the future—our solar-powered, turn-of-the-millenium, age-of-global-brotherhood, and peace-for-all-mankind future, hold for us? Not much. Certainly not any optimistic ideals. The future's just not what it used to be. And it's not going to get any better, either.

Nuclear war, or at least the fatal abuse of nuclear weaponry, seems inevitable. World famine is highly probable. And what can we, the shining lights of tomorrow, do about it? Nothing.

"That's awful!" you exclaim. You're right. The future *is* awful; awful to think about, awful to try and do something about, and coming awfully fast. Those happy summer days of the 70's are over; now it's time for the long, cold winter of future shock.

Go forth, brave young women and men! Forge a brave new world for the generations yet to come!

Fat chance.

20 Wonderful Predictions for 1980 That Never Came True (1899-1959)

1. Atomic-powered planes, trains, and automobiles.
2. Electronic light ("light without light bulbs").
3. Intercontinental mail missiles.
4. The economically useful desalination of seawater.
5. Robot servants.
6. Flying automobiles.
7. Low-cost electricity from the Aurora Borealis.
8. Atomic batteries.
9. Eradication of cancer and tuberculosis.
10. Low-cost, pre-fab suburban housing.
11. Electric airplanes.
12. Remote-control dentistry.
13. Cremation by law.
14. 120 mph electric monorails.
15. The "two-airplane" middle-class family.
17. Capsulized food.
18. The abolishment, by public demand, of smoking and alcoholism.
19. Strictly enforced noise laws in all cities.
20. No wars.

33 Things That Will Be a Part of Our Future and Are Very Depressing

1. Particle-beam weapons ("death rays").
2. The DC-10.
3. Joey Travolta.
4. The jet stream is shifting southwards and the whole earth is getting colder and will continue to do so for as long as we live.
5. A "Mork and Mindy" spin-off.
6. "Killer" satellites.
7. By the time you reach retirement age, there will be too many old people and the entire social security system will collapse.
8. Higher album prices.
9. The death of Walter Cronkite.
10. Larger world deserts. The Sahara alone will gobble up another 50,000 acres next year.
11. A staggering national debt. Soon, the United States will have spent $500 billion that doesn't even exist.
12. Nostradamus's predictions.
13. Whoever is President in 1980.
14. Books about the Beatles written by their children.
15. The phrase "History repeats itself."
16. A worldwide increase in volcanic activity.
17. Continued unbalanced world population growth. Populations in the countries with the least

food and the most fanatical governments are rising faster than ever.

18. 1984. One hundred of George Orwell's 130 predictions have already come true.
19. Iran will have nuclear "first strike" capabilities within five years.
20. A better than 50 percent chance that your marriage will end in divorce.
21. The impending major earthquake in California.
22. More teenage alcoholism.
23. Nuclear waste disposal. We've been creating nuclear waste now for 35 years, and we still don't know how to get rid of it.
24. The draft.
25. More see-through vinyl clothing.
26. More gas line murders.
27. More snuff films.
28. The rising acidity in rainwater. In some parts of the United States it has already attained a pH level of 4 to 4.5—equal to that of orange juice.
29. SALT III.
30. McDonald's 35 billionth hamburger.
31. More teenage pregnancies. Already two out of every ten high school girls in America are pregnant. Some 60 percent of them are not married.
32. The August, 1982, alignment of the five inner planets.
33. The end of the world. Most of the earth's major religions predict some sort of global disaster within the next 15 years.

Four Very General, Very Depressing Predictions (And Some Helpful Hints)

1. Someone, at some time in the future, is going to set off a nuclear bomb and kill a lot of people. The only way that absolute universal nuclear disarmament is going to take place is if (a) so much of the earth is destroyed in a nuclear conflict that the capabilities for countries to support nuclear weaponry is nullified, or (b) if a mass antinuclear movement sweeps the earth. Unfortunately, the only thing that makes the latter probability likely is if somebody sets off a nuclear bomb and kills a lot of people.

2. The world is headed for some sort of major, biological disaster. The earth is one huge system in which every event that takes place affects something else to some extent. Assholes punch out ceiling tiles in the Student Center, the Student Center runs over it maintenance budget and ups the Student Center fee, assholes get angry at the raised Student Center fee and punch holes in the ceiling tiles.

   Various negative elements worldwide in scope are increasing geometrically (factoring themselves; i.e., population and nuclear wastes).

   Now, if you combine these propositions—that the world is a single, interrelated system and that certain worldwide negative elements are increasing geometrically—a logical conclusion is that the world is heading toward some sort of interrelated disaster. Example: A homeless Palestinian, seeking shelter in a salt mine, accidentally opens up a can of waste plutonium and kills half a million people. It could happen.

3. A combined biological and man-

made Armageddon. Pessimists are a funny lot. Some argue that the world will end in famine, some say that its tombstone will be the mushroom cloud. True, nuclear war can destroy the civilized world before famine does, but that does not mean that both can't occur. Example: The pressures of population on scarce resources lead to minor wars, depleting the population but devastating the land. This in turn causes more crop failures, disease, and famine, until, eventually, nuclear war breaks out. Watch India for this one.

4. The nations that have the most potential to alter the world's course are those of the technological persuasion. Theoretically, it is possible that technology will solve a large portion of the world's problems in our lifetime while allowing us a high standard of living and a good amount of freedom. However, such solutions cannot be developed under today's, or in any foreseeable future's, system of world economics—containing, as it does, too many complexities to allow such a massive, economically disruptive renaissance to occur. Even if it did, it is doubtful that the social or political movements needed to sanction such work would ever exist. Example: If the only thing that would convince the governments of the United States and the USSR not to have a nuclear war were to have a nuclear war, then the question of whether or not it would be economically wise to ban all nuclear weapons would be nullified.

Some Good Investments for the Future

Chinese ceramics and gold. Gold is preferable, as it is more easily bartered. Platinum is almost as good. A four-wheel-drive truck with a good reinforced suspension and a second gas tank would make a fine investment, as it would enable you to get into places where no one could spot you (even from the air). A second language, such as Russian or Chinese, would be helpful. Investments in manufacturers of sweaters (new

ice age) and paraffin (effective neutron radiation shield) would be helpful in allowing you to stockpile more gold and platinum. Above all, don't get too used to living comfortably. Wash in cold water, eat canned foods (better yet, become a vegetarian), and stop using your heat and air conditioning. Limit your light bulb usage to one per evening. Get back to nature. After all, we all may have to eventually.

Afterthought: What if Philadelphia Were Nuked?

Why would the Ruskies (or whomever) want to waste an ICBM on the City of Brotherly Love? The answer manifests itself in the several major refineries which line the Delaware River and supply much of the petroleum needs of the northeastern United States. These qualify as prime industrial targets for any aggressor and would require at least a 20-megaton commitment to assure destruction.

How would you be affected by this? Well, the attack would probably be called unannounced, in which case you would have about 25 minutes' warning before the entire Delaware Valley was turned into a sheet of glass. If you had access to a car, you might get five or ten miles out before the roads became hopelessly jammed (figure on another one or two miles on foot before the bomb hits).

A 20-megaton hit in Philly would dig a crater 20 stories deep, instantly vaporize one million persons with a fireball four times hotter than the sun, and generate 1000 mph winds that would toss burning trucks around like giant Molotov cocktails as far as ten miles (your approximate location) from the blast site. Lighter objects, such as concrete blocks, would of course travel much farther. More than half of Philadelphia's population would be dead within 24 hours, with most of the survivors seriously contaminated enough to die inside of a month or, at the very latest, by year's end.

And what if, by some chance, you did survive? In order to make the area habitable (within, say, 40 years), everything that came in contact with the radiation would have to be either thoroughly cleaned (such as buildings and streets) or destroyed. All the topsoil and organic material within the affected area would have to be removed and stored someplace for a thousand years or so until it became usable again.

By which time, of course, you would be dead.

Uncertainty
explained by Ogden Nash

The Heisenberg Uncertainty Principle
Must not be forgot,
For sometimes it's here,
And sometimes

SICK TIMES

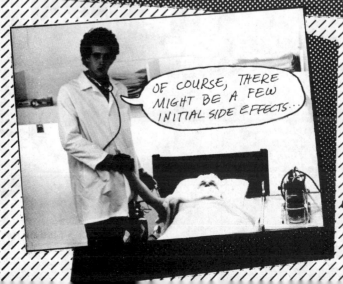

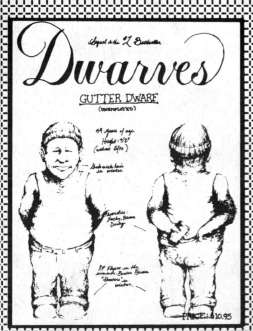

The Florence Henderson Generation

Madonna and Toaster

Do you remember the sensational seventies? The Alaska Pipeline. Wilbur Mills. Fanny Foxxe. Bruce Lee. *The Sting*. Acupuncture. Smilely face buttons. Archie Bunker. Howard Cosell. Elizabeth Ray. Chad Everett. Risk. *The Godfather*. Three Dog Night. Tom Eagleton. *The French Connection*. Mark Spitz. "Keep on Truckin'." *American Grafitti*. Nerf balls. Rhoda Morgenstern. Clackers. Odd-Even Gas Rationing. Star Trek Conventions. Sam Ervin. Panama Red. Glen Campbell. *Future Shock*. Skylab. Uri Geller. Robert Redford. David Cassidy. P.O.W. bracelets. Iron-on T-shirts. Pie throwing. Streaking. *The Poseidon Adventure*. *Towering Inferno*. Killer bees. The Bump. *The Exorcist*. *Jaws*. Patty Hearst. John Dean. Adidas. Earth shoes. Clogs. Platform shoes. Halter tops. Neil Sedaka. Elton John. *Tommy*. The Carpenters. Pet rocks. Trash compactors. Ozone. "I can't believe I ate the whole thing." Jogging. Kung Fu. The Hustle. Sensurround. *The Great Gatsby*. Bruce Jenner. Dorothy Hamill. "Please don't squeeze the Charmin." Deep Throat. Count Chocula. Pong. Hot pants. Hank Aaron. Barbara Streisand. "Flick my Bic." Jesus Freaks. Pringle's. "Dyn-O-Mite!" Giant TV screens. *Jonathan Livingston Seagull*. Mood rings. The Amazing Kreskin. The Bermuda Triangle. Toe socks. Leisure suits. Helen Reddy. Tatum O'Neal. Tony Orlando & Dawn. Cher & Greg. John Denver. "Adam-12." Ironside. Mannix. Cannon. Jim Croce. "Stairway to Heaven." Black Sabbath. Cat Stevens. *New Times*. Yes. *I'm OK, You're OK*. *Last Tango in Paris*. Erich Von Daniken. Herbal Essence shampoo. Backgammon. Boz Scaggs. Rodney Allen Rippey. Mason Reese. Tic-Tacs. Cum-gum. Frozen yogurt. L'eggs. Ziggy. Bubble Umbrellas. Wolfman Jack. Cheech & Chong. *High Times*. Head Shops. Microwave Ovens. WIN buttons. The Bicentennial. "Hey Mikey, he likes it." Pop rocks. Mr. Pibb. The Fonz. Laverne & Shirley. *Roots*. Miss Lillian. Son of Sam. *Saturday Night Fever*. Studio 54. Olga Korbut. The B-1 bomber. Barbara Walters. Lucite. Viking. Voyager. "Wild and Crazy." *Annie Hall*. Lynyrd Skynyrd. Sex Pistols. *Annie*. Larry Flynt. The Bee Gees. *est*. Bruce Springsteen. "May the Force be with you." Vans. Skateboards. Roller disco. Keith Moon. Billy Beer. *Close Encounters*. Roman Polanski. Freddie Prinze. *Airport 77*. Secretariat. Seattle Slew. Muhammad Ali. Leon Spinx. Laetril. *Equus*. Charo. Swine flu. *Rocky*. Boston. Red Dye #2. Margaret Trudeau. Wings. Shaun Cassidy. Moonies. Kiss. Saccharin. String bikinis. Gucci. Hamilton Jordon. Donna Summer. "You deserve a break today." Betamax. Rupert Murdoch. Decriminalization. Mary Hartman. The New York Blackout. SST. Squeaky Fromme. Karen Ann Quinlan. Hatch-backs. Martin Mull. Farrah Fawcett. Johnny-Can't-Read. Freddy Silverman. Spaceship Earth. Linda Ronstadt. Abba. Idi Amin. "Voulez-Vous Coucher avec Moi." Anita Bryant. Grape Kool-Aid. Angola. Abe Beame. Pope John Paul I & II. Tom Snyder. *M*A*S*H*. George Jefferson. *Kojak*. Angie Dickinson. Adrienne Barbeau. Gary Gilmore. *Playgirl*. Sylvester Stallone. *The Rocky Horror Picture Show*. *People*. *Hustler*. "The Gong Show." Paraquat. Donny & Marie. "Have it your way." Diane von Furstenberg. John Irving. Toast-R-Ovens. Sidney Sheldon. Harold Robbins. Fleetwood Mac. The Gang of Four. Jacuzzis. Disposable razors. Cloning. Quaaludes. Free-basing. Elvis Costello. Three Mile Island. Le Car. Bette Midler. Food Processors. "Love Boat." "Fantasy Island." Foto novels. Black holes. "Go for it!" Space Invaders.

Some people said we were trendy and consumer oriented. That opinion never caught on. Have a nice day!

The Trouble with Jeannie

Major Tony Nelson relaxed in his favorite easy chair and slowly sipped his Moa-Moa Punch while enjoying the laziness of a Coco Beach afternoon.

"Master, what are you doing?" Jeannie bounced gleefully into the living room.

"Oh, nothing much, just watching this old *Star Trek* episode," answered Tony, indicating the TV with his punch.

"What is it about?"

"A starship far in the future," Tony said drowsily, "They explore new worlds."

"It looks exciting. Would you like to be there, Master?"

"Yeah, sure, Jeannie." Tony absently nodded.

Jeannie smiled, crossed her arms, and blinked.

"What? What are you doing, Jeannie? Stop!"

The Enterprise was moving away from Delta Epsilon 4 at a cruising speed of warp factor one. Captain Kirk sat at the bridge. Mr. Spock toyed with the ship's computer.

Suddenly, Kirk felt an additional presence. He turned in his chair. His mouth dropped. Chekov turned to Sulu. Mr. Spock looked up and, raising an eyebrow, said, "Fascinating."

Before them stood Jeannie and Major Tony Nelson.

"Spock, what's going on here? Who are these people?"

"Unknown, sir. Tricorder shows some form of humanoid life."

"Of course we're humanoid!" declared Tony, glaring at Jeannie. "My name is Major Anthony Nelson. Jeannie here blinked us aboard."

"Major?" queried the Captain. "Dressed like that? How did you get aboard my ship?"

"Captain," interrupted Spock. "The Computer shows Anthony Nelson to be a fictional character from a 20th century earth television series, and the girl apparently has some sort of magical powers."

"That's quite correct," Jeannie said.

Kirk paused momentarily. "Spock, could this be a trick?"

"Unknown, sir. I'm working on it now."

"You just blink?" asked Uhuru.

"Yes, I'll show you!"

"Spock. Damage report," Kirk commanded.

"Sensors indicate none, Captain. However the presence of seven additional humans on deck four has been detected."

Kirk slammed his fist into the chair panel. "Security: to the bridge, on the double!"

The elevator door whizzed open and seven mismatched humans paraded onto the bridge.

"Professor, where are we?" asked the Skipper.

"Apparently not within the boundaries of planetary confinement at the present chronological measurement."

"Yeah, and maybe we're in outer space," said Gilligan.

"Oh, I'm not dressed for outer space at all," moaned Mrs. Howell.

"What a ship!" exclaimed Gilligan. "I'll bet I know how to get us back home," he said while throwing some switches on the console.

"Stop!" shouted Kirk. "Quiet, all of you!"

Everyone froze. A long silence spread over the bridge.

"Now who in the world are you?" Kirk asked, pointing to the pudgy man in the blue shirt and cap.

"I'm the Skipper of the S.S. Minnow. Gilligan, Mr. and Mrs. Howell, Ginger, the professor, Mary Anne, and I have all been shipwrecked on a small uncharted island in the Pacific for quite some time now. We were all eating some of Mary Anne's coconut cream pie when. . . ."

"Security, sir."

"Send these two to the brig," said Kirk, "and be careful; the girl blinks."

The guards escorted Tony and Jeannie from the bridge.

"Perhaps we should have tried the Vulcan mind meld on the girl," suggested Spock.

"Fascinating," said the professor, studying Spock at a closer range.

"Fascinating," said Spock, raising an eyebrow while eyeing the professor.

"PV=nRT," said the professor.

"w=((LC)-1-(R/2L)2)½," declared Spock.

"Yabadabadoo!"

"Gee, Fred, how are we going to explain this to Wilma and Betty?"

Kirk wheeled around. "Spock . . . who are they?"

Spock turned to the tricorder. "These two aren't carbon-based units at all. They're a completely different life form. They seem to be animated. If my calculations are correct, and I believe they are. . . ."

"No, they aren't," interrupted the professor, pointing to the computer display. "That x term should be positive. You can't raise it to a half if it's a negative quantity."

"I'm taking the absolute value,"

said Spock. He turned to Kirk. "Captain, you would have found it quite advantageous to have persisted in monitoring the proceedings of the intergalactic vessel in which we are contained," Spock continued, picking up one of the professor's idiosyncracies.

"What?" asked Kirk.

"You should have been watching the road, Jim."

"We're deep in the heart of Klingon space," said Mr. Chekov.

"Mr. Sulu, set a course for Starbase Four, warp factor six."

"Yes sir."

"Scotty," commanded the Captain into his chair panel, "give me everything you've got. I want shields on full."

"Aye Cap'n."

"Red alert," bellowed Kirk, "this is not a drill. Repeat: this is not a drill."

"Cap'n, she can't take it anymore," spoke Scotty over the communicator panel.

"Where's Mrs. Beasley?" asked Buffy Davis.

"Settle down everyone!" ordered Kirk. "Order! Order please!"

"Ham and cheese on rye!" said Gilligan.

The Skipper took the cap from his head and used it to hit Gilligan.

"The Enterprise is down to impulse engines, we're deep in the heart of Klingon territory, and the bridge is full of television characters. What could possibly be worse?"

"Klingon ship within sensor range, Captain."

"Thank you Mr. Spock," Kirk replied. "Uhuru, all hailing frequencies open."

"No response, sir."

"Not to worry, Captain," announced Thurston Howell III. "I'm sure they'll understand this." He waved a wad of bills. "The universal language!" he chuckled and marched bravely into the elevator. "Come along, Lovey."

"Sir," interrupted Uhuru, "the Klingons are attempting visual contact."

"Put it through, Lieutenant."

The screen quickly faded from the unchanging starfield to the face of the Klingon Commander. "Traveling through enemy territory, are we, Captain Kirk? That could be considered an act of war, eh Captain?"

"I get it!" Fred spoke up loudly, nudging Barney. "This is one of Joe Rockhead's practical jokes! Joe's getting pretty good at these!"

"So!" interrupted Maxwell Smart dramatically while stepping off the elevator. "It's the old Zap-me-from-Control-headquarters-onto-the-bridge-of-the-Enterprise trick."

"Captain," spoke the Klingon. "I've just been informed that you transported two humans aboard to bribe us. We're keeping the woman for our own purposes and returning what's left of the man."

A pile of charred ashes was beamed through to the transporter room.

"Captain, the situation is critical," said Spock. "We could attempt the Corbomite Maneuver."

"That's a good idea," agreed the professor.

"We could hold a carnival to raise money!" suggested Buffy Davis.

"That's a good idea, too," Gilligan added.

"I was in a movie like this once," purred Ginger, "and we just surrendered and were taken to a planet of handsome men."

"That's a good idea too," Gilligan added.

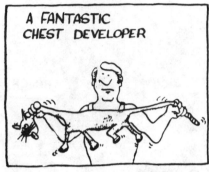

"But little buddy," said the Skipper, "they can't all be right."

"That's a good idea, too, Skipper." The Skipper fought to contain himself.

"What's to become of us?" asked Mary Anne.

"I'm afraid," answered Kirk, "we're all going to perish."

"Well at least we're not going to die!" said Gilligan.

"Sure 'nuff," Jed Clampett said, sitting on the steps to the bridge whittling a wooden stick.

Gilligan disappeared into the elevator.

"Security, to the bridge," ordered Kirk. "I'm responsible for the lives of four hundred and thirty eight crewmen, and there are enough people on the bridge to play a decent game of touch football." He turned to the screen. "We've contacted Starfleet command, Commander," he warned.

"At this very moment you are completely surrounded by Federation ships."

"Nice try, Captain, but it looks like you're at the end of the line," said the Klingon Commander.

"Would you believe two boy scouts, a vile-smelling horse, and a book of trading stamps?" asked Maxwell Smart.

Suddenly a blaring red alert signal was triggered on the bridge of the Klingon ship. The Commander was instantly briefed by one of his crew.

"I believe, Captain Kirk, that you and your ship have just about run out of time."

Suddenly, Gilligan stumbled out onto the screen. He was on the bridge of the Klingon ship.

"Wow! What a neat ship you guys have!" Gilligan exclaimed and he began to throw all sorts of switches on the control panels.

"Stop him!" shouted the Commander.

"Self-destruct in 20 seconds," announced the Klingon ship's computer.

The Commander turned to Kirk. "This cannot be. You have defeated us! This is impossible!"

"Sulu!"

"Sir?"

"Warp factor eight, get us out of here!"

"Aye, aye, sir."

The Enterprise pulled away swiftly, and within seconds, the Klingon ship exploded, creating a silent but mighty ball of flame and fury.

"Well, that certainly was a close call," Kirk said relieved, sitting back in his chair as the Enterprise headed toward the neutral zone.

"Golly, just wait till Sergeant Carter hears about this!" Gomer exclaimed.

FIFTH PERIOD

Three Pages of Lists

Six Bad Uses for Cinderblocks

1. Back scratcher.
2. Paperweight.
3. Pacifier.
4. Pillow.
5. Sponge.
6. Record Cleaner.

Eight Freak Accidents

1. Drowning at foam rubber city.
2. Paper cut from Silly Putty.
3. Great Dane slips on Crisco, negligee tears, vibrator impales postman.
4. Geology professor slips on icy sidewalk; 723 die.
5. Town of Stolix, Mass., caught in a sleeping bag zipper.
6. Look in mirror and see Bob Keeshan.
7. Television explodes while you're out salting slugs.
8. Find Ricardo Montalban in glove compartment.

Six Animals That Would Have Gone Extinct If They Had Existed In The First Place

1. The Backpack Kangaroo—
Instead of pouches this unfortunate marsupial used bookbags, losing its young when it hopped.
2. The Needle Snake—
Had a rigid backbone and could not crawl forward.
3. The Lava Bat—
Could not fly anywhere since it was always born within solid rock.
4. The Peruvian Flatheaded Condor–
Thought it could fly. It couldn't.
5. The Balloon Shark—
Was lighter than water and couldn't swim beneath the surface.
6. The Panamanian Two-Headed Frog—
Tore itself in two when it jumped.

Seven Things You're Told Not To Do and What Will Happen If You Do Them

1. Putting powdered soap on hands without wetting them first . . . Leprosy.
2. Opening wrong side of bandaid . . . Yeast Infection.
3. Buying yogurt after the expiration date . . . Crib Death
4. Peeking to the next page of SAT's . . .Dyslexia (for two years).
5. Failing to put Social Security number on registration form . . . Strapped to a Titan II missile.
6. Folding an IBM computer card . . . Silent treatment from Art Linkletter.
7. Failing to shake really well before using . . . Fusion of synapses.

Three Fatal Hiccough Remedies

1. Hold your breath for twenty minutes.
2. Drink a glass of water in a war zone.
3. Jump out a thirty-story building with a paper bag over your head.

Thirteen Worst Opening Pick-Up Lines

1. You know, if you cut off your arms you'd look like Venus de Milo.
2. Are you incredibly beautiful, or is it just my chemotherapy?
3. Sorry, I thought you were a moose.
4. Your place or my car?
5. Quick! How many psalms are there?
6. Ontogeny Recapitulates Phylogeny.

7. Wanna come up to my place for a pizza and a fuck? What's the matter, you don't like pizza?
8. You know, you look better without my glasses.
9. What's a slut like you doing in a classy joint like this?
10. Um . . . er . . . I . . . um . . . er. . . .
12. Why is it that the really beautiful girls are all assholes?
13. Your body is like haiku in motion.

Four Futile Methods of Fishing

1. Empty lake through a straw.
2. Grope underwater with your hands.
3. Move to Nevada.
4. Go water-skiing with hooks on your ankles.

Seven Qualities That Make Babies Disgusting

1. They vomit and spit up cheese.
2. They defecate in their clothes.
3. They're bald.
4. They're fat.
5. They drool.
6. They babble unintelligibly.
7. They grow into bratty two-year-olds.

Fifty-Two People You Wish Had Been Taken Hostage by the Iranians and Never Returned

1. Gloria Vanderbilt
2. Chuck Barris
3. Jesse Helms
4. Liberace
5. Ernie Bushmiller
6. McLean Stevenson
7. David Susskind
8. Gay Talese
9. Florence Henderson
10. Brooke Shields
11. William Shockley
12. Bill Cullen
13. Uri Geller
14. Jerry Falwell
15. Brett Somers Klugman
16. George Will
17. Buzz Aldrin
18. Frank Perdue
19. Marlin Perkins
20. Neil Diamond
21. Pete Best
22. Sylvester Stallone
23. Gus Hall
24. S.I. Hayakawa
25. Joe Garagiola
26. Jody Powell
27. Eldridge Cleaver
28. DeForest Kelly
29. Toni Tennille
30. Strom Thurmond
31. Abigail Van Buren
32. Fabian
33. Rona Barrett
34. Mr. Bill
35. Edwin Newman
36. Werner Erhard
37. Carly Simon
38. Abe Beame
39. Oral Roberts
40. Barbara Mandrell
41. Alvin Toffler
42. Brent Musberger
43. Kenny Rogers
44. Larry Hagman
45. Anita Bryant
46. Ruth Buzzi
47. Erma Bombeck
48. Phyllis Schlafly
49. Alexander Haig
50. Pete Rose
51. Milton Friedman
52. Don McLean

NO FRILLS

Travel

Dentistry

1. Leophobia: Fear of reading *War and Peace* and not understanding the ending.
2. Tripleletterscorophobia: Fear of being reincarnated as the letter "G" in a game of Scrabble.
3. Aibohphobia: Fear of palindromes.
4. Yawniphobia: Fear of people who brag about their high school sports teams.
5. Billionsandbillionsofintergalacticaphobia: Fear of people who impersonate Carl Sagan.
6. Phaphaphaphobia: Fear of stutterers.
7. Sankaphobia: Fear of being advised by Robert Young.
8. Coincidiphobia: Fear of running into your father at a house of ill-repute.
9. Lacostephobia: Fear of Perrier.

Five Unacceptable Ways to Make Cheese

1. Take milk and throw it into a river.
2. Grind up cheesecloth.
3. Put a cow on a rollercoaster.
4. Put yogurt in a microwave oven.
5. Sift through the garbage can behind a pizzeria.

One Phrase to Induce Paranoia

1. "Do you always eat like that?"

Eleven Things Erik Estrada Forced His Wife To Do

1. Bowl in the nude.
2. Vote Republican.
3. Dress up like Eleanor Roosevelt and push him around in a wheelchair.
4. Root for the Padres.
5. Floss the teeth of his old Army buddies.
6. Attend P.T.A. meetings at elementary schools.
7. Drink Windex.
8. Do Bette Davis impersonations at parties.
9. Participate in spelling bees at the homes of aging Hollywood starlets.
10. Appear on the *Mike Douglas Show* with a piece of spinach stuck in her front teeth.
11. Watch *CHiPS*.

Fifteen Things Nobody Would Notice Vanishing Off The Face Of The Earth

1. Jokes about elephants who walk into bars.
2. Cellophane toothpicks restaurants put in sandwiches.
3. Parsley.
4. The Gabor Sisters.
5. 12-year-olds who call you up at 3 AM and ask if you have Prince Albert in a can.
6. Sea-Monkeys.
7. Smokey and The Bandit lunchboxes.
8. Crayon sharpeners.
9. Movies about Roller Disco.
10. Dial-A-Joke.
11. Mickey Mouse telephones.
12. Fuzzy Dice for rear-view mirrors.
13. Mood-rings.
14. Slinkies.
15. Rich Corinthian leather.

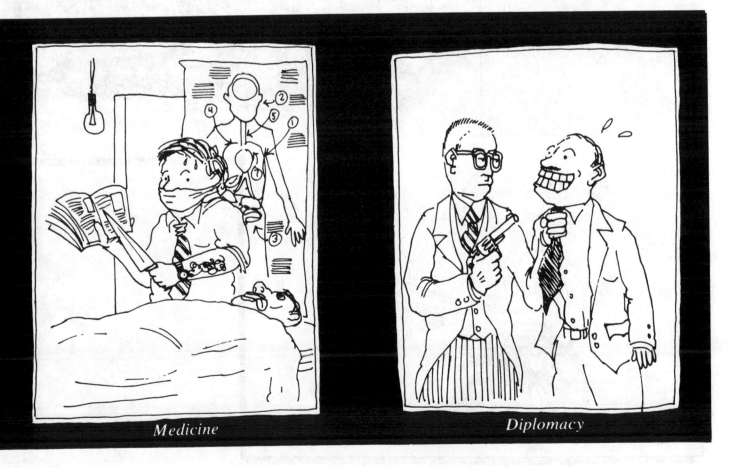

Medicine

Diplomacy

Catastrophes

**Cher: I was a
Hostage of Love**

**How Tony Orlando
Made a Bundle**

■$1.00

People
weekly

THE HOSTAGES

Day 42 of Freedom

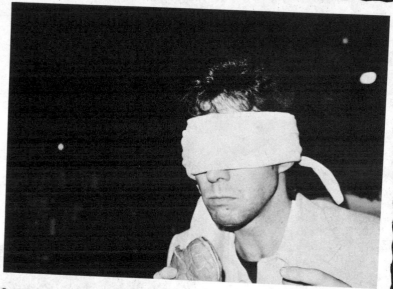

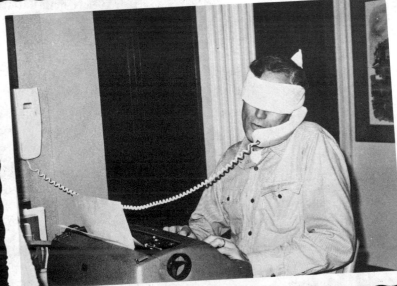

How Are
They Holding Up?

As the 110-year-old patient at the East Limping Brook Nursing Home opens his official-looking letter and reads the contents, he gives a frenzied cry, his heart racing out of control to a furious nine beats a minute. Nurses and interns race to his aid, their respirators and oxygen tent ready, diagnosing a massive, perhaps terminal, cerebral hemorrhage. But there is no real cause for alarm. Leopold Van Zandt, '88, Princeton University's oldest living graduate, has merely received an invitation to his class's 89th reunion, and God willing, Leopold is sure to be there.

Van Zandt is perhaps the most dedicated alumnus the university has ever seen (with the possible exception of H. L. Cheesburg, '08, who willed his entire estate and eight of his vital organs to a university scholarship fund and donated the rest of himself as fertilizer for the campus-wide resodding project). In his later years he has been easily recognizable leading the annual "Parade" of the classes down Prospect Avenue in his motorized wheelchair with fluorescent orange-and-black racing stripes, waving merrily to the throngs of "townies" who come out every June to witness the ludicrous spectacle.

But Van Zandt's health has been fading recently, and the still-breathing centa-decagenarian appears to be drawing near the end of a long and unproductive life. With senility rapidly advancing, the ex-scholar has been reduced to a veritable mental cripple, engaging in long and rambling conversations with his cream-of-wheat.

Even more embarrassing have been his solo trips back to Princeton the last few summers. In 1976 he showed up at the annual reunions of Lehigh, Yale, Middlebury, Duke, and the East Brunswick Secretarial School before a Good Samaritan escorted him to the right place and then stole his freshman beanie.

Nevertheless, "where there's a will, there's a way," as Van Zandt wheezes, and rest assured that, come June 2nd, the old codger will be carrying his luggage out to his waiting station wagon, staggering under the heavy suitcases while the nursing home staff hides in the bushes, convulsed with laughter. Should Leopold get to Princeton, he's in for a cruel surprise. Thaddeus Wigglesmith, '89, Leopold's collegiate companion and fellow co-manager of the junior varsity tricycle team, died of heart failure this spring when called by "Dialing for Dollars," leaving Van Zandt as the sole Princeton alumni representative from the Grover Cleveland era.

Future plans? Van Zandt says he plans to avoid "strenuous exercise" in the future, such as breathing or watching television, in the hope that he'll be able to hang in there for just 11 more years, when he can head back to Old Nassau for the biggest reunion of all—the magical 100th.

BIG BAD ERNIE "PSYCHO" JONES SERVING 693 YEARS IN PRISON IS THE STEELERS' NEW SENSATION

In the rough and brutal world of pro football, there is hardly a man more feared than 6'7", 285-pound Ernie "Psycho" Jones, all-pro defensive tackle for the Pittsburgh Steelers.

"The man is a killer," says NFL commissioner Pete Rozelle, and nobody, least of all Ernie, would deny it. For the fact of the matter is that Jones *is* a killer—a convicted killer who is currently serving five consecutive life terms in solitary confinement in Trenton State Prison with absolutely no chance of parole. Every Sunday morning during football season, however, a part of a unique work-release program, the hulking convict is permitted to leave the prison in an armored truck and take his place on the Steeler's front line, along with Dwight White, Mean Joe Greene, L.C. Greenwood, and two armed guards who must be handcuffed to him at all times.

The home crowd roars in approval and referees often look the other way in fear of their lives as Bad Ernie seeks to improve upon one record after another that he himself set: most punters crippled, game and season; most career-ending tackles made after the final gun; and what he regards as his finest achievement, most quarterback fatalities, game, season, and lifetime. Ambulances and priests are on constant patrol around the playing field, ever ready to whisk a player off to intensive care or deliver the last rites, depending on how long it took the refs to pull Ernie away from his victim.

Each day Pittsburgh fans flock to the football Hall of Fame in downtown Canton, Ohio, to gaze awestruck at the stuffed remains of Bengal quarterback Kent Cooke, struck down by Psycho late in a promising rookie season, and now on permanent display behind a glass case. A bronze plaque commemorated the youngster as the "11th 1st-round draft choice killed by Jones in a single season—new all-time record."

Defensive captain Ernie marches his highly-disciplined unit onto the field.

Ernie reacts unfavorably to a penalty called on him by a courageous ref.

Ernie now must play all games handcuffed to two corrections officers after storming the stands last November and killing six jeering teenagers with his bare fists.

It has been a long climb to the top for Psycho Jones. He was born the son of a poor dirt farmer in Trenton, New Jersey, whose frustration at being unable to command higher prices for his dirt caused him to beat the boy unmercifully each night with a tire iron. Prison psychiatrists think this might have had some bearing on Ernie's failure to develop "a particular fondness of the man" and in fact might indeed have been at the root of his wild sniper attack at age three that sent him to his first juvenile institution and on the road to a life of crime and football.

The massive tackle has matured "a helluva lot" since his rookie playing days, according to his coach Chuck "Noodles" Noll. "At first the guy was unbelievably wild—it took us six games to convince him that tossing grenades at opposing players was illegal under NFL rules. Even now he forgets himself occasionally and lobs one into their huddle when we get too far behind." By the end of last season, however, the uniformed Panzer had become an inspiration to his teammates and was unanimously elected defensive captain in an open ballot.

In prison Ernie divides his time between working out in the weight room, reading the bible, and making television commercials (he recently received $5,000 from Gillette for shaving his head on camera with a Track-2 razor blade). His fellow inmates are awed by his success and watch his exploits every Sunday on TV in the prison recreation room, though loud cheering often results in beatings or shock treatments from over-eager prison guards.

"Ernie's a real right guy and we're proud as hell to have him here," says Prison Warden Wanter Grunge. "With good behavior he'll be outta here in 100 years. We're gonna miss him."

"This ain't a checkers game," Ernie screams as Bengal quarterback begs for mercy. "This is football!"

"We know we've got a real hit on our hands," says Penny. "But one minute you're up, the next minute you're down. We'll try not to blow it."

HOLY BAZONGAS! THE "PETER'S PIECES" GIRLS ARE TV'S NEWEST SMASH, AS ABC GAINS A BIG RISE IN ITS AUDIENCE

Penny Pelvic-Thrust, Anita Hand-job, and Sandy Underwear have been having the time of their lives since their ABC action-adventure-sex series, "Peter's Pieces," became a hit in the ratings this fall. But it is a fact that being a part of the current number two television show (and rapidly closing in on "Bowling for Dollars") can be a bit of a hassle as well as a lot of fun, as our buxom heroines have long since discovered. Shooting the series seven days a week beginning at 4:30 A.M. and ending at midnight doesn't give the girls much time for social lives and often leaves them physically and mentally strained: Last week all production was shut down when Penny Pelvic-Thrust's beautiful hair began showing signs of split ends.

Above all, the sheer danger involved in filming intense action-ad-venture sequences is what gets to the girls the most. The three beautiful stars play private eyes, or "Pieces" in the detective argot. Each week the "Pieces" receive a dangerous assignment from Peter, an unidentified middle-aged Filipino who never reveals what he looks like, but shows up at the "Pieces" office occasionally, wearing a paper bag over his head to incite their curiosity.

In this particular episode now filming, J.F. Dillban, multi-millionaire hot pretzel tycoon and owner of the Bay Bombers roller derby team, is found murdered in his mansion, a skate key protruding from his back. The key is traced back to the Bay Bombers, whereupon Penny, because of her penchant for indoor sports, is selected to impersonate a roller derby star and infiltrate the club. Meanwhile Anita is attacked by

a man with a fire extinguisher, so that her tight clinging pants-suit clings even tighter, and Sandy, the "plainest" and brainiest of the group, sits in the office searching for a sci-entific formula to improve her complexion.

In the first of several hair-raising sequences in the episode, Penny discovers that the brakes in her '77 Peugeot have been tampered with and hurtles into an oil truck on the L.A. Freeway at 110 miles an hour. Luckily she escapes without harm, although the truck driver, who ironically turns out to be the same man who drained her brake fluid, is blown up. This scene, plus the roller derby sequences in which Penny was knocked to the floor several times by bull dykes twice her size were "terrifying experiences" for the voluptuous young actress, who broke down in tears twice on the set and wildly threatened to stop using Wella Balsam unless stunt women were provided for her in the future. ("It was a crazy, impulsive threat. I could never have gone through with it.")

For all their flossy TV image as sexually hep females, Penny, Anita, and Sandy are actually very disturbed women. On the set and at home recently, the three of them talked about their lives.

Anita, the ex-porn star

Anita is a Texas Rose, the daughter of a Houston dentist whom she calls "the most disgusting person in the world." Unable to stand her father's habits of clipping his toenails, and swabbing his ears with Q-tips during dinner, Anita left home at age 16, hoping to find stardom in New York. Checking into the Collingwood Hotel in the heart of the city, Anita found it difficult to break into legitimate theater but quickly attracted the attention of the Rhimebeck Brothers, the noted mail-order tycoons specializing in 8 mm films and rubber goods.

"I admit there wasn't much acting talent necessary for those films," concedes Anita, who made some 116 shorts over a four-year period (her personal favorite, "Pam's Eager Lips," won her the 1974 hottest new mail order talent award), "but it certainly gave me a lot of exposure." Indeed, it culminated in her being called out to Hollywood by the producer of "Peter's Pieces" for a "Try out" for the role of one of the three voluptuous detectives—a role she won virtually overnight.

Anita now lives alone in West Hollywood (her three-year marriage to George Rhimebeck broke up after he insisted on putting their 2-year-old daughter in mail-order films), and has no hobbies or interests.

Sandy, the sophisticate

"I'd like to be Katharine Hepburn," allows Sandy Underwear. Indeed, the most sophisticated "Piece" does have a hint of Kate's intensity, though none of her charm or intelligence. Still, Sandy likes to think of herself as an intellectual, citing her high school equivalency diploma, her ICS degrees in plumbing and air-conditioning repair, and her certificate of completion from the Evelyn Wood Speed-Reading Dynamics School.

Penny, a gourmet cook, loves to please Lee in every way she can. Here she serves up a double helping of his favorite dish.

Sophisticated, educated Sandy loves showing off her ICS skills. Here she displays a fine air-conditioner disassembly job and tries to figure out what to do next.

A native of Birmingham, Alabama, Sandy acted out her dreams in the family garage before nearly asphyxiating from gasoline fumes, then moved outdoors and acted out her dreams on the family front lawn. This continued for several years until she moved out onto the sidewalk, where she was immediately discovered and sent off to be a "Piece" in Hollywood.

A swinging single, Sandy is often seen around town attempting to get the autographs of many of Hollywood's leading men, and speed reading fan magazines in her spare time.

Penny, the sex goddess

With two hit shows in the family and little spare time between them, Penny Pelvic-Thrust and her "Bionic Tool" husband, Lee Thrust, "Take it whenever we can get it. Last week we did it in front of a Grand Union on Hollywood Boulevard. The week before it was on the crosstown bus during rush hour. Everybody who sees us loves it. It's their own fantasy come true."

It is this wholesome, all-American sexiness that makes Penny the most popular "Piece" with the public, and the trio's emerging superstar. The Penny Pelvic-Thrust full-color poster that features her sucking suggestively on her revolver is the best-selling pin-up of all time, and Penny Pelvic-Thrust toothpaste, t-shirts, showermats, and vaseline have also been selling like hotcakes.

Penny majored in sociology at University of Texas, and graduated Phi Beta Kappa. The secret, she says, was "getting to know my sociology professors extremely well, and giving some of the old ones a new lease on life in the process." She met her husband, Lee, star quarterback of the UT football team, under a sofa at his Gamma Summa Dumma Frat House and has been "in heaven" with him ever since.

None of that Women's Lib stuff for Penny, who claims that she had never even heard of the ERA until she blundered into a feminists' rally on her way home from the set. "I always thought it had to do with pitching," she grins, exposing the pearly white teeth she must brush eight times a day under a special clause in her contract. She is a total wife to Lee and subscribes to the philosophy that "if God had wanted the two sexes to be equal, he would have invented Stayfree maxi-pads for men."

Take out a pencil. No, that's a pen—a *pencil*. Good. Now sharpen it. No, no, the *other* end. All right. Now look at the maze of letters below. The average People reader can do it, and with this list of clues you should be able to circle all 20 hidden names. The average *People* sleuth should be able to identify 10 or more names. The average laboratory rat can identify 8.

```
C H E R C H E R C C
H C C E C H E R H H
E H Q H C H E R E E
R E Z C E C H E R R
B R C H E R W H C C
O C H E R E H C H H
C H E R R E H C E E
H C R C H E R H R R
E C H E R C H E R Q
R E H C C H E R X P
```

Clues

1. "The Sonny and—Show"
2. Hit singing team, Sonny and—
3. Chastity's mom
4. TV singer-comedienne
5. Sonny's ex-wife
6. CBS female superstar
7. Greg's ex-wife
8. —Bono Allman
9. Former Mrs. Bono
10. Former Mrs. Allman
11. Half of old musical team
12. Boob-tube songstress
13. Sang "I Got You Babe"
14. Sonny's old love
15. Long-haired television temptress
16. Had hit show with Sonny
17. Married Macon rock star
18. Divorced Macon rock star
19. Short for Cherilyn
20. *People*'s favorite four-letter word

Answers to last week's puzzle:

```
N I C H O L S O N N
N I C H O L S O N I
N I C H O L S O N C
N I C H O L S O N H
N I C H O L S O N O
N I C H O L S O N L
N I C H O L S O N S
N I C H O L S O N O
N I C H O L S O N N
Q P Z R E D F O R D
```

217

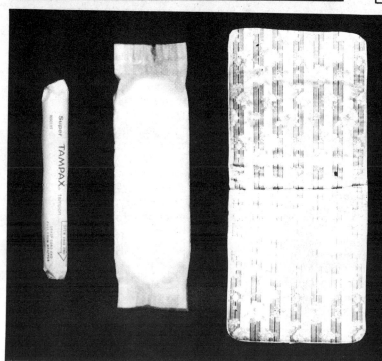

Billy Bombs. "He was without a doubt the most disgusting celebrity we've ever had on this show," says Peter Marshall, describing Billy Carter's five-day fiasco as a "Hollywood Squares" replacement for Paul Lynde, who was out sick all week with menstrual cramps. Carter, according to Marshall, "acted with a total lack of responsibility" by consuming two cases of Schlitz Beer in his dressing room before the show and then staggering blindly onto the set, requiring the assistance of four NBC ushers to get to his seat. Carter further reviled the studio audience by responding with loud, guttural burps to every question, whether or not it was directed at him, and put a sudden end to the first day's taping when midway through the show he leaned out over his square, clutched his stomach, and booted on Rose Marie some ten feet below. "Get him out! Get him out!" screamed emcee Marshall, as two NBC security officers immediately rushed the smashed good ol' boy off the stage, while an apologetic technical director attended to the startled Miss Marie with a wet washcloth.

Buried Treasure. They're capitalizing on everything these days. Art James has been slated to host the new ABC prime-time game show, "The Jimmy Hoffa Treasure Hunt," in which contestants race against the clock in search of the remains of the late labor leader. Moving to a different garbage dump, construction site, river bed, rock quarry, or tidal basin each week, James provides each contestant with a pickax, a shovel, and a set of scuba gear if they are searching under water, and gives them exactly one-half hour to try and dig up any or all of Hoffa. Prizes range from $25,000 to a Hamilton Beach Blender. Noted mob boss Tony "Pro" Provenzano has signed a contract with ABC to act as consultant to the program, responsible for weeding out those contestants who might have prior knowledge of Hoffa's whereabouts. "It's the second big 'Hoffa' contract I've signed," says the affable racketeer.

Barry's Roots. The latest national fad of tracing back one's ancestry, inspired by Alex Haley's smash best-seller *Roots*, has even spread to the United States Senate, with somewhat unexpected results. Distinguished Senator Barry Goldwater (R-Arizona) began investigating his genealogy last month and was in a state of shock this week after discovering that he is an 8th generation, direct-line descendant of Komuba Mobutu, a Zambian tribal chieftain who was captured by British slave traders in 1712 and shipped to America in exchange for three quarts of molasses. Mixed breeding gradually erased all traces of Goldwater's African ancestry, and the Senator had been misled until now into thinking that he came from a long line of White Anglo-Saxon Protestants. The overwrought Goldwater has since destroyed his entire collection of African jewelry and his son's complete set of "Earth, Wind, and Fire" albums and nearly killed an ABC representative who approached him about appearing with Andrew Young, Alex Haley, and Julius Erving on a "Great Black Faces of the '70's" TV profile show later this month.

Furthermore. To bolster sagging ratings on the ABC Evening News, the network is trying a completely new approach. Beginning Monday, an ABC spokesman announced, Barbara Walters will appear on the air wearing a filmy pink negligee and several thick layers of rouge and mascara, and will whisper the news seductively amid erotic sighs and moans while co-anchorperson Harry Reasoner pants loudly in the background. "The viewers obviously want more from Barbara than the staid, newsy delivery they're getting," explained the spokesman, "and our policy is to give the viewers what they want. If this doesn't work, we'll have to can Walters and put Reasoner in the negligee. We're willing to try anything once."

Weekend Gifts !!!

Here to satisfy all your shopping needs, every item listed can be obtained by mailing check (no stamps, please) and return address to *Weekend Gifts,* Box 5050, Hanover, N.H.

You're in on the action (radio-action, that is) with a Seabrook Nuclear Power paperweight that actually glows in the dark. So lustrously radiant you'll want to handle it with lead gloves. Hurry, before supply decays! $1.00 per megaton. $4.95

Flu-Away

Protect your household from swine flu with this handy swine-flu detector. It will make you proud again. (Comes in plain brown, Republican wrapper.) $68.95

Know Your Veggies

Vegetable embosser can put your name into any organic food product . . . 100 Julienne Fries (comes in plain brown wrapper). $9.95

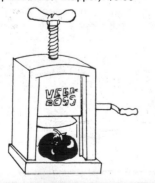

It Only Hurts a Minute
Canker Sore Remover

But it's worth it to use this Canker Sore Remover. No expensive cosmetics, no messy ointments or painful file work, and NO WAITING!!! Complete with cord or detachable battery pack $5.95

Bug Away!!!

Kills bugs automatically! Formerly available only to professional exterminators . . . quick, clean, efficient. No more powders, pastes, and sprays. $59.99

No More Sticky Fingers

With the aerosol sugar dispenser complete with no-stick child guard pump. Makes life a little sweeter. $.79

Come Out or the Linen Closet

With these handsome monogrammed "His & His" towel sets. $12.95

Don't Lose Your Grit!

Keep old issues of *Grit* magazine in this handy dispenser. Mounts anywhere . . . one indoor car racing set. Order NOW. $12.95

Announcing . . .
Leisure Suits for Dogs!

Man's Best Friend deserves to look his best for those fashionable swingle-doggy parties at the Country Club. Snappy styling. Perfect with Hawaiian batik top and pucka choker. Watch Fido grab for all the gusto in his livable double-knit suit. He'll be top dog at the kennel in any one of three (3) colors: creamy beige, mint/avocado green, pastel black. White patent leather shoes standard. Specify size. Next month: golf carts for the family pet! Just $7.99 for the doggy leisure suit

★ Amazing Research ★
★ Discovery! ★
Elastalace!

Just one lace ties both shoes. Says former President Gerry Ford: "I love it. It gives me the freedom I need without making me struggle with two shoelaces every morning. It's making me proud again." $.50 per pair

Products for the Frozen North

Down sleeves, sun-down-glasses, down bikinis, down corn plaster . . . all items in set, $75 down

Credits, Acknowledgments, and General Gobbledegook

As with any large-scale venture, we faced inevitable large-scale problems in putting this book together. The *Princeton Tiger*, for instance, refused to give us reprint rights until we bought them a chauffeured limousine and a lifetime supply of Perrier. But that obstacle was easily overcome when the *Temple Spice* came to our aid, generously presenting us with a chauffeured limousine and lifetime supply of Perrier on the condition that some of their more lackluster material be squeezed into the book.

When it came to editing (known in polite circles as censorship), you can rest assured we threw artistic integrity to the wind and ruthlessly cut material to pack everything in, placate the publishers, cheapen the product, and sell our audience short. We cleaned up the grammar, corrected the spelling, omitted the deadwood, plucked some of the metaphorical fuzzballs off our proverbial sweater, and carelessly left the four-letter words intact.

Unfortunately, Holt, Rinehart and Winston's lawyers approve of copyright violation only between consenting adults. We were all set to run a provocative photo-funny using GI Joe and Barbie, but Mattel and Hasbro refused to give us permission (since we'd be causing irreparable damage to the image they spend millions to create). So we're left tipping our hats to GI Joe's untarnished reputation. The same goes for the Man from Glad.

Since our stuffed-shirt society does not take kindly to college humor magazine editors who clip photos from other sources and print them without asking permission, we had to pay the price and go the legal route. That's the rationale behind excluding some of the tastier topless shots from Chapter 8. In some cases, original photographs could not be located. To accurately recapture the precise look of the originals, these photos were painstakingly restaged to the tune of eight and a half million dollars on location in Paris, London, Heidelberg, and Secaucus, New Jersey.

Without further ado, we bid heartfelt thanks to the college humor magazines and many individuals listed below who granted us permission and gave their lives so that we might reprint their material under one cover. Thanks to their tireless efforts, the flag of democracy shall forever wave, until some wiseacre runs a brazier up the flagpole in its place.

Credits (in Order of Appearance)

Front Matter

"Contents of Table" by Martha Keavney and Lois Dilivio. Copyright © 1979 *Colgate Harlequin*.

"Dartmouth Jack O'Lantern" cover copyright © 1975 by *Dartmouth Jack O'Lantern*.

"Punchbowl" cover by John Auerbach. Copyright © 1975 *Pennsylvania Punchbowl*.

"Cornell Lunatic" cover by Joey Green. Copyright © 1980 *Cornell Lunatic*.

"M.I.T. Comic Book" cover by Brian Bradley. Copyright © 1975 *MIT Voodoo*.

"Chaparral" cover by Perry Vasquez. Copyright © 1980 *Stanford Chaparral*.

"The Saturday Evening Pelican" cover by John Farley. Copyright © 1979 *California Pelican* (Berkeley).

"The Wag" cover copyright © 1979 *Hamilton Wag*.

"Datebook" cover by Jay Martel. Photo collage by Perry Vasquez. Copyright © 1981 *Stanford Chaparral*.

"Pravda" cover copyright © 1980 *Duke Pravda*.

"Wednesday Is Sundae" copyright © 1980 *St. John's Common Good*.

"Official Homecoming Program 1979" cover by Joey Green. Copyright © 1979 *Cornell Lunatic*.

"Venue" cover by Doug Kirby. Copyright © 1976 *Glassboro Venue*.

"The Princeton Tiger" cover by Jonathan Bumas. Copyright © 1976 *Princeton Tiger*.

"Rubber Teeth" cover by Rick Rodstrom. Copyright © 1980 Northwestern *Rubber Teeth*.

"Columbia Jester" cover by Donna Tsufra. Copyright © 1978 *Columbia Jester*.

Chapter 1. You're So Immature

"I miss the old days" drawing by Bruce Handy. Copyright © 1978 *Stanford Chaparral*.

Introduction by Joey Green. Copyright © 1978 *Cornell Lunatic*. Drawing by Bruce Handy. Copyright © 1979 *Stanford Chaparral*.

"Jack and the Beanstalk" by Jeremy Wolff. Except "Catcher in the Beanstalk" by Joey Green. Title photograph by Joey Green. Copyright © 1979 *Cornell Lunatic*.

"ISSN" drawing by Joey Green. Copyright © 1979 *Cornell Lunatic*.

"Hey Kids! Make Us Rich" by Joey Green, Barry Kushelowitz, and Steven Weinreb. Drawings by Joey Green. Copyright © 1979 *Cornell Lunatic*.

"Murders in Pooh Morgue" by Jay Grover-Rogoff. Copyright © 1975 *Pennsylvania Punchbowl*.

"Stayin' Alive" drawing by Douglas Johnson. Copyright © 1980 *Cornell Lunatic*.

"Public Toilet Terror" by Kenneth Gruskin. Copyright © 1981 *Cornell Lunatic*.

"Baby Showers" drawing by Lois Dilivio. Copyright © 1979 *Colgate Harlequin*.

"Savory Seuss" copyright © 1979 *Hamilton Wag*.

"Billy the Kid Baxter" copyright © 1979 *Cornell Lunatic*.

"Me and Bogey" by Jay Martel. Copyright © 1980 *Stanford Chaparral*.

"Baby/Lawsuit" drawing by Stephania Martin. Copyright © 1979 *NYU Plague*.

"Great Scenes from Childhood" by Brooks Clark. Copyright © 1977 *Dartmouth Jack O'Lantern*.

Chapter 2. If You Don't Stop Matriculating You'll Go Blind

Chapter 3. Sex, Drugs, and Bowling

Green. Copyright © 1978 *Cornell Lunatic*.

"The Joy of Television" by Mark Palmer, Joel Drucker, and John Farley. Drawings by Jocelyn Bergen. Copyright © 1981 *California Pelican* (Berkeley).

Chapter 4. Help, Martha, I'm Being Absorbed

Drawing (page 98) copyright © 1978 *Cornell Lunatic*.

Introduction by Gus Bernard. Copyright © 1980 *Cornell Lunatic*. Drawing by Bruce Handy. Copyright © 1978 *Stanford Chaparral*.

"Your Vacation in New Jersey" copyright © 1978 *Cornell Lunatic*.

"You Starring in a Typical Day" by Bruce Handy. Copyright © 1978 *Stanford Chaparral*.

"Head Eraser" by David Eisenberg. Copyright © 1979 *Stanford Chaparral*.

"Where Foreigners Come From" by Bret Falk. Copyright © 1980 *California Pelican* (Berkeley).

"To Tell the Truth" drawing by Robert Leighton. Copyright © 1980 Northwestern *Rubber Teeth*.

"Metamorphic Rock" drawings by James Hu. Copyright © 1976 *Stanford Chaparral*.

"Spiral" by Michael Aronson. Drawings by Douglas Johnson. Photograph by Michael Aronson. Copyright © 1980 *Cornell Lunatic*.

"Fly" drawings by Dave Lyon. Copyright © 1979 *Stanford Chaparral*.

"The Night Grandfather Turned Into a Horse" by Seth Biser. Copyright © 1980 *Cornell Lunatic*.

"On No! It's the Polish Shell Game" copyright © 1977 *St. John's Common Good*. Photographs restaged.

"Chrysler" ad by Gus Bernard. Copyright © 1979 *Cornell Lunatic*.

"Poorcourse" by Derek Krause. Copyright © 1980 *California Pelican* (Berkeley).

"Bitter, Cynical Humor" by Martha Keavney. Copyright © 1979 *Colgate Harlequin*.

"Vacuum Cleaner Crisis" by Robyn Ewing. Copyright © 1981 *Cornell Lunatic*.

"Origori" by Brian E. Bradley and Larry Appleman. Copyright © 1977 *MIT Voodoo*.

"Spider" drawings by Whitehead. Copyright © 1970 *Texas Ranger*.

"How to Become a Millionaire" by Howard Mermel. Copyright © 1978 *Penn State Froth*.

"The Invincible Elephant Man" by Adam Castro. Drawings by Douglas Johnson. Copyright © 1981 *Cornell Lunatic*.

"The Los Altos House of Toast Annual Report" by Barry Parr. Photographs by Jim Gable. Drawings by Perry Vasquez and Barry Parr. Copyright © 1980 *Stanford Chaparral*. "House of Toast" ad by Mike Wilkins. Drawing by William Fox. Copyright © 1979 *Stanford Chaparral*.

Chapter 5. Apathy on the March

Apple photographs copyright © 1978 *Emory Spoke*. Photographs restaged. Introduction by Bruce Handy. Drawing by Hilary Brown; copyright © 1976 *Princeton Tiger*.

"INCAR" by Michael Aronson. Copyright © 1980 *Cornell Lunatic*.

"The Military" by Joey Green. Photographs by Michael Frawley. Copyright © 1978 *Cornell Lunatic*.

"Humor in Uniform" copyright © 1970 *Columbia Jester*.

"Teddy Agnew" ad copyright © 1974 *RPI Unicorn*.

"Notes from Underground" by Walter Kloefkorn. Copyright © 1975 *Stanford Chaparral*.

"Strike" drawing by Cary Mazur. Copyright © 1970 *Princeton Tiger*.

"Geese at War" by Martha Keavney. Photography by John Palomaki. Copyright © 1980 *Colgate Harlequin*.

"Symbionese Liberation Army" ad copyright © 1976 *Berkeleyan*.

"Any Word from the Governor" drawing by Stephania Martin. Copyright © 1978 *NYU Plague*.

"Zapruder Family Scrapbook" by Dave Lyon and Jay Martel. Photographs by Jim Gable. Copyright © 1980 *Stanford Chaparral*.

"Olivia Wadsworth" ad by Brad Brinegar. Copyright © 1975 *Dartmouth Jack O'Lantern*.

"Jer" by Douglas Steiner. Drawing by James Holder. Copyright © 1979 *Stanford Chaparral*.

"Energy Police" ad by Douglas Kirby. Copyright © 1975 *Glassboro Venue*.

"Borealis" by Steve Adolph, Jay Martel, Bruce Handy, and David Eisenberg. Photographs by Jim Gable. "Brothers All" drawing by Jay Martel. Copyright © 1980 *Stanford Chaparral*.

"Conservative Student Body" ad by Barry Parr. Copyright © 1976 *Stanford Chaparral*. Photographs restaged.

"Ted Kennedy's Stand Up Comic Routine" by Joey Green. Copyright © 1980 *Cornell Lunatic*.

"A Mine is a Terrible Thing to Waste" ad by Joey Green, Barry Kushelowitz, and Jeremy Wolff. Photograph by Michael Frawley. Copyright © 1978 *Cornell Lunatic*.

"Let's Capitulate to the Russians" by Neil Steinberg. Drawings by Robert Leighton. Copyright © 1980 Northwestern *Rubber Teeth*.

"Zen and the Art of Motorcycle Misrepresentation" by Jay Furst. Copyright © 1975 *Princeton Tiger*.

"Boat People" by Joey Green. Copyright © 1980 *Cornell Lunatic*.

"America's 1980 Olympians" ad by Douglas Steiner. Photograph and drawings by Peter Stamats. Copyright © 1980 *Stanford Chaparral*.

"Invest Mints" ad by Jon Good. Copyright © 1979 *California Pelican* (Berkeley).

"Our Nation's Armpit" by Jeremy Wolff. Copyright © 1978 *Cornell Lunatic*. Drawing by Rick Rodstrom. Copyright © 1980 Northwestern *Rubber Teeth*.

Chapter 6. Fun With Carcinogens

Introduction by David Cohn. Copyright © 1981 *Cornell Lunatic*. Drawing by Dave Lyon. Copyright © 1981 *Stanford Chaparral*.

Photograph page 170 by Jim Gable. Copyright © 1979 *Stanford Chaparral*.

"The Greatest Hits of Modern Psychology" by Brooks Clark, Peter Reissman, and James M. Lattin. Drawings by Vincent Tam. Copyright © 1976 *Dartmouth Jack O'Lantern*.

"Conditioning" drawing page 177 conceived by Henry Mazzeo and illustrated by Richard Gardner. Copyright © 1951 *Columbia Jester*. This 1951 cartoon doesn't belong in a collection of college humor from the 70s and 80s. But it has been called the most frequently reprinted illustration in the history of college humor, so why fight city hall?

"Ms. Ogyny" by Jonathan Bumas. Copyright © 1976 *Princeton Tiger*.

"Gravity" ad by Bret Watson. Drawings by John Jackson. Copyright © 1979 *Princeton Tiger*.

"Flushed Organ" by John P. Auerbach. Copyright © 1975 *Pennsylvania Punchbowl*.

"Sartrek" by Rob Holbrook. Drawings by Derek Mueller. Copyright © 1980 *Stanford Chaparral*.

"Clown in a Crazy House" by John Beahm. Copyright © 1979 *California Pelican* (Berkeley).

"Jupiter I" drawing by Greg Collins. Copyright © 1976 *Columbia Jester*.

"Lightbulb" drawing by Tom Gibb. Copyright © 1975 *Penn State Froth*.

"Donut Gag" by Ron Harnar. Copyright © 1975 *Penn State Froth*.

"Tru-Life Space-Age TV Game Show Tales" by Mark Voglesong. Drawings by Don Lyles. Copyright © 1980 *Glassboro Venue*.

"Digital Bell Tower" collage by Joey Green. Photograph by Russ Hamilton. Copyright © 1978 *Cornell Lunatic*.

"Greetings from the Moon" by Douglas Kirby. Copyright © 1979 *Glassboro Venue*.

Chapter 7. The Florence Henderson Generation

Models

George Acosta, Judy Baruch, Cynthia Bond, Missy Brinegar, Chris Caruso, Lucy Castellucio, Mickey Clark, Matt Colona, Alan Corcoran, Brad Davids, Ed Desch, Beth Eiserman, Elsie, Leigh Engelhardt, Rebecca Engelking, Robyn Ewing, Nancy Follender, Michael Frawley, Joel Friedman, Carlo Galluccio, Elizabeth Gavin, Jo Goldberg, Barbara Green, Douglas Green, Robert Green, Bruce Handy, Brad Hennenfent, Mark Hoebee, Rob Holbrook, Dave Holt, Rob Hunter, Bill Jennings, Douglas Johnson, Barry Kates, Judy Kaplan, Gary Kroeger, Lucia LaRocca, Gloria Lee, Nathan Leiberman, Henry Lowenstein, Sally MacNichol, Pat Magee, William McGill, Patty Mengler, Michael Nowack, Henry Price, Ricardo, Barbara Richard, Bill Rogers, Wayne Rullan, Jeffrey Seeman, Erica Shames, Martin Sidrow, Chris Spear, Ray Steinman, Victor Venning, Wali Waiters, Andy Weber, Donna Wilkinson, Jill Witlin, David Wrobel, Bob Zazzali.

Thanks To:

Cricket Allen, Mark Amidon, Michael Aronson, Talya Baharal, Art Baxter, Tom Beurkle, Mark Blechman, Gilbert Borman, Kent L. Brown, Jackie Cantor, Katie Carpenter, Adam Castro, Christopher Cerf, Rachel Christmas, Brooks Clark, Clifford Cook, Mr. and Mrs. Corcoran & family, Tim Cornell, Bill Craver, Jay Cross, Anne Demeray, Keith Deterling, Lois Dilivio, Robert Dinsmoor, Steve Dorsky, Richard Dyckman, Loyd Edmonds, Linda Ednrzyiwski, Melvin B. Endy, Jr., Carol Fein, Dan Fiorella, Finger Lakes Music, Shary Flenniken, Michael Frawley & family, William H. Fox, Stanley Gerin, John Gernand, Howard Gershen, Michael Gessel, Andy Gold, Amy Sue Green, Douglas Green, Michael Green, Dale Grossman, Ken Gruskin, Mr. and Mrs. Handy & family, Peter Heller, Tony Hendra, Amy Hill, Bruce Hilsberg, Michael Hogan, Douglas Johnson, Scot Johnston, Michelle Kay, Trina Kassler, Chris Keavney, Martha Keavney, Steven Kessler, Douglas Kirby, Edwin Kohler, Erik Kriss, Lorna Kriss, Lucia LaRocca, Robert Leighton, John Lewin, Scott MacIsaac, Vanessa Malcarne, Andy Mantis, Daniel Margulis, Richard Marini, Jay Martel, Henry Martin, Stephen Mazur, Tom McCormick, Howard Mermel, Rebecca Moss, Mary Ellen Muzio, David Nettles, Bonnie Norton, Dirk Olin, P.J. O'Rourke, Barry Parr, Karen Peltz, Bob Reed, Rafe Reisenman & the Brooklyn Co-op, Eric Rosedale, Barbara Rosen, James D. Ross, Ruff, Steve Rubenstein, Alan and Sherry Salzman & family, Martin and Andrea Salzman & family, Bill Smith, Smokey, Chris Spear, David Stanford, Douglas Steiner, John Stevens, Bill Townsend, Peter Tubman, Mark Voglesong, Bret Watson, Stefanie Weiss, Mike Wilkins, Dororthy Wilson, Peter Wirth, Jill Witlin, Jeremy Wolff, David Woronov, Al X.

Special thanks to my agent, Helen Merrill, for her constant encouragement and for making it all happen.

Superduper thanks to our editor, Natalie Chapman, for putting up with our shennanigans, busting her chops, letting us crank up the stereo, and risking her job.

Many thanks to Jo Goldberg for her invaluable help, for her friendship, and for always picking up the check.

Love to my family, whose support, patience, and understanding has been an undying source of encouragement, inspiring this overly sentimental postscript.